Getting StartED with Netbooks

Nancy Nicolaisen

friendsof

an Apress® company

GETTING STARTED WITH NETBOOKS

Copyright © 2009 by Nancy Nicolaisen

ISBN-13 (pbk): 978-1-4302-2501-0

ISBN-13 (electronic): 978-1-4302-2502-7

Trademarked names may appear in this book. Rather than use a trademark symbol with every occurrence of a trademarked name, we use the names only in an editorial fashion and to the benefit of the trademark owner, with no intention of infringement of the trademark.

Distributed to the book trade worldwide by Springer-Verlag New York, Inc., 233 Spring Street, 6th Floor, New York, NY 10013. Phone 1-800-SPRINGER, fax 201-348-4505, e-mail orders-ny@springer-sbm.com, or visit www.springeronline.com.

For information on translations, please e-mail info@apress.com, or visit www.apress.com.

Apress and friends of ED books may be purchased in bulk for academic, corporate, or promotional use. eBook versions and licenses are also available for most titles. For more information, reference our Special Bulk Sales–eBook Licensing web page at http://www.apress.com/info/bulksales.

Credits

President and Publisher:
Paul Manning

Lead Editor:
Ben Renow-Clarke

Technical Reviewer:
Ann Tan

Editorial Board:
Clay Andres, Steve Anglin, Mark Beckner, Ewan Buckingham, Gary Cornell, Jonathan Gennick, Jonathan Hassell, Michelle Lowman, Matthew Moodie, Duncan Parkes, Jeffrey Pepper, Frank Pohlmann, Douglas Pundick, Ben Renow-Clarke, Dominic Shakeshaft, Matt Wade, Tom Welsh

Coordinating Editor:
Jim Markham

Copy Editor:
Tracy Brown Collins

Compositors:
MacPS, LLC

Indexers:
John Collin

Artist:
April Milne

Cover Designer:
Kurt Krames

To S.E., my adventure travel consultant, of course.

Getting StartED with Netbooks

Nancy Nicolaisen

an Apress® company

Contents

About the Author

 **Nancy Nicolaisen** is an author, researcher, and former computer science professor specializing in mobile and embedded device technologies. She's provided mobile device education materials, analysis, and strategy consultation to Apple, CBS Interactive, Symbian Foundation, Intel, Microsoft, Time Warner AOL, Information Today, and other global players in the mobile connected device space.

About the Technical Reviewer

 **Mary Ann C. Tan** has experience in many fields, including slinging regular expressions, watching Linux servers, writing telecom billing systems, developing GUIs for a telecom testing company, being an obsessive-compulsive spreadsheet user, and arguing about machine learning. She is learning Italian and German, teaching Hiligaynon, but has forgotten most of her Mandarin. In her free time, she teaches felines Cat-Kwan-Do and sings videoke to survive the Manila night. She manages build processes, source code repositories and software development teams in her day job.

Acknowledgments

I've written many books, been published in a variety of languages, and have been read by people from all over the globe. I've been a researcher and a computer science professor. I've worked with everything from computers in satellites to computers that do their job thousands of feet below the surface of the ocean. I've enjoyed a stimulating, interesting career. And all of this while leading a comfortable, secure life. So, I wrote this book because of my mother's rule:

"Those who do well ought to do good."

I've certainly done well by educating my software engineering colleagues, students, and clients, in the deeper matters of computing technology. This book, however, is written for a completely different audience: complete netbook beginners. It is my effort to do good.

In all of my time in the computer industry (decades, and quite a number of them...), the netbook technology is the first one I've seen that, in the hands of everyday, non-technical people, has the potential to dramatically, rapidly, and decisively defeat some of the worst human problems that plague our world. A unique confluence of technology, economics, and social factors, netbooks are superlative tools for improving education, providing distance delivery of healthcare, and creating transformational kinds of community in places where people can solve their own problems if barriers of distance and politics are rendered meaningless.

In writing this book, I meant to help readers understand the basics of buying, using, and building upon netbook technology to accomplish their goals. But people like me will only truly appreciate the real power of the netbook technology when typical consumers, educators, and activists take them in hand and innovate, create, and connect. Which is why I wish to acknowledge the creative, proactive people I have yet to know, that will impress us all with the uses to which they put this watershed technology.

Introduction

Timing makes this book unique. Mobile-connected culture has been a relatively exclusive club up to this point. Because it has almost entirely been based on smartphones — expensive, quirky, non-standard, walled garden gadgets — its growth has been stulified by fragmentation on every level. In contrast, netbooks offer a populist solution: inexpensive, dependable, and benefiting from a huge head start in software applications, peripheral devices, and web-based services that were built for desktop or laptop computers, but can be easily reused by netbook owners. Even in a weak economy, netbooks have taken off in Asia and India, and show every indication of following suit in North America.

In this book, I set out to make you a better, savvier consumer of a technology that can transform your day-to-day life in some pretty important ways. But I don't assume that you already know a lot about this kind of computing or, for that matter, any kind of computing. I was guided by the idea that if you want to get started, I want to help you do it. So here are all of the steps, with nothing left out. Use this book as your resource if

- you are considering buying a netbook to shop intelligently, find a best-fit solution, and get maximum value for the dollar;
- you already have a netbook, but you need a jumpstart with basic netbook features, software, and services; or
- you want to quickly become a "power user" in areas of specific interest (cloud content, gaming, and the like).

Netbooks and the lifestyle they can create for you are really as much a cultural phenomenon as a technical one. For this reason, the concept for this book is based on two templates: *Consumer Reports*, where readers receive actionable, balanced evaluation of the strengths and weaknesses of various products and services, and Stuart Brand's landmark 1970s opus, *The Whole Earth Catalog*. The idea here is that netbooks are a radical social and cultural shift in the making; they are more than an incremental advance in the miniaturization of ordinary computing devices.

So, it's pretty simple. Use the information between these covers to understand the personal significance of the fastest growing technology niche in the global consumer electronics space. I want to help you shop for, use, and enjoy your netbook. I want to help you be more productive, healthier, safer, and better connected. I want you to have a wonderful new entertainment option, but also new learning opportunities. And most of all, I want to welcome you to the emerging global connected community that will transform this twenty-first century.

Chapter 1

Getting the Best Fit and Value

This chapter will help you understand two things about netbooks: what you are buying and, perhaps as important, *what you are buying into*. In more or less the same way mobile phones have changed our ideas about when and where we can connect with *people*, netbooks are about to change our ideas about our connectedness to *services, information, and a global culture of ideas*.

As netbooks proliferate in diverse geographical, social, and economic circumstances around the world, they will enable something far more profound than the ability to do word processing or watch television wherever we feel like it. *Netbooks will enable and accelerate the emergence of "real-time," global, intellectual, and cultural communities of interest*. Wow. That was an eye-full.

How about this instead: by owning and using a powerful, affordable, and incredibly mobile netbook, you'll get to enjoy relationships and experiences of an entirely new sort. Here's why: netbooks are what are known in the technology business as *convergence devices*. Convergence devices let us use a single tool to do all the jobs it used to take two or more tools to do. Netbooks are convergence devices because they amplify your self-reliance and let you do things you want or need to do, but without being tightly coupled to a bunch of infrastructure that is difficult or expensive to get. This is big stuff, and sometimes hard for people to get their minds around, which is why there is a certain amount of confusion regarding the netbook niche at this early point in its history. As an analogy, think about a Swiss Army knife: whittle a stick to roast the hot dog, use the bottle opener on the accompanying beer, and have a toothpick handy for after dinner.

More than one pundit (and probably a lot more than one skeptical husband, wife, parent, or boss) has publicly voiced doubt. "There is no *there* there," they say. "What can you possibly do with a netbook that you can't already do with a top-end mobile phone or laptop computer?"

Pretty obviously, nothing.

Herein lies the subtlety, because that is a reasonable answer to the question, if you are hung up on answers. Usually, though, the key to understanding anything is asking the right *questions*.

So let's return to our Swiss Army knife analogy. What's a Swiss Army knife good for? You already own a bottle opener and a full-sized fork, so you don't *need* it for the hot dog roast in the previous example. Similarly, nobody would build a *house* with a Swiss Army knife, even though they come with a usable little saw, a screwdriver, and a tiny drill. And what about, say, an appendectomy? The knife has tweezers, a sharp blade, and a sewing tool. But clearly, when you want to build a house, you'll get some full-sized tools, genuine big iron, and go to town cutting up plywood and so forth. If you need your appendix removed, you'll call a surgeon.

These are, of course, silly comparisons, but they do make a point. We inherently and intuitively know that a Swiss Army knife is a useful thing, not so much because of *how* it is useful, but because of *where* it is useful. With the sole exception of U.S. airport TSA security lines, a Swiss Army knife can be useful to have no matter where you are. It is a powerful, convenient, darn handy thing, if you are somewhere far from the kinds of resources you need to do a small but critical job. In fact, you are *empowered to wander far from the supports of civilization and comforts of technology* if you carry the trusted "fix any problem in a pinch" tool. (And yes, I could probably just as easily have used duct tape in this example.)

Similarly, the unique and wonderful thing about a netbook is that it can do much, though not all, of what your mobile phone or laptop can do, in a whole lot more places, with more flexibly, and more affordably. With a netbook, you are more than adequately compensated for what you sacrifice in absolute computing power over a traditional laptop.

Netbooks beat laptops because

- you get more and easier portability because of netbooks' light weight and small size;
- you get up to four times the battery life than with a standalone computer;
- you get up to twice the battery life when using the netbook to connect to the Internet;

- you get access to the same applications and user interfaces that are familiar to you, whether you are a diehard Windows partisan or a Linux user;
- you get the ability to make phone calls and do video conferencing over the Internet for little or no cost, with dramatically increased convenience and flexibility;
- you get the opportunity to use cloud-based services that are secure, powerful, and cost-efficient (we tell you all about cloud computing in Chapter 2), so your tiny netbook can do virtually all the heavy lifting that a more costly and cumbersome laptop can do; and
- you get it all really, really inexpensively.

Here's what a netbook gives you that your mobile phone isn't brilliant at providing:

- You get a much better quality screen, so that you can actually see and enjoy content created for the desktop or television.
- You don't have to have a costly wireless plan to send and receive data, even in vast quantities.
- You have complete flexibility in terms of which applications and even which operating system you want to use.
- You can make Voice-over-IP (VoIP) phone calls to just about anywhere and hold videoconferences for practically nothing, with no ongoing commitment.

All this said, as a matter of practicality, I think it very unlikely that I will get rid of my mobile phone any time soon, and I have no intention whatsoever of relinquishing my laptop. But I have to admit that after a surprisingly short time, I have become completely dependent on my netbook. For traveling, the netbook has no equal. And netbooks take the sting out of equipping kids for a connected mobile future, because these devices are truly affordable, and the total cost of ownership makes them a no-brainer for just about any family. Through the sheer convenience of being able to productively use time when you are stuck somewhere you really didn't anticipate being, a netbook pays for itself inside a week. (You read it here first: when netbooks take off with enterprise, public transportation use and vanpooling are going to skyrocket. Who will want to waste valuable commuting time behind the wheel, when you could be watching your favorite television program or finishing that quarterly report?)

Enough of this glib stuff. Read this chapter to get yourself started, both with netbook computing and with a truly connected mobile lifestyle. Here's what you'll learn:

- To be a savvy shopper. Make sure you end up with the device that fits your needs and your budget, by understanding how to read and interpret netbook product specifications.
- Know who manufactures netbooks, and what their products' strengths, weaknesses, and price points are.
- Find out where you can get hands-on experience with netbook devices before you make a buying decision.
- Have a clear idea which features you need from your netbook so that you can narrow the field of candidates before you go shopping.
- Know how and where to shop to get the lowest possible price on these (mostly) already inexpensive devices.

Getting the Lowdown: Read and Understand Netbook Manufacturers' Specs and Technical Product Info

The key to a happy, satisfying netbook experience is doing your homework before you shop. Precisely because netbooks are in their infancy, there isn't total agreement on what makes a device a "netbook," how it should behave, or what it should or shouldn't be able to do. Basically, it's a jungle out there.

You need to be equipped with an all-important savvy shoppers' tool: the ability to read and understand the full implications of manufacturer's published specifications for the devices they market as netbooks. Here are two reasons why this is true:

- If you take into account all the customizations, service options, and configurations in which netbooks are manufactured, there are currently *hundreds* of netbook products from which to choose. Today, there are less than 10 credible, large-production-run netbook vendors, but this number will probably increase until the market becomes saturated and devices become commoditized. So, lesson number one is that this is a really diverse, diffuse market.

- Lesson number two is actually a side effect of lesson one. Because there are so many vendors, so many versions of devices, and such a broad range of prices, capabilities, and features, it is very unlikely that you'll be able to get hands-on experience with all of the candidates you want to consider. Remember also that these little boxes are constantly being enhanced, improved, and tweaked, so even if you get to see and touch one this week, its sleeker, faster cousin may be available when you decide to buy. The only real way to know whether a netbook will meet your needs is to be able to extrapolate from published specs. For example, if you plan to buy a Linux netbook, chances are you care a lot about *which* Linux. Similarly, if you plan to buy a Windows-based device to use for mobile business processes, security considerations may send you to a netbook vendor that offers the right kind of configuration and support options.

ExplainED

Let me be clear on one thing here. I don't advocate "waiting to see what is coming." Definitely, whatever it is will be super. But what's available now is really terrific, too. Netbooks are more than just "ready for prime time." They are defining and enabling a new sort of prime time. So you'd be missing out if you defer a purchase just because there might be something better coming soon, because no matter when you buy, there will always be something better just around the corner.

Netbook Specs: What They Mean, Which Ones Matter to You, and When to Ask More Questions

A couple of years ago, a multinational consumer electronics company commissioned a full-fledged scientific study, complete with PhDs and everything, to discover what people actually do with the instructional manuals that the company had been shipping with its products. The researchers reported results by nationality, and this is what they found: in Germany, people generally open packaging, read all the documentation, and only then attempt to actually use the product. In Italy, people generally just get right down to business with the item they bought, and throw both the documentation and the packaging away. In the United States, we have sort of a hybrid approach. We get stuff out of the box, try to use it, and only consult the directions if there is a problem. We like this story because it is a perfect depiction of when and why people are willing to learn things.

Basically, most people don't mind learning things that seem like they'll be fun. (And the national differences in the study say more about what people think might be fun than they do about anything else.) It is very difficult to make a case of any sort that the average person will have "fun" reading the technical specifications for a small computer, and for this reason almost no consumer ever *does* read them. Given that stark reality, I am not going to try to make netbook specification perusal fun for you. I *am,* however, going to make this something that *you can do fast,* which is the next best thing.

Think of it this way: engineering specifications are *meant* to be dry. This is because each fact in a spec is actually a precise, unambiguous, yes-or-no answer to a particular question. The key to being good at reading and evaluating specs is to understand which question each spec implies, and to know if the questions being posed matter to you. Using this approach, product specs become a resource for looking up information pertaining to your key concerns, and thus give you a quick, authoritative tool for deciding whether a particular netbook will actually work for you.

For the purposes of getting up to speed on reading specs, we'll use those specs published for the Asus series of devices as examples in this chapter. ***This is not because Asus makes the "best" netbooks.*** The best netbook is always and only the one that works best for you, in your particular circumstances. Rather, there are a couple of especially useful things about the Asus product specifications site. First, shopping this company's products is complicated, because there are so many of them. This mirrors what you'll experience when you evaluate the broader netbook market place. Second, Asus provides a comparison-shopping tool for its own products. This gives you a chance to do a side-by-side comparison of important device specs you'll be using when you shop. Using this tool, it becomes apparent that small differences in product configuration can have a big impact on whether a given netbook will be the right choice for you.

System Characteristics

This category of information describes the installed operating system, main processor brand and model, amount of runtime memory (RAM), amount of storage for files and media, and the types of external peripherals you can connect. This last item is key, because if you want to be able to use your netbook with USB devices, flash cards, and the like, you'll need to understand what's supported on a given device and what's not. This is one of the most inflexible characteristics of any hardware design, so it's a key buying decision point.

ExplainED

Key Shopping Terms and Abbreviations:

RAM: RAM actually stands for Random Access Memory. That's useful trivia for your local pub quiz, but in all honesty, you'll never need to know it. All you need to know is that when someone talks about a computer's memory, what they mean is its RAM. The computer relies most heavily on this kind of memory to do actual, ongoing work, such as running applications and the operating system, painting the screen, and driving devices such as speakers, modems, cameras, and the like. RAM is used for storing things that the computer only needs to keep temporarily. Think of RAM as the computer's chalkboard. It uses it to make calculations and store notes, but at the end of the session it's wiped clean. The amount of RAM in a computer is more or less fixed at the time you buy it. While it can be expanded and upgraded, this can be costly, and you might need a professional's help. For this reason, you don't want to buy a computer that has less RAM than you need right this minute, plus a litte extra to allow you to grow. So why not just go big, and max out the RAM? A couple of reasons: it takes battery power in proportion to its size, produces waste heat in proportion to its size, and quickly increases the cost of a system.

Storage space: This is where the computer holds permanent data, such as your files, photos, and applications. Your netbook comes with some fixed amount of storage space, but it is far less limiting than built-in RAM, because it is very easily and transparently expanded. For example, you could use flash cards, thumb drives, secure digital drives (SDDs), and a variety of other means of storing your data. How you weigh storage memory and size in your buying decision is mostly a matter of convenience and preference.

External peripherals: You can connect a lot of things to your netbook using standard USB technology, but you can also connect things such as external monitors or televisions with VGA Out. This makes netbooks really great command and control centers for multimedia productions and intelligent, user-tailored learning tools. If you want to do things of this sort, specialized connectivity options are a key buying factor.

Start by learning which operating systems a netbook comes with, because chances are you'll have a definite preference about this. For example, in Figure 1-1, you see that the smallest of the Asus netbooks is Linux only. (You can explore these resources in more depth here: http://usa.asus.com/products_compare.aspx). This may be a deal breaker for you if you have a strong Windows preference or you have to work with some Windows-only applications.

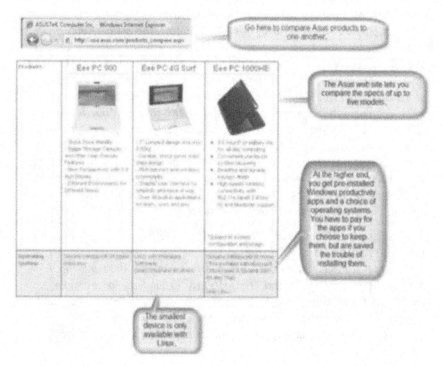

Figure 1-1. Learning about operating system and preinstalled software options using the Asus Product Comparison web site.

Next, find out how much RAM and data storage you'll have (see Figure 1-2). These features matter because they determine what your netbook will be able to do and how well it will perform certain tasks. For example, if you like to download music, you need a fairly large amount of data storage, because audio files tend to be large. If you like to watch streaming video, you may need a fairly large amount of RAM (1GB or more), because this will help keep video playback smooth and continuous.

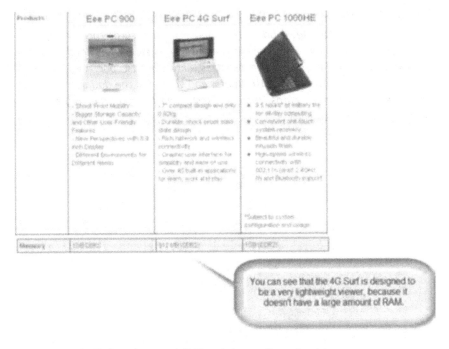

Figure 1-2. Find out how much RAM and storage the netbook has.

You need to know how much data the netbook can store *locally*. Asus (and other vendors) offer cloud-based data storage that vastly enlarges the amount of data to which you have access, but you can only interact with this storage while connected to the Internet. Sometimes these expanded storage numbers are advertised in a way that makes it seem like they are going to be right there on the device all of the time. When you are using the netbook *offline,* the only data and applications you'll be able to access are the ones that are physically stored on the device. If you want to do things like watch downloaded video or listen to music, you'll need fairly beefy local storage. Note that you might be able to compensate for lack of local storage if the netbook supports common external storage media, such as USB drives or flash cards.

There are various ways of describing how much storage a netbook offers, as shown in Figure 1-3. Generally, access times will be fastest for built-in storage like hard disk drives and solid state drives. See the sidebar later in this chapter.

ExplainED

Flash cards: (Nope, not the kind for learning multiplication tables!) Flash cards are small, durable, solid state memory storage cards that are often used with digital cameras, handheld computers, music players, and mobile phones. They come in several shapes, sizes, and storage capacities, and are prized for their convenience, sturdiness, and value for the dollar. You may also see them called PC cards, compact flash, smart media, memory sticks, or secure digital (SD) cards.

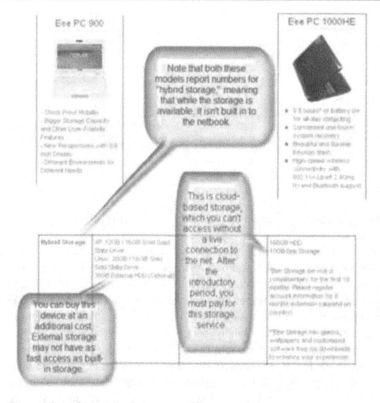

Figure 1-3. Looking at local storage options.

ExplainED

What's the difference between a hard disk drive and a solid state drive (SSD)? Basically, two words: moving parts. Hard disks are stacks of thin metal disks, which are mounted on a spindle and coated with a veneer of metallic oxides. When a computer "writes" to a hard disk, it does so by creating tiny areas of magnetism in the metallic veneer for each "bit" it records. In order to read the data back off the disk, the drive spins (like a DVD or CD) under a read head that senses the varying magnetic states of tracks in the veneer and converts these back into data. This is important because it means in order for your data to remain intact, the integrity of the veneer must be nearly perfect. If you drop a hard disk drive or treat a computer roughly while it is operating, it is possible to damage the coating and corrupt or destroy the data recorded. Hard disks have gotten fairly sturdy over the years, but they are still the weakest link in any mobile device, which is why a lot of people prefer to avoid them and use SSDs instead.

SSDs aren't actually "drives" at all, because they have no moving parts. The reason they are called drives is to help consumers understand their purpose. SSDs are composed of chips not unlike those used for RAM, but they are non-volatile, which means that they store information even if the computer is powered off, rebooted, or the battery runs completely down, and they typically aren't quite as fast as the chips used for RAM. They make a computer very, very much more durable, lighter (because there is no requirement for a motor to spin disks or a cooling fan), more battery efficient, and usually, noticeably faster.

A netbook is potentially a very powerful mobile office or media display device, so chances are you'll eventually want to be able to connect yours to all manner of peripheral devices: headphones, webcams, speakers, screens, storage media, and the like. The ability to make these connections is one of the few things you really can't change about your netbook. Either it comes with built-in support or you are out of luck. Think ahead about the different connection options you may want to have: USB for most devices, VGA for screens, audio jack for headphones, Ethernet ports for wired Internet, and so on (see Figure 1-4).

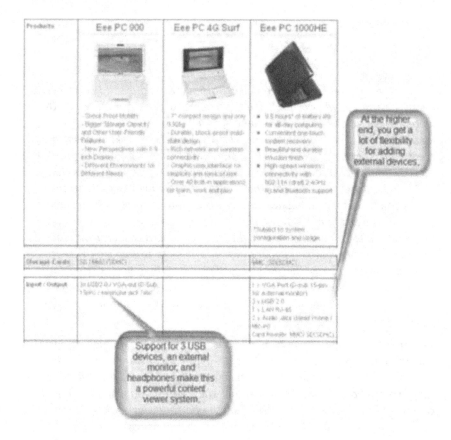

Figure 1-4. Find out what sort of devices you can connect to the netbook before you buy, because you can't retrofit support that is missing or inadequate to your needs.

Physical Characteristics

Physical characteristics include things like dimensions, weight, and battery type. Battery type matters because it determines how long the device can go between charges and how much it will weigh. (The battery accounts for at least half of the netbook's overall weight.) Weight and size matter a lot, and it's worth talking about the differing measurements manufacturers use to report their specs, as seen in Figure 1-5. (Is this done on purpose, to dissuade direct comparison? Don't know). Keep in mind when shopping that 1 kilogram equals approximately 2.5 pounds, and 1 inch is about 2.5 centimeters.

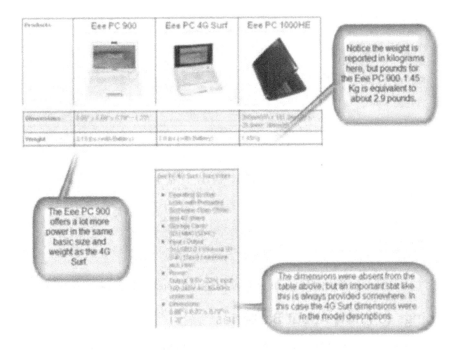

Figure 1-5. The size and weight of a netbook has everything to do with how portable it is on the one hand, and how usable it is on the other. This is a key trade-off decision for most people.

Aside from impacting weight, battery technology is a key feature of netbooks. Lithium ion batteries have many advantages over other technologies and are widely used for small mobile devices. See Figure 1-6.

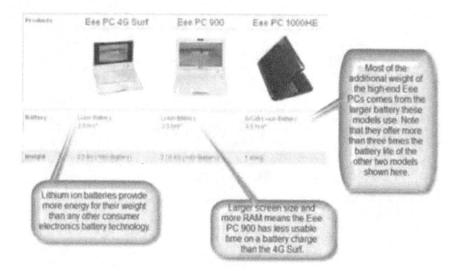

Figure 1-6. Battery technology is another important consideration to make.

Things to Know About Batteries

Lithium-ion (Li-ion) batteries are popular for use in netbooks because

- they are easily molded into most any shape and size, so they efficiently fill space in the devices they power;
- they are much lighter than other batteries of the same chemical type;
- they do not suffer from the battery memory effect, a property which can dramatically impair the charge retention ability of a battery if it is recharged improperly by the user; and
- they have a low self-discharge rate of approximately 5% per month, meaning that once charged, they don't lose significant amounts of charge from sitting around unused.

Li-ion batteries do have a couple of disadvantages, though. First, their "freshness" matters. Although a charged Li-ion battery doesn't lose charge by sitting around, its capacity to take a charge lessens over time. The older it is, the less charge it can take. Also, heat accelerates permanent loss of charging capacity, and all computers generate excess heat. After a certain period of time and use, you'll have to replace a Li-ion battery, regardless of the number of charge cycles it has experienced.

Things to Know About Screens

When it comes to screens, size matters. At the small end, netbooks screens measure about 7 inches diagonally. At this size, if you set your web browser to display an entire page (the browser window displays a whole page at once, without requiring scrolling), fonts are extremely compact. For all but those users with the best vision and in the best lighting conditions, text will be very difficult to read. In addition, ordinary video production techniques begin to break down as screen sizes get much smaller than this, which means that a 7-inch screen might not provide a good viewing experience for streaming video, because the playback window may not get to use the entire screen. Figure 1-7 shows examples of screen specs.

Bottom line: screen size preference is a very personal choice, because more than any other single thing, it defines both *usability* (in terms of the visual experience) and *portability* (because extremely small screens help achieve lighter weight and extended battery life). Hands-on experience is the only possible way to determine which is going to deliver the right combination of features and user experience for you.

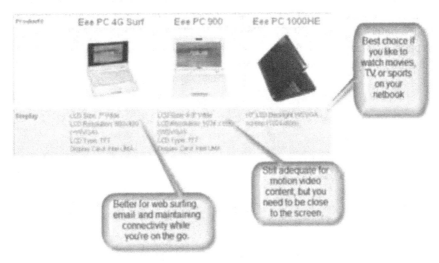

Figure 1-7. If you like to watch a lot of motion video, go for a screen of 9 inches or larger.

Things to Know About Keyboards

Keyboard size is often expressed in two ways for netbooks: the overall dimensions and as a percentage of the size of a normal desktop or laptop keyboard, exclusive of the numeric keypad. Usability research has shown that with less than 90% "standard" keyboard size, productivity apps such as word processors and spreadsheets become much more difficult to use. On a netbook, the keyboard will be something between 85 and 96% of the size of a typical laptop keyboard. For some people, this is extremely critical, either because they use the keyboard extensively, especially the numeric keypad, or they have large hands.

This has been sort of a "hot button" issue among reviewers, and the discussion can be confusing. Here's why: by definition, in the United States, a "standard" keyboard has either 101 or 104 keys. However, many laptops use abbreviated sets of keys, resulting in smaller keyboards. What is fairly uniform across laptops and desktops is the *size of an individual key,* which has largely been determined by the size of an average fingertip. Netbooks, at least the smaller ones, reduce the size of individual keys, which can take some getting used to. If this is a consideration for you, your key resource in the specs is the overall dimensional measurement of a given model. If you can't actually touch a device before you buy, try arranging your hands in keyboarding position inside a space the size of a candidate's keyboard and see if you like the feel. Figure 1-8 shows examples of keyboard specs.

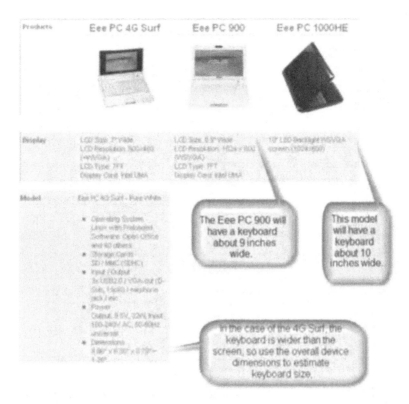

Figure 1-8. For most netbooks, the keyboard is about the same width as the screen. The exception to this rule arises when the device has a very small screen.

Connectivity

These specs tell you where and how you'll be able to connect to the Internet; which accessory devices you can use, such as headsets; and which peripherals you can add on (think printers, digital tablets, supplementary keyboards, and screens). These specs also indicate what you'll have to consider when making sure that access to your device and data are properly secured. See Figure 1-9.

Figure 1-9. Types of connectivity provided by a netbook may be an important factor in buying decisions, particularly for business.

It is not uncommon for premium devices to include connection by infrared (IR) port as well. It's not for everybody, but IR support has some advantages: it is less susceptible to eavesdropping or unintended pairing than Bluetooth; it is less subject to interference than the wireless ends of the spectrum; and it is a really spiffy way to cordlessly connect to peripherals like printers and mice.

Another really great high-end feature, and one you should definitely consider if you can find a device that has it and that meets your other requirements, is IEEE 802.11n wireless networking support. This new wireless networking standard builds on previous 802.11 (802.11b or 802.11g) standards by adding the ability to move data much more quickly and be far less vulnerable to "noise." This can be a really big advantage in places where there are a lot of electronic devices working or where your contact with a wireless hotspot is susceptible to interference.

Media Support

Screen size, resolution, color characteristics, and audio quality have everything to do with how much you'll be able to use and enjoy your netbook for entertainment, gaming, and video "telepresence" purposes. *Telepresence* is a recently coined term for a convergence of technologies that helps providers such as medical personnel, teachers, and professionals deliver services and collaborate using videoconferencing, shared desktop technology, and remote sensing instruments.

Types of connectivity provided by a netbook may be an important factor in buying decisions, particularly for business. See Figure 1-10.

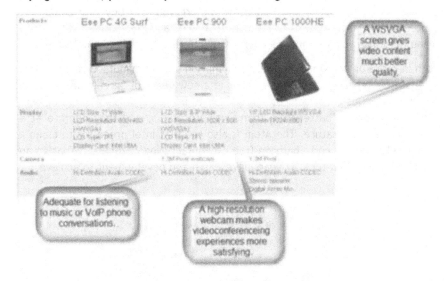

Figure 1-10. The quality of content viewing and creation experiences depend on the media capabilities of the netbook.

Green Technology

You can vote for a healthy environment with your dollars. In fact, you can do more to improve the state of the planet by being a discerning consumer than you can by almost any other means. Most manufacturers provide information about how well and how broadly they comply with existing environmental guidance and regulation.

One of the leaders in creating green options for netbook is Hewlett Packard (HP), and its list of environmental compliance and green product design certifications is truly impressive. Though the HP MiniNote netbooks are definitely at the high end of the price spectrum, it is gratifying to know that some of that cost went into making a product that is safe, clean, and has a lifecycle design that is both green and sustainable.

Another exciting green technology to keep in mind is Intel's Atom processor (see Figure 1-11). The processor is the heart of the computer, it is what performs all of the key tasks: running the operating sytem and all of the applications, telling the hard drive what information to store, recognizing when a new peripheral is attached, and so on. The processor draws a lot of power from the system, because it's constantly in use, and it generates a lot of heat, meaning that it may need a dedicated fan to cool it. There is another big green problem with processors, and that comes before you ever buy your computer: processors are incredibly tricky things to make, and they usually demand a manufacturing cycle requiring dangerous chemicals such as lead and halogen.

Both in terms of its own low power consumption and its manufacturing process, Intel's Atom processor is the forerunner in a new genre of "green" information technologies. Designed from the ground up to be power misers, Atom devices can achieve longer battery life than rival processors, and they operate at a much cooler temperature. The Atom is also the first Intel processor to claim a completely lead- and halogen-free manufacturing process. That's an accomplishment that took six years of research and development to achieve.

Figure 1-11. Consumer choices matter to the environment. Intel's low power, low heat Atom processor is the greenest CPU ever built.

The Shopping List: Define Your Needs and Expectations and Buy Smart

Before you set out shopping, take the time to arm yourself with a clear-eyed analysis of what you want to accomplish with your new netbook. Not only is there a broad spectrum of uses for which these tiny powerhouses are designed, but they come with matching price tags. There is no point in paying for more than you will realistically need from your device. Netbooks are likely to become commoditized very quickly, so buy what you need right now, even if you will outgrow it in the future. Chances are, next year's netbooks will have interesting new features and declining price points that will make it easy to accommodate your growing sophistication and skill level. In this section, I outline several basic patterns of use. These highlight shopping considerations and spell out what you do and don't need to comfortably, productively, and enjoyably use your netbook for some common activities.

I have also included tables in Appendix A for comparing the different netbook models. In the shopping points tables for each type of netbook user, the tables tell you where to look in the published specs for a given product to find out whether a netbook will fit your needs. Using these tables, you can narrow down to a few candidates on the web. After you do so, you can go have a hands-on look at your favorites, fully equipped to be in charge of your choice. This is a really good way to head into a brick and mortar electronics retailer, because it is easy to be confused and overwhelmed by the claims of sales people.

Lowest Cost

For some of us, it simply comes down to a matter of dollars and cents. If you want a netbook, but need to absolutely hold the line on the budget, chances are you'll be looking at a device with a 7 to 8-inch screen, exclusively solid state storage, and a keyboard that is about 86% the size of that of a full-sized laptop. As of the time of this writing, there are devices in this class that sell for well under $200. In most cases you'll get a version of Linux on a device in this price class.

My advice to you, *and this is strictly my opinion,* is that there is no reason for anyone to be intimidated by Linux these days. Particularly in the case of Ubuntu, Linux is easy to learn and use, with a graphical user interface not unlike that of Windows or Mac. There are tons of free apps of all sorts available for Linux, including things like word processing, database, and spreadsheet tools. Because they were first popular in Asia, where consumers tend to be extremely price-sensitive, most of the pioneering netbooks ran on one sort of

Linux or another, because it cost manufacturers very little to use it. This means that as far as the netbook platform goes, Linux is mature and time-tested operating system.

Lightest, Smallest, and Leanest

There's an old joke in the software engineering business, and it's often seen posted on the wall of engineering labs. It's funny because it's still true, and will always be true. It reads

- Good
- Cheap
- Fast

Pick any two.

Indeed, if you want the lightest, leanest, leading-edge netbook, it's going to cost you. This is a choice for someone who prizes style, power, and up-to-the minute technology, and is willing to pay for it. For the best of breed in this niche, you may well be looking at something in excess of $1,000. I've tested a couple of the devices in this class, and I have to admit they are extremely hard to part with when I receive the dreaded FedEx return label.

Entertainment: Music, Movies, Television, Sports, and News

Netbooks shine as a convergence technology, especially where entertainment is concerned. Their screens are big enough that you can watch and enjoy a movie or television show, provided the ambient lighting is good and you aren't far away. They are incredibly convenient for this purpose, because you can watch a few minutes when you have time and then return later and pick up where you left off. Most have decent audio, and some of them have phenomenally good audio.

Basically, netbooks were designed with content viewing as a key use, and so you can find a device that gives you a really nice media experience in almost any price class. As you scale up in cost, you start to see enhanced features, like the ability to output digital video to another device or to drive additional external speakers. If you plan to do several things with your netbook, chances are good that this will be the easiest of all the potential uses to satisfy.

Kids and Families

This use pattern is distinct from most of the rest because it assumes the netbook is probably going to be shared among family members. There are several good reasons for doing this, and I heartily encourage you to think about doing this if you feel it could work in your clan. First of all, it is less expensive to own one device than many, and by this I don't simply mean the initial purchase price. There are always hidden and unanticipated costs of ownership for computers: multiple copies of software licenses, add-on hardware like headsets or game controllers, and the like. Having one batch is cheaper, and there is nothing wrong with learning to share or take turns. Second, and of more particular importance in cases where preteen and younger children will be using the netbook, if you all share a family device, it will be a good deal easier for you to monitor your children's surfing habits and contacts. It is impossible to overstate the importance of this sort of supervision, and it is going to seem far less intrusive to kids if you are sharing a netbook. (Parents, please do read and ponder Chapter 7. There are some unfortunate but sobering facts to be learned there that will help you keep your children and teens safe from others, and from themselves.)

Travelers

Next to one of those "good the world over" credit cards and the right pair of shoes, there is nothing more essential to pack when you are taking off for a trip of long duration than a netbook. You can literally roam all over the world, including to remote places, and keep your life, your business, and your trip on track with a trusty netbook in your satchel.

It is prolix to say that when you travel, in many places, the local criminally entrepreneurial set is sizing you up as a potential victim. For this reason, you want to make sure your netbook and its contents are as hard to steal as you can make them. Many models come equipped with devices that make them easy to lock down, either when they are traveling around in your luggage or when you have them out and are using them. In addition, it is very much worth taking steps to make sure that if the netbook is lost or stolen, nobody can cull useful information from it. I recommend choosing a netbook that either has integrated support for biometric logon identification (usually a thumbprint reader) or can be configured to use a third-party key like a USB device.

This kind of secure logon is known as *two-factor authentication*. Authentication means that you can definitively prove who you are. The *two-factor* part means you *have* something (like the USB key or your thumb) and you *know* something (like a password). If you take care to store the USB key away from the netbook, this is a very simple, virtually unbeatable method of securing your data.

Students and Teachers

Some of the most impressive academic innovations to come down the road in a long while are being built on a foundation of netbook hardware and cloud-based instruction, reference materials, and enrichment curriculums. In the UK, this effort is achieving impressive results with netbooks designed using the Intel consortium's Classmate PC Reference design. These programs are supported with extensive teacher training and preparation and are helping meet the needs of kids in underserved areas or underperforming schools. In the United States, the Fresno, California union school district has launched a pilot program using 10,000 HP netbooks to help kids there catch up and to receive enrichment instruction in advanced subjects.

By the time this book goes to press, it is a safe bet there *won't* be a program like this near you. However, these examples are instructive. It has never been cheaper, easier, or more important to give children access to the best education they can get. Netbooks are the most cost-effective way to do this we've seen yet. With the right planning, training, and supervision, these devices can be a boon to students in their preteens and older. If you have a kid going off to college and can't spring $1,000 on a fancy laptop, buy them a netbook instead. (They may not be able to pop in a DVD to watch a movie, but then that wasn't why you wanted to see them in college in the first place, but on the other hand you can always buy them an external combo drive.)

Most kids can benefit from information that may help keep them safer on the Internet, and to know how to avoid the more predictable Internet blunders. Please read Chapter 7 for more on keeping kids safe on the Internet.

Field Research

Because they are off-the-shelf, mostly standard platform, netbooks have more to offer field researchers in the natural and social sciences than anything that's burst on the scene since accurate, low-cost GPS. It is no overstatement to say that there are many studies that can be dramatically extended in their reach or are even being made possible by the price differential between netbooks and laptops. Depending on which devices you pick, you might be able to equip more investigators using netbooks and cloud-based services than you could using laptops and licensed local copies of software tools.

Backpack Journalists

Netbooks are key tools for backpack journalists, partly because they are powerful and conveniently mobile. In less sanguine settings, they have the advantage of being relatively easily concealed. It's important to understand the limitations of a netbook for these purposes. For example, you can certainly use them to record interviews, in some cases to take photos, or to capture short video segments and assemble these into digital compositions for web-based distribution. They are less well suited to any heavy duty editing or manipulation of data intensive content.

If you are involved in the sort of journalism that has the potential to be very controversial, consider getting a netbook that supports biometric logon or two-factor authentication. (See the section "Travelers" earlier in this chapter.) This way, if your netbook is lost, stolen, or confiscated, you have a better chance of retaining control over your information and your sources' identities.

Gamers: Multiplayer Mobile Gaming

Chances are, the die-hard mobile gamer already has something optimized for that purpose in a way that a netbook isn't now and won't be anytime soon. This kind of use is a classic case of convergence, though. If you are a student trying to stretch your dollars as far as they'll go, you'll get more for your money with a netbook that can help you study, entertain you, and provide a little gaming on the side as well. In addition, gamers that currently play connected mobile games based on phones could save a good deal of money in airtime charges by switching to web-based play.

Eldercare

As the world population ages, strains on elder-caregiver resources loom. Research has shown that most elders do best and are happiest if they can remain in their own homes as long as possible. It is also far and away the preference of this population to live independently. Simple, easily portable, and always-on, netbooks provide a platform for systems that could vastly improve the ability of caregivers to monitor and support larger numbers of in-home elders, ensure that key medications are taken on schedule, and frequently assess the status of fragile elders.

Until institutional programs and supports arrive, netbooks could be just the resource elders and adult children need to stay in touch. They can provide an easy and visual connectedness; perform as a central repository for medical records and prescription information; maintain up-to-date contact information;

and help caregivers and elders keep track of events such as doctor's appointments. Setting an elderly relative up with a netbook equipped for VoIP, video conferencing, email, and Internet access could be the best investment you make toward their well-being and your peace of mind. See Chapter 4 for more on setting up Skype and other applications.

Public Safety/Public Service Delivery

No one who was old enough to sit in front of a television at the time of Hurricane Katrina, the Virginia Tech Massacre, or the Santa Barbara wildfires has any doubts about how important communication is in a time of crisis. Netbooks have the advantage of being relatively direct and low tech as security solutions. Most can connect to the Internet via Wi-Fi or Ethernet cable. Many are Bluetooth-enabled, providing a short-distance networking protocol that has a reach of around 30 feet and the advantage of being completely silent and inconspicuous. In an institution like a school or hospital, netbooks can connect to wireless hotspots on a private network. Most have cameras and many can capture video and audio.

In addition to allowing first responders to provide rich, complete, and timely status information to remote support, netbooks can provide important coordination by letting people caught in perilous situations know about additional threats or routes to safety. They can also provide a conduit for the delivery of emergency medical advice, probable arrival time of health and safety responders, and tactical advice. Netbooks are better suited to this purpose than laptops, because of their small size and long battery life.

Mobile Productivity

Mobile productivity tools can pay for a netbook in a week if you commute using public transportation or fly frequently. The key difference between a netbook and a laptop for purposes of getting things done on the road is how much *longer* you have to get them done using your netbook, and the convenient portability. If you are working offline, you can count on up to six hours from the better netbooks. To me, what's better still, is that although I may not use the six hours in a single stretch, I am far less likely to get powered off using the netbook intermittently over an extended period of time than I am if doing the same things with a laptop. The reason this matters is that I can sometimes go several days without having to find a place to stop, plug in, and recharge. This, in addition to its lighter weight and smaller size, just makes me more willing to pop my netbook into a purse or backpack so that I can stay connected using odd bits of time. Dragging a laptop around seems pretty onerous by comparison, at least on a day-to-day basis.

What makes the netbook solution attractive is that there are a lot of cloud-based services I can use on my netbook that deliver every bit of the sophistication, power, and flexibility of any application I have running at home on my "big iron" systems, but I don't have to worry about storing (or licensing or updating) these applications on my netbook. I can get all of this as a service, either free or for a nominal fee from vendors who not only specialize in providing high availability application services, they also back up my data and offer a six sigma guarantee (a statistical measure of quality that says there will be about 3.4 defects per million opportunities to perform a task) on *its* availability and integrity. See Chapter 3 to learn more about these services.

Business: Mobilize Your Business Processes

Netbooks offer businesses a terrific opportunity in terms of using a relatively inexpensive, standard mobile computing device to extend services; evolve siloed custom solutions for automation; exploit new wireless technologies such as smart cards and Radio Frequency ID tags; create robust mobile solutions for environments where wall power is inaccessible, rarely available, or dirty; and open new markets, based on inexpensive, pervasive computing presence (think health care, chain of custody tracking for shipping, and food and drug safety). This is all made possible because the netbook's confluence of low price, low power, and low barriers to mainstream PC software developers makes many new genres of mobilized applications possible in the near future.

From a solution architect's point of view, exploiting the strategic value of netbooks is a straightforward matter of identifying their strengths and matching them to potential areas of business process application. If current solutions are Windows-based, retargeting these apps to netbooks won't incur any retraining costs to get users up to speed, nor is the burden of support and administration likely to climb. In terms of purchase price performance, netbooks outperform traditional laptops and notebooks by at least two to one, so you halve acquisition costs on the first day. The more capable netbooks are very flexible in terms of network connectivity and external device support.

Netbooks give workers who spend a lot of time in harsh or remote environments a big advantage, because they can function for significantly longer on a charge.

Business: Lowest Total Cost of Ownership

One of the big, near-term trajectories for netbooks is enterprise use as thin clients in mobile business process support solutions. Using netbooks to cheaply mobilize user-facing components of distributed apps, for example a web-based front end to an enterprise inventory database, offers big benefits. As a client device, they have far greater power, flexibility and sophistication than similarly priced smartphones, and web-based solutions can eliminate airtime charges associated with phone networks. Another big advantage of netbooks as business process support tools is that they logically and functionally mesh with existing server side administrative tools and policies. The most popular products will run either a Windows system, XP Vista, or Windows 7, or variants of Linux. All of these enjoy mature, robust, fully integrated security models, making them targets of choice for mobilizing enterprise apps. In contrast to most smartphone and PDA-based enterprise solutions, Atom devices are relatively easy to administer, configure, secure, and provision.

From a software developer's point of view, there are only two significant differences between netbooks and other PCs: display size and power management issues. These are both key considerations, as no application can expect to be successful on a netbook-class device without solid, well-designed strategies for each. However, this still allows extensive reuse of existing i86 business logic; some existing interface design; and much of existing security policy and implementation. Infrastructure reusability translates to reduced testing cost and rapid deployment for enterprise apps mobilized on netbooks. These factors combine to make netbook apps the safest, most predictable, and most fiscally conservative path for mobilizing traditional enterprise client server systems.

Best Spots for Hot Deals on Netbooks

I've discussed a lot about the different types of netbooks available, so now I'm going to look at the best places to buy them. A lot of the netbook manufacturers have great direct sales sites, and many can be found in brick and mortar outlets including Best Buy, Costco, Staples, and Office Max. However, it just seems to make sense to shop for your cloud-based information and media appliance in the cloud. Here are three really good bets for finding a deal and getting a feel for what the price competition on various devices is at any given point in time.

Amazon.com

You'll find a really large, though not comprehensive, population of netbooks for sale at Amazon.com (see Figure 1-12). If you buy a new device, Amazon has a peerless reputation for delivering quickly and standing behind what it sells. If you choose a used or refurbished product, it's more of a case of "buyer beware."

Figure 1-12. Amazon.com carries a huge variety of netbook products and buy options.

Pricewatch.com

You probably need to be at least mildly geeky to like Pricewatch.com (see Figure 1-13), but it is absolutely the last word in deal shopping when it comes to computers, peripherals, and parts. Prices in the netbook space are either so competitive or so rigid that you may not gain tons of discounts by going this route, but it's worth a look, especially if you may need to add some cool but esoteric gadgets to your netbook kit.

Figure 1-13. Pricewatch.com updates its list of prices and suppliers several times a day.

EBay and Other Third-Party Used Netbook Outlets

If you are shopping on price alone, the temptation to buy used or refurbished products is going to be huge. Computers are notoriously subject to sticker shock, so the discounts can be really deep. There is always the chance you'll get a real steal, but if you don't get a long guarantee and iron clad return option on the battery, chances are good you'll get burned going this route. The problem with used netbooks (or smartphones or other battery powered devices) is that it is difficult to tell whether you have a dying battery until you've had a device for a while. Replacing a battery is typically pretty costly, so any savings you get on the purchase price will be wiped out if this is necessary. Unless you are certain about the condition of the equipment or have a no-questions-asked return policy, it's wisest to buy new.

Meet the Leading Netbook Manufacturers And Their Products

In this section we'll cover the leading manufacturers of netbooks and give you the lowdown on what to expect from them and any pros and cons to going with one brand over another. More and more manufacturers are jumping on the netbook bandwagon, so you may encounter more names on the Net than you'll find here, but this list will cover the current market leaders.

Acer

Acer has made a name for itself in the broader PC and laptop market by delivering value for the dollar, and it is right on course with strategy in the netbook space as well. As of this writing, Acer's Aspire One netbook series prices out at or below the nearest equivalent of its direct competitors. Like the netbook lines of other vendors, Acer's Aspire One model offers lots of optional features and enhancements. Direct competitors include products from Asus, Dell, and MSI Wind. The Aspire One series comes in a variety of colors, and this is one frill that is probably well worth taking advantage of, particularly if you are shopping for kids. These little netbooks are such a bargain that lots of them will be popping up at school, libraries, and the like. The personalization features make it a little easier for your netbook to look distinctive, in case it gets set down next to a similar box. You can find Acer Aspire specs at us.acer.com.

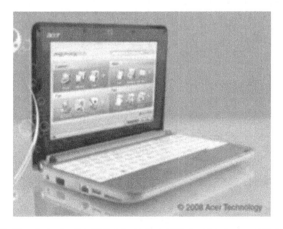

Figure 1-14. The Acer Aspire One comes in a variety of colors and is a value packed little unit, with the lowest price points in its class.

Asus

Asus offers consumers more personalization and feature options than any netbook manufacturer in the space. See Figure 1-15. You literally can design exactly the solution you need, want, and are willing to pay for. This is a great advantage if you are considering one or two features that are characteristic of high-end netbooks, but don't want to shell out for the rest of the kit because you may not be able to use it all.

Shopping the Asus product line is a job in itself, but luckily Asus provides a really useful product comparison chart that lays out each of their two dozen or so netbooks in a way that makes it (relatively) easy to see where your range of choices should map out.

You can find that chart here: `http://event.asus.com/eeepc/comparison/eeepc_comparison.htm`

It is downloadable in PDF format, and I recommend doing this. If nothing else, it will sharpen your spec-reading skills. (Um, yes I *am* kidding....) The real reason I recommend downloading the Asus specs is so that you can print them. This is such an extensive amount of information that you'll want to go over it with a highlighter to identify the models you are going to consider. If you are like most people, you'll find that there are probably a few things on your wish list that don't add a lot of cost to the system you think you need, but would provide a lot of added productivity or convenience. You can find Asus specs at www.asus.com/products.aspx.

Figure 1-15. Asus Eee PC 904HA netbook features a9 inch screen and all day battery life.

Dell

The Dell Inspiron series has a lot of nice features, and competes at the more affordable end of the price spectrum with Acer, Asus, and MSI Wind products. See Figure 1-16. However, all other things being equal, give this brand a hard look if you care about environmentally friendly products and proactive technology leadership.

Dell has made significant investments in corporate green-ness, pioneering a consumer electronics recycling program along with big-box office supply vendor Staples. In many cities you can drop off unwanted electronics at Staples locations for safe disposal. This is no small deal, because an old fashioned CRT monitor can contain up to 10 pounds of lead. Most computer chips (of which there are dozens in each and every system) contain the basic ingredients for an instant, stir and serve toxic cocktail of heavy metals: just add ground water and jostle around. Which is, of course, exactly what happens when computers and peripherals get pitched into a landfill or dumped offshore. You can find the specs for Dell's Mini 9 at www.dell.com/content/products.

Dell has of the following programs to make sure that technology manufacturing is as benign as possible:

- It allows for the free return of all Dell-branded equipment. In addition, Dell has programs that accept any make or model of computer, monitor, printer, or peripheral.
- Dell also offers customers free donation programs for unwanted functional computers. (This one depends on where you live.) You can donate your used or unwanted computer to the National Cristina Foundation (NCF). NCF aids disabled and economically disadvantaged children and adults in your community. NCF picks up your computer at your doorstep, repurposes it, and then Dell gives you a 10 percent discount off your next software or peripheral purchase.
- Dell designs its own manufacturing processes to minimize carbon footprint, waste, toxic solvents and other nasty effluent. They choose suppliers and partners at least partially based on their use of the same sort of practices and accountability.

Figure 1-16. Dell's Mini 9 comes in a variety of fun finishes.

Hewlett Packard

HP's Mini-Note series, shown in Figure 1-17, is designed for enterprise and educational markets. These devices are extremely customizable and offer a lot of options that make them easier to integrate into enterprise or institutional infrastructure than some of the more consumer-oriented devices. One particular strength of the Mini-Note series is its emphasis on security. Standard features include:

- configuration control hardware
- memory change alert
- ownership tag
- setup password
- power-on password
- Kensington lock slot

HP gives a respectable performance in the environmental friendliness category. The company has an encyclopedic listing of the national and international energy conservation, clean manufacturing, and recycling directives with which it complies posted on its Mini Note site.

It wouldn't be an HP if it didn't have some snazzy, leading edge technology, and this product line has one that many traveling business people will find very convenient. You can do a 90% recharge of the Mini-Note in about 90 minutes, using HP's Fast Charge technology. The system has to be off (meaning you can't charge this fast while you are actually using the thing, but are plugged into wall current), but this is still pretty impressive. Who hasn't drained the battery on a laptop late at night, and turned in without remembering to recharge? With the Mini Note, you can get a good charge in about the time it takes to get a start on the day. You can find the Mini Note specs at www.hp.com.

© 2009 Hewlett Packard

Figure 1-17. The HP Mini Note is a premium entrant in the netbook space. It's a very high quality product, and offers business and institutional users a high degree of customization and support.

Intel Classmate PC Reference Design

Intel doesn't actually manufacture the Classmate PCs, but it did create this *reference design* for low-cost laptops (aka netbooks), and more specifically, low-cost laptops designed to be used for educational purposes. A *reference design* is a pattern that someone else can use to build a system. Intel's Classmate PC design has enabled several third-party manufacturers to produce standardized, low-cost netbooks and label them with their own brands. Most are variations of the reference design to some degree, which allows the manufacturers to compete on feature sets and customization instead of setting up "race to the bottom" price competition.

Key features of Classmate PC-based netbooks are:

- They can be used like a digital tablet or like an ordinary laptop. When opened like a laptop, the screen swivels 180 degrees so that a single Classmate PC is easily shared among students.
- High-end Classmate PCs offer an 8.9-inch touch screen.

- Standard OS software let's students write or draw directly on the screen.
- The built-in web cam rotates 180 degrees, so that if students share devices, they can all take part in a remotely delivered lesson or interaction.
- The Classmate PC is designed for portability and durability, is somewhat drop-proof (tested to 60 centimeters), and has a built-in handle and spill-resistant keyboard.

Classmate PCs can run either Linux or Windows XP Professional operating systems. Intel's reference design didn't include any features that definitely mandate a specific operating system. Many of these devices will be sold in the developing world where there is no existing Windows bias and where a few dollars difference in price can be compelling for consumers, so this was intentional, and designed to promote global adoption. Broad adoption decreases manufacturers' cost through economies of scale.

Figure 1-18. Intel's newest reference design for the Classmate PC features a design that allows the device to be used either as a tablet or as a traditional notebook. This allows the Classmate PC to be more easily shared among students.

Intel actively collaborates with educators and governments worldwide to ensure teachers are ready for Classmate PC netbooks in the classroom. See Figure 1-19 for one such collaboration in the U.K. Through joint efforts with its educational partners, the company develops and funds programs and reference designs for professional training of K through 12 teachers; math and science curriculum delivery; and community oriented distance-learning programs. Collectively, these programs constitute the Intel Learning Series, and include the hardware, software, and services to meet the needs of students and educators worldwide. To make these resources broadly available, Intel has invested heavily in comprehensive research on ethnographic and human factors, real-life use contexts, and collaborative local solutions. The Intel Learning Series designs are brought to specific niches of the global market as useful products and services, customized by local technology companies. Intel collaborates with its niche and locale-specific manufacturers and service providers, making sure the right infrastructure, external accessories, and software support the students and teachers that use them.

Read more about Classroom PC reference design specs at www.classmatepc.com/.

Figure 1-19. **Netbooks are taking hold as tools for delivery of education in countries around the world. This portal serves children through the UK with math and science curriculum enrichment and remediation.**

Lenovo

The Australian government just announced an initiative in which it will buy Lenovo IdeaPads for *every* student in Grade 9. Students get to keep the computers if they finish Grade 12. This is a pretty stunning commitment to a single vendor, and I have to admit it had me wondering, until I started looking into the features this line offers. Lenovo IdeaPads are feature rich and midrange in price, so if you are shopping exclusively for the killer deal, don't read this. It will make you cry. If you are willing to spend 30 percent more than the rock-bottom netbook costs you can get some or all of this:

- An energy efficient 10.1-inch LED backlit WSVGA screen.
- Dolby headphone technology with surround sound.
- A multi-touch navigation pad that allows you to enlarge, reduce, and edit images by drawing with your fingers.
- A nearly full-sized keyboard.
- The Lenovo Quick Start software platform that enables quick and easy access to frequently used apps such web browsers, email, Skype, and the like, *without* waiting for a full system boot.
- Lenovo's VeriFace face recognition software, which lets you make your face your password.
- Lenovo OneKey Rescue System, which restores your system from a crash or virus with one click.

This company also has a very credible environment friendliness stance. They extensively use recycled materials in their manufacturing process and also provide numerous options for consumers in managing lifecycles of computing equipment. You can find IdeaPad's specs at shop.lenovo.com/us/notebooks/ideapad

Figure 1-20. The Lenovo IdeaPad integrates a fixed position web cam to make video conference calls over the web a richer experience.

MSI Wind

In its most basic form, the MSI Wind is manufactured by Micro-Star International, a Taiwan-based computer hardware manufacturer best known for desktop computer motherboards. The name *Wind* stands for Wi-Fi Network Device. In a way, the MSI Wind occupies something like the same space as the Intel Classmate PC reference design. Although MSI sells the device directly to the public, it sells a lot more of them to other computer manufacturers who customize them for locale-specific markets and sell the Wind under other product names.

Given the fact that MSI really isn't that consumer-oriented a company (at least in terms of its North American businesses), you need to dig a bit to appreciate the finer features of the MSI Wind line of devices. One absolutely unique, stand-out feature the MSI Wind offers is *screen-magnifying technology*. Users can magnify words and images displayed on a region of the screen to make them more readable. This is obviously a key benefit for those with less than perfect vision, but it has other uses as well.

It's going to take web page designers a while to catch up with exploding populations of smartphones and netbooks. Redesigning web pages to be reasonably useful across a tremendous range of screen sizes is a big job. Until this task is handled, you can expect that some of your surfing experience to be sub-par. When important items of information (think maps, large tables, and images) don't display properly on the smaller screen of a netbook, being able to magnify a particular region could make information a lot more accessible to the average person.

If you are looking at the low-end of the netbook price spectrum, MSI Wind offers appealing value for the dollar. Their lowest priced model comes in a significantly below $300, *and* you get a 10-inch screen and keyboard for this price. If you are price-sensitive, enjoy a good cloud-based media experience, and aren't set on having the smallest box, the low-end Wind would be a good choice.

Green Literacy and the Three Rs: Reduce, Reuse, Recycle

We can each do things to make the earth a little less burdened by waste and pollution, and we can start doing them right away. Number one on that list of important, personal action items is to make informed, responsible choices when we buy high-tech items. There are some netbook manufacturers that hold themselves and their suppliers to an extremely high standard of environmental stewardship, and design products and manufacturing processes with sustainable environmental principles in mind. They take a proactive, hands-on approach, and make sure that computers are recycled or repurposed appropriately. At the very least, these pioneers deserve your respect, and probably your dollars as well.

The lesson here is that if you want to make a responsible selection both in *choosing* a future netbook and *choosing the future for your netbook when it is no longer serviceable,* you need to have a plan. Taking unwanted technology products to the annual "we recycle everything" day in your town is probably just a recipe for dumping the problem somewhere else and making yourself feel better. If you didn't buy from a vendor with a lifecycle management plan, there are still some useful resources that you can tap into.

The United States Environmental Protection Agency's (EPA) eCycling programs provide education and information about local eCyclers. If you need to dispose of old electronics (and this includes things that are not actually computers, such as microwaves, coffee pots, clock radios, and the like), they have a tool that will help you find a nearby solution. If you suspect recycling shenanigans, you can report them to the EPA. The EPA monitors the organizations and resources it posts on its eCycling portal. This isn't an absolute guarantee of integrity, but these recyclers do submit to a higher degree of scrutiny than most.

Another good option if you can't recycle your old technology is to pass it on to someone else who can benefit from it. The NCF is a not-for-profit organization that supports education and training for the disadvantaged and handicapped using donated technology. NCF matches donors and beneficiaries, giving new life to computers and technology equipment that has become obsolescent in its first place of use. Not only does this keep tech gear out of the waste stream, it has created a stable foundation for tech education in places where it is most needed.

Looking Ahead

Now you are set to realistically define your needs and shop for the right netbook. In each price range there are a lot of solid choices and much variety. Though you can do a dizzying number of things with a netbook the day you bring it home, the real power of these little boxes is in how you can customize and personalize them. In the next chapter I discuss add-ons and services that can help you turn your netbook into the ultimate personal entertainment appliance, a traveling office, or a social movement in a backpack.

Chapter 2

Getting Connected

What is the point of a netbook? The Net, of course! Among the most important aspects of netbook computers is how easy they make it to get connected, anywhere. In this chapter, you'll learn how to connect. The following topics are covered:

- Configuring Bluetooth
- Connecting to a 3G network
- Connecting to a wired network
- Connecting to a wireless network

Configuring Bluetooth

No matter how you connect your computer to the Internet, it may be necessary to use Bluetooth, especially if you want to connect your cell phone to your computer. So before I start talking about the way you connect your computer to the Internet using 3G on your cell phone, I'll talk about Bluetooth configuration.

This chapter is adapted from Chapter 3 of Sander van Vugt's Ubuntu Netbooks, Apress, 2009, and uses Ubuntu screens for the examples. However, the process is similar on Windows or other Unix systems, so readers on all platforms should find this information quite useful.

You can tell that your computer has Bluetooth if a Bluetooth icon appears in the panel at the top of the screen. If it doesn't, from the Preferences menu, open the Bluetooth item to access the available Bluetooth options (see Figure 2-1).

NotED

Some brands of netbook manufacturers don't have an internal Bluetooth adapter. For instance, the popular Acer Aspire One lacks this feature. If you haven't yet bought a netbook computer, make sure the one you buy has Bluetooth—it's a very convenient feature.

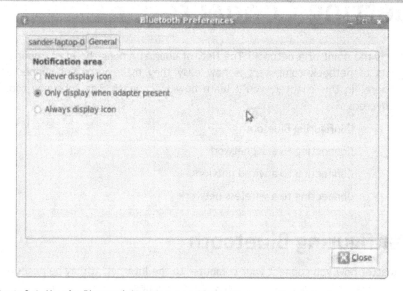

Figure 2-1. Use the Bluetooth icon to set up Bluetooth connection options.

The Bluetooth Preferences item offers two tabs with configuration options. First, you can specify when the Bluetooth icon should appear. The default setting displays the icon in the panel only when a Bluetooth adapter is present. You should probably keep it that way, because it offers the most convenient means of setting up a Bluetooth connection and it makes sense not to show the icon if no Bluetooth adapter is present. If for any reason you prefer not to use this option, select Never Display Icon if you never want to see the Bluetooth connection menu, or Always Display Icon if you always want to see it, regardless of whether an adapter is present.

After you specify whether you want to see the connection icon, you can specify visibility settings on your computer's configuration tab. In this window, you can configure two items. First is the visibility of your netbook computer. Other people who want to establish a link to your computer need to be able to see your computer before they can access it. If you want to exchange files with someone else, and the other person asks how to connect to your computer, you may choose to make your computer visible.

Be aware that Bluetooth visibility imposes a security risk; if your netbook is visible, anyone can try to make a connection to your computer—and you probably don't want that. If you need to make your computer visible so that others can connect to it, I recommend using the Temporary Visible option so you don't forget to turn visibility off again. When you do this, you can also specify how long you want your computer to be visible. Figure 2-2 shows the slide bar you use to define the amount of time your computer should be visible. The default value of 3 minutes is normally a good suggestion; 3 minutes should be long enough for others to connect to your computer.

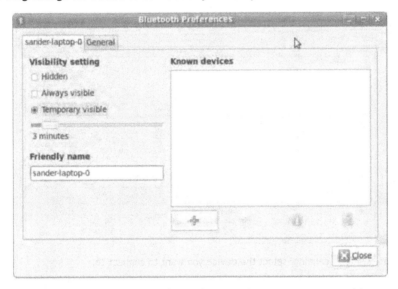

Figure 2-2. If others need to make a Bluetooth connection to your computer, it's a good idea to make it visible only temporarily.

To make a connection to your mobile phone so that you can use it as a modem to get on the Internet, you don't need the Visibility setting. Just click the + sign in the Bluetooth Preferences window to add the new Bluetooth connection. Doing so starts the Bluetooth Device Wizard, which in its first step shows a welcome message. In this window, click Forward to proceed.

Your neighborhood is now checked for available devices. Several devices may appear; if this is the case, make sure you wait until scanning for devices is complete. When it is, you should recognize the correct device by its name (see Figure 2-3).

Figure 2-3. After scanning, select the device you want to connect to.

Now, select the device. Use the Automatic PIN Code Selection option; it generates a PIN code for you automatically, which you need to use on the device to initiate the connection. When this PIN code is displayed, click Forward. At this point, you should see a message on your cell phone, indicating that your computer wants to establish a connection. Accept this request, and enter the PIN code that was generated by your netbook. Doing so initiates the connection (see Figure 2-4).

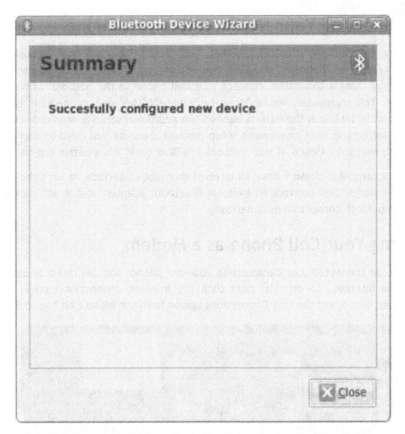

Figure 2-4. After you accept the incoming connection and enter the PIN code, your Bluetooth connection is established.

Connecting to a 3G network

Imagine that you want to be able to connect no matter where you are. In that case, using a 3G network is probably your best option. 3G works over virtually any cell phone network, so the setup requirements are minimal.

There are different ways to connect to a 3G network. The easiest way is to use the 3G available on many modern cell phones. You'll read about configuring this in the next section. Another method is to connect a 3G USB dongle to your netbook. When you do this, the configuration is similar to the configuration with a mobile phone.

Connecting Your Netbook to a Cell Phone

Before you can dial in to the Internet, you need to connect your netbook to your cell phone. Basically, you have two options: using USB or using Bluetooth. If you're using a USB cable, connect your cell phone to the netbook with that cable. Your computer will automatically detect the new connection type. Connecting by USB is the easiest method—no additional setup is required—but it may not be the most convenient setup method, because you need to carry an additional cable. Hence, if your netbook has Bluetooth, it's a better option.

If your computer doesn't have an internal Bluetooth interface, it isn't the end of the world. Just connect an external Bluetooth adapter, and it will pick up the Bluetooth connection automatically.

Using Your Cell Phone as a Modem

If you've connected your computer to your cell phone, you can use it to dial in to the Internet. To do this, right-click the Internet connection icon in the toolbar, and select the Edit Connections option from the menu (see Figure 2-5).

Figure 2-5. Select Edit Connections to create a new connection.

The Network Connections window offers different options to establish a network connection, depending on the type of connection you need. Because you're trying to initialize a mobile broadband connection, choose the Mobile Broadband tab and then click Add to set up the Internet connection using your cell phone (see Figure 2-6).

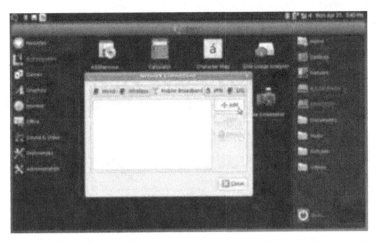

Figure 2-6. You can create the 3G network connection using the Mobile Broadband tab.

The New Mobile Broadband Connection Wizard opens. This wizard shows you its welcome message; click Forward to proceed. In the next step, enter the connection details for your service provider. First, select your country; next, select your provider from the list of available providers (see Figure 2-7). Then, click Forward to proceed.

Figure 2-7. First select your country, and next select the provider for your 3G connection.

In the Summary screen that appears (see Figure 2-8), you see the country and provider you selected. You also have the option to enter a name for this connection. If everything is correct, click Apply to save your changes.

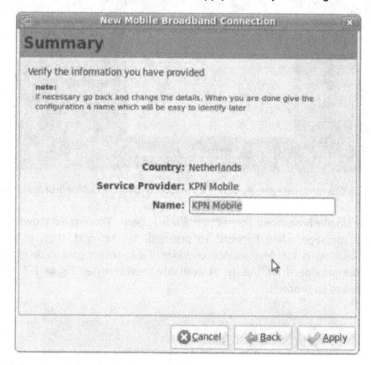

Figure 2-8. If the settings in the Summary screen are correct, click Apply to save them.

Your cell phone is ready for use as a modem. Right-click the network connection icon, and select the new connection type. You can now start working on the Internet.

Connecting to a Wireless Network

Another way to get connected is to use a wireless network. A wireless network typically is fixed around an access point, which is referred to as a *hot spot* if it's in a public place, but you can also your own wireless network at home. This access point is connected to a wired network that often offers high-speed access to the Internet.

Wireless networks are owned by someone. You'll find them in many public places, like airports and hotels. Some wireless network owners charge you a fee to connect, and others don't. In exchange for the access fee, you often get a connection that is decent and performs well. But many people have a wireless network at home, which makes using your netbook very convenient. Netbooks are great for a surfing on the sofa or looking up recipes on the Internet in the kitchen.

In addition, if you travel a lot, wireless networks are the way to get connected. Cheap Internet access using 3G networks often stops at the borders of your country; while you're travelling, 3G network access may become (extremely) expensive. Wireless, on the other hand, is often available for free; and if it isn't, you at least know that you can keep the cost under control.

Wireless Networking Background

When you connect to a wireless network, you need to know something about its background. First, there are commonly two types of wireless networks: networks with and networks without security. This security is normally enforced using encryption. With encryption, the data you send (including passwords) is scrambled before it's sent over the air, which makes it impossible for other people to intercept what you're sending. You should try to always use encryption when you connect to a wireless network.

You'll find unsecured wireless networks in some private environments and badly protected public places. You should avoid them, because other people can read the data you're transmitting. This means there's a chance that bad people are present and sniffing the network to see if any interesting data passes by—for example, wireless users' credit-card numbers and personal passwords.

Wireless security is usually based on a password (also known as the *encryption key*), so you need to know the password to get connected. This isn't always practical in a public place—what's the use of a password if anyone can call the front desk of your hotel to ask for it? Nevertheless, a bad password is better than no password at all. A password requirement is more common in private places. There are different kinds of passwords that need to be entered; some are defined in the Wired Equivalent Privacy (WEP) protocol, and others are defined in the Wi-Fi Protected Access (WPA) protocol.

ExplainED

WEP is old-school encryption for wireless networks, and it can easily be cracked. However, it gives some amount of protection, so use it if nothing else is offered. If possible, it's much better to use another form of encryption. Currently, WPA2 is the most secure and most popular method to protect your wireless network.

When you're setting up a connection, you need to know which password type the wireless network of your choice is using. The owner of the network can provide this information. Before you start, make sure you have the answers to the following questions. If you do, you can proceed with the next section:

- Does your wireless network require you to enter a password (key) or anything like that?

- If so, what is the password?

- Does the wireless network use the WEP or the WPA protocol?

You may encounter cases where you have to authenticate at some other level. For example, the wireless network itself may be open, but you have to authenticate to a proxy server that enables your Internet connection. This method is used quite often in paid wireless networks, such as those in hotels, airport lounges, and other public places. You should be aware that such a network offers no protection whatsoever (so your data may be intercepted by someone else). These public wireless networks only have you authenticate on the proxy so they can make you pay for using the Internet connection.

Connecting to the Wireless Network

To connect to the wireless network, begin by clicking the network connection icon in the toolbar. If the wireless network isn't hidden, you'll probably see it listed (see listing 2-9). Select it.

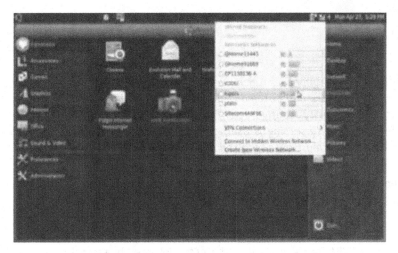

Figure 2-9. If the wireless network of your choice isn't hidden, select it to make a connection.

If the network of your choice is protected, you're prompted to enter a key or a password. The exact options that are available depend on the network you're connecting to; hence, you may not see all the options listed in this section when connecting to a particular network. You can find different security options in the drop-down menu at the Wireless Security option, which opens automatically if authentication is required (see Figure 2-10).

Figure 2-10. The Wireless Security option that appears depends on the kind of security the wireless network of your choice is using.

NotED

In most cases, Ubuntu determines what kind of security is used on your wireless network and automatically offers the options that are relevant for that security configuration. In some cases—especially if a less common security setting is used—it may offer you the wrong option. In that case, you must enter the required information.

If the settings for your wireless network aren't detected automatically, you can specify them yourself. The following security options are available:

- *WPA & WPA2 Personal*: This option comes up automatically if the wireless network of your choice uses WPA for its security. In this case, you need to enter a password to connect.

- *WEP 40/128-bit Key*: This is the classic protection used for wireless networks. You'll probably need to select this if your password (the key) consists of numbers and letters *A-F* only.

- *WEP 128-bit Passphrase*: Use this option if you've obtained a real password.

- *LEAP*: LEAP is a very specific protocol. You'll find it in business networks that use Cisco hardware to establish network connections. Try this option if neither WEP 40/128-bit Key nor WEP 128-bit Passphrase works.

- *Dynamic WEP (802.1x)*: This solution also isn't used often. You'll find it in some business networks. Try it if none of the other options work out well.

Depending on the option you select for security, you may see some other options as well. For instance, if you select WEP as the authentication option, you need to specify the authentication type. You can choose between Open System and Shared Key authentication; in almost all cases, you need the Shared Key authentication option, where you enter a secret key that the administrator of the wireless network gives you. A WEP network may use more than one WEP key. If this is the case, you may need to specify which WEP index you're on, to ensure that you're using the correct authentication credentials. The Shared Key authentication option is used when the administrator of the network configures different WEP keys, which is sometimes done to differentiate between groups of users. In any case, WEP is getting increasingly rare these days, because WPA security is much better and supported as good as WEP.

Connecting to an Unlisted Wireless Network

If the wireless network of your choice is in the list of available networks, connecting is easy: select the network, and enter your authentication credentials. If it's not, there are two options to make the connection manually:

- *Connect to Hidden Wireless Network*: Use this option if the administrator has deliberately hidden the wireless network you want to connect to.

- *Create New Wireless Network*: Choose this if for any other reason that isn't completely clear, you can't connect to your wireless network.

You can find both of these options at the bottom of the menu you see after clicking the network connection icon in the toolbar.

Connecting to a Hidden Wireless Network

One way to secure a wireless network is to hide it. This form of security is old school and not very effective, because nowadays many tools exist to find a hidden wireless network. Nevertheless, if the administrator of your wireless network has hidden the network, you can set up a connection by adding the wireless network by hand. The following procedure describes how to do that:

1. Click the network access icon on your computer's toolbar. Select Connect to Hidden Wireless Network from the menu. This opens the window shown in Figure 2-11.

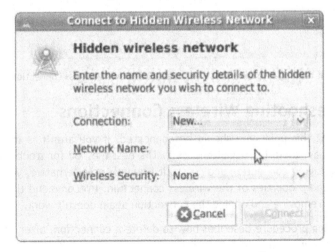

Figure 2-11. Enter the network name and security option to configure access to a hidden wireless network.

2. Select the New Connection option. Next, enter the name of the wireless network (ask the administrator) and the type of wireless security the network is using.

3. Click Connect to automatically connect to the wireless network.

Creating a New Wireless Connection

If for some reason, the options just described don't work, you can add a new wireless connection. To do this, click the network connection icon on the toolbar, and select Create New Wireless Network from the menu. Next, in the window shown in Figure 2-12, enter the name of the network and the wireless security mode you want to use, and click Create. You're immediately connected to the wireless network you just created.

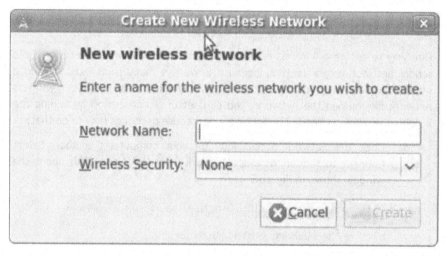

Figure 2-12. If nothing else works, you can create your own wireless connection.

Troubleshooting Wireless Connections

Normally, at this point you should be connected. If you aren't, some limited options are available for troubleshooting. The best method for troubleshooting is to remove your connection and create it again. As an alternative, you can try to modify the properties of the wireless connection. I recommend that you do that only if removing and adding the connection again doesn't work.

The following procedure describes how to delete a connection, after which you can use the procedure from the previous section to create the connection again:

1. Right-click the network connection icon on your computer's toolbar. From the menu that pops up, select Edit Connections.

2. In the Network Connections window, select the Wireless tab (see Figure 2-13). This brings up a list of all the wireless networks you've ever selected.

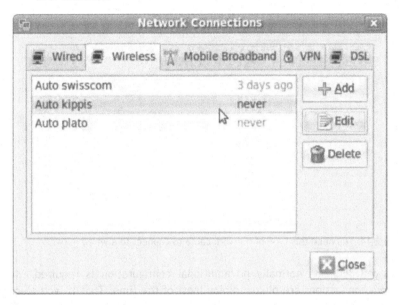

Figure 2-13. On the Wireless tab, you have access to all wireless networks you've ever accessed.

3. Select the wireless network you're having problems with, and click Delete to remove it from the list. All of the configuration used in the past is removed, and you can try connecting again.

Connecting to a Wired Network

Most network connections today are wireless. Nevertheless, if you want the best possible performance and reliability, it's always better to take a network cable and connect your netbook to a wired network. Let there be no misunderstanding about the cables. You can't use just any cable—you need to connect a specific unshielded twisted pair (UTP) network cable to the RJ-45 socket on your netbook. Not sure what kind of cable that is? No problem; Figure 2-14 shows you exactly what you need.

Figure 2-14. You need this type of network cable to connect to a wired network.

After you connect, normally no additional configuration is required. Wired network connections are plug-and-play most of the time. That is, you plug the network cable into your netbook computer, you automatically receive all of the configuration required to connect to the network, and you can start using the Internet. But sometimes it's useful to find out the properties of the network connection you're using. To check, right-click the network connection icon (which now looks like two small computer screens instead of the vertical bars you see for a wireless connection). From the menu, select Connection Information. This brings up the screen shown in Figure 2-15.

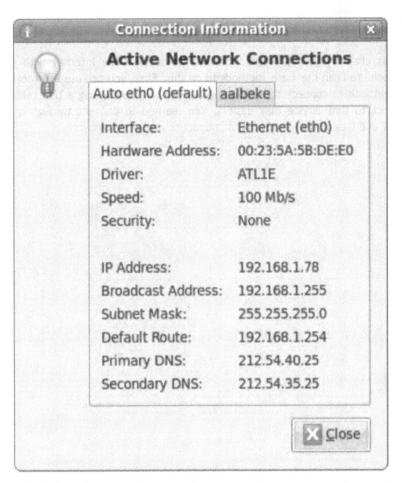

Figure 2-15. Using the Connection Information menu option, you can see all properties your network connection currently is using.

For you, this configuration may mean nothing. But for a network expert who is trying to help you get your network connection up and running, this is useful information indeed. It shows all the addresses you're using to connect to the network, which is very helpful if you're having trouble connecting. Make sure you know where to find this information if you need it.

Summary

In this chapter, you've learned how to connect to the Internet with your netbook. You can use many methods to do this. First, you can use Bluetooth on the netbook to connect to an external device (although using a USB cable to connect to that device may easier). You learned to connect through a cell phone and then you learned how to connect to a wireless network.

Chapter 3

Hands-On Power Shopping: Best of Breed Tools for Today's Netbooks and the Cloud Lifestyle

Let's assume you've had the perfect *veni vidi vici* netbook shopping experience, and are now happily getting to know your new mobile device. First, it is worth emphasizing that if you never buy a single additional service, subscription, or peripheral, you can get tons of benefits and enjoyment from your new netbook. That said, by adding key gadgets and using cloud-based tools and services, you can dramatically expand the richness and capability of your connected mobile lifestyle. You can learn more about cloud-based office and productivity apps in Chapter 4. Most of them have free versions or generous trials.

In this chapter I describe some unique devices and services that can make your netbook a ticket to near total geographic freedom. You'll be able to do more, and in more places, than you ever thought possible. I've grouped the devices by categories such as usage, connectivity, and entertainment. It's worth mentioning that you can expect just about any USB-based device to work with both Windows and Linux operating systems, but there will be exceptions for those that don't have Linux drivers or that don't work reliably on certain netbooks.

Tips for Bargain Hunting and Finding Novel Items

In this chapter, I describe a variety of novel items, useful gadgets, and a few definite must-haves. The thing about finding this stuff is that it doesn't necessarily throw itself into your path, precisely because it is often designed to meet the needs of people in special circumstances or of whimsical tastes. I've included screenshots of products and provided the URLs of where I discovered them, as well as information that may help you find your way to related services.

Here's something to remember when doing any sort of shopping on the Internet, but especially when you are scouting out technological solutions to what may be an unusual problem or need. If you are willing to go a little off the beaten path to find the unusual things you think you want or need for a better netbook experience, chances are you'll get better prices, fresher ideas, and more targeted tech gadgets. Use common sense when making online purchases, but by all means explore. Look beyond Amazon.com and eBay, and you'll find interesting, early-cycle, attractive deals.

Here are a few places to look for a broad variety of merchandise. Some of these definitely fall into the "quirky" category.

- **Pricewatch.com:** This site is the best source of screamin' deals I personally know of when it comes to gadgets, computers, and hardware. I've used it to equip my software engineering lab for more than ten years, and have yet to be disappointed. Once or twice I've had to return things that were broken in shipment or were the wrong item and received polite immediate response. Pricewatch.com is actually a sort of clearinghouse, so there are a large number of individual vendors, and prices and products are updated frequently.
- **Shopzilla.com:** This is a good place to do comparison-shopping, if the item you are looking for is fairly common.
- **Overstock.com:** This is a site that can have unbelievable bargains, but it is sort of an online garage sale, in that it has constantly changing inventories of electronics.

Note that for each item listed in this chapter, I have included a price. This almost goes without saying, but just to be clear, prices fluctuate rapidly. Prices may have changed since the time of writing. Use them as a guide, and for budgeting purposes.

Connectivity

Connectivity devices allow you to take advantage of networking to the wider Internet, among groups of netbooks and wired computers, or to set up local networks that share resources such as printers, scanners, and the like.

Bluetooth Wireless Mouse

http://usb.brando.com

$25.00

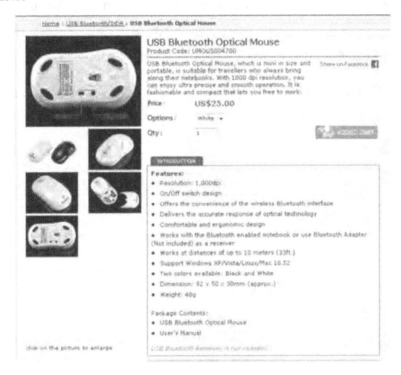

Uses

This accessory is suggested for the following:

- Backpack print journalism
- Business, lowest Total Cost of Ownership (TCO)
- Business, mobilizing
- Field researchers

Features

If you have to do a lot of typing with your netbook, chances are you'll want a mouse. Most netbooks will have a track pad, which performs the same function as a mouse, but a lot of people find a mouse easier to use. The downside of a mouse is portability. A mouse works best on stable surfaces, so it won't be as handy when you're using your netbook on the go. But a mouse is perfect if you're sitting at table. This one is small, light, and easy to use. You definitely want wireless connectivity in a netbook accessory mouse, and this one works off a Bluetooth connection. If your netbook is Bluetooth-enabled, this is a no-brainer. If not, you'll have to add Bluetooth support with a USB adaptor (see the following item). Otherwise, most wireless mice come with their own USB receivers for connecting to your netbook. Most have a storage space in the mouse itself where you can keep the receiver when you're traveling.

Bluetooth / IrDA Adapter

http://usb.brando.com.hk

$30.00

Uses

This accessory is suggested for the following:

- Backpack journalism
- Business, mobilizing
- RFID

- Field researchers
- Public safety workers

Features

Flexible connectivity is key with a netbook, and this device provides you two extra options for connecting to Bluetooth or infrared (IR) peripherals and devices. In a certain respect, it's an advantage to set up these forms of connectivity as add-ons. Then you have them available when and where you want them, but you don't have the additional security worry of making sure your netbook isn't "invaded" by surreptitious access through a networking device you forgot to turn off. (Bluetooth devices are particularly vulnerable to this sort of compromise, and there are documented cases of identity thieves cruising airports, conference facilities, and the like looking for Bluetooth "open doors.")

Verizon MiFi 3g Router

moremobileInternet .com

$59.99

Uses

This accessory is suggested for the following:

- Backpack journalism
- Business, mobilizing
- RFID
- Field Research
- Public Safety

Features

When I saw this little device, it was love at first sight. Being able to set up your own wireless access point on a whim, wherever you are, is a wonderful tool for teachers, journalists, researchers, and any form of collaborative content development. It is an inexpensive but serviceable device; however, note that you need to have a mechanism set up to pay for your use of Verizon bandwidth. You can either set up a regular monthly plan that has a predefined ceiling on bandwidth use (after which you get whacked with a pretty considerable rate for exceeding your limit) or you can pay as you go on a daily basis.

Belkin USB Hubs

http://catalog.belkin.com

$15.00 to $50.00

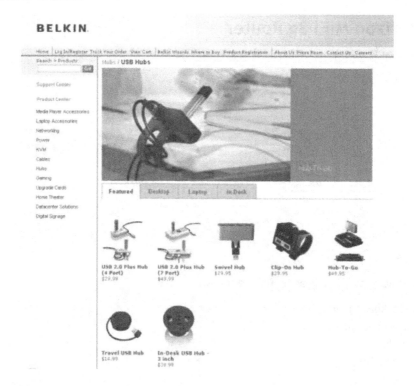

Uses

This accessory is suggested for the following:

- Backpack journalism
- Business, mobilizing
- RFID
- Elder care
- Field research
- Public safety
- Kids and families
- Musicians

Features

USB hubs are similar in concept to power strips that convert one electrical outlet into five or six. The thing to remember with a USB hub is that you can plug a lot more things in, but you can't necessarily use them all at once and expect them to work well.

This is a convenience item that will be handy if you are in a situation where you just need more connectivity than the typical two or three USB ports a netbook has. If you really load up with external USB devices, you can expect battery life to take a pretty steep nosedive. This may be an accessory you use most when you have access to wall power or an easy way to quickly recharge your netbook.

Accessories and Entertainment Services

One of the biggest markets initially targeted by netbook manufacturers was the content consumer. Netbooks are very well suited to providing mobile entertainment right out of the box, but you can certainly enhance your experience with a few well-chosen entertainment-oriented add-ons.

USB Chocolate MP3 Player 2GB

http://usb.brando.com.hk

$39.00

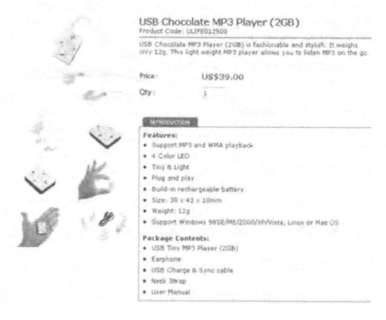

Uses

This accessory is suggested for the following:

- Travelers
- Kids and families
- Entertainment
- Musicians

Features

This is a really economical little device that pairs well with a netbook. You can use the netbook to load the player with your favorite music. If you travel with kids, they can download audio books, music, podcasts, and so on using the family netbook, which gives you a very inexpensive alternative to iPods. You don't have to commit local storage and you can revise the content of the player easily and often. If you have a giant library you want to access while you travel, consider storing the full library in a cloud-based repository. This way you sacrifice neither variety nor mobility.

USB TV Tuner

www.avermedia.com

$39.96

Uses

This accessory is suggested for the following:

- Elder care
- Travelers
- Kids and families
- Entertainment
- Public safety

Features

This is an absolutely sensational tool for making your netbook the go-to convergence device for kids and elders, or for general information delivery purposes. It's cheaper and more convenient than putting a television in every room in the house.

Apple AirTunes

www.apple.com

$79.00

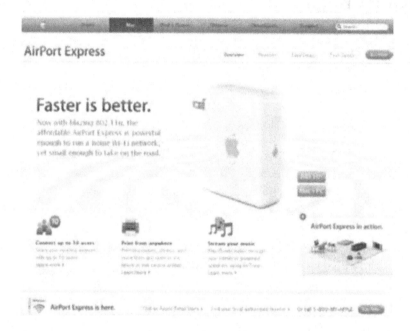

Uses

This accessory is suggested for the following:

- Backpack journalism
- Travelers
- Kids and families
- Entertainment
- Musicians

Features

AirTunes uses the content of your iTunes library and wirelessly relays it to any stereo or set of speakers in the vicinity. You plug the Apple AirPort Express into a wall outlet near the speakers you want to use, then cable the speakers to the Airport Express. Aside from being great for flexibility of listening at home, this is also a pretty light traveling setup for parties and events, as you can easily travel with just your netbook and a light Airport Express unit and have an instant stereo wherever you go.

ATH-PRO5MSA Stereo Headphones

www.audio-technica.com

$119.00

Uses

This accessory is suggested for the following:

- Backpack broadcast journalism
- Entertainment
- Musicians

Features

Sound quality is key for audio content production, and these headphones have professional quality noise cancellation features that enable you to hear exactly how your audio will sound to content consumers.

Netflix Watch Instantly

www.netflix.com

Price varies

Uses

This accessory is suggested for the following:

- Travelers
- Kids and families
- Entertainment

Features

Netflix Watch Now movies are provided to subscribers as part of the overall DVD-by-mail service. Typically (though this fluctuates from time to time) you get one hour of movie-viewing for every dollar of per-month subscription cost.

The glitch is it doesn't include the entire Netflix catalog. You may need to browse around a bit to find something you are excited about viewing, and the movies and television shows on Watch Now do tend to be older. Many netbooks also have TV-out capabilities that allow you to view content from your netbook on the big screen at home.

Amazon Video on Demand

www.amazon.com

Price varies

Uses

This accessory is suggested for the following:

- Travelers
- Kids and families
- Entertainment

Features

Amazon.com offers this video-on-demand service for users who want to rent or purchase premium first-run content. Rented movies must be viewed within three days of purchase, and must be watched in their entirety within 24 hours of the first time the user pushes "Play." You get to see the full show (either movie or episode) without interruption by commercials.

Health and Safety Equipment and Accessories

If you've ever watched an ambulance crew at work, you know that after paramedics create a safe and secure environment for a patient, their next priority is to methodically and accurately build a record of status information about the person's condition and communicate this to a doctor in an emergency room. A solid record of observations over time is key to the doctor's ability to rapidly and accurately diagnose a patient and render appropriate care.

The difference between *most* people and an EMT, of course, is that ambulance staff deals with difficult, shocking situations every day, and are trained to cope with them. Gathering patient status data (blood pressure, heart rate, and the like) accurately while waiting for help to arrive or deciding whether to seek emergency care is pretty far beyond most people's level of poise under pressure. However, if you have a netbook and fingertip Puls/Ox in your backpack, you can whip it out, set it up, and let it record data while you handle more immediate needs. In so doing, you have preserved information that may help a lot with the care of the ill or injured person.

Likewise, for chronic illnesses like diabetes, stability and routine are everything. Making it easy for a person to keep status records for themselves leads to much better care and evaluation of their true condition.

Glucose Meter USB Adapter

www.drugstore.com

$29.99

Uses

This accessory is suggested for the following:

- Elder care
- Home health
- Public safety

Features

This adapter kit lets you connect a One Touch Glucose meter to your netbook via a USB cable. You can save the data locally or transmit it to a caregiver over the Internet. This is a key piece of support equipment for elders living independently and trying to manage their diabetes, or for distance delivery of healthcare and monitoring services.

Blood Pressure Cuff

usb.brando.com.hk

$57.00

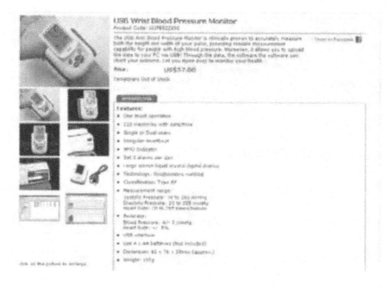

Uses

This accessory is suggested for the following:

- Elder care
- Home health
- Kids and family
- Public safety

Features

This little unit gives fairly accurate, though not absolutely definitive, vital signs status monitoring information. It reports blood pressure and heart rate measurements, can store data for up to two users, and has a USB interface that allows data to be downloaded to a computer. Like the Glucose Meter and the O_2 Saturation Meter that follow, this small, inexpensive device can easily be fashioned into a basic distance delivery health monitoring setup for shut-ins, people who have mobility difficulties, or for people who are being isolated for surveillance when serious infectious disease is suspected.

Oxygen Saturation/Heart Rate

www.echostore.com

$139.99

Wireless Pulse Oximeter CMS–50E, CMS50E, Wireless Oxygen Meter

Wireless pulse Oximeter CMS-50E, CMS50E, wireless Oxygen Meter, Oxygen Meters, Oxygen Meter Level

FDA 510K Approved
Free Advanced Analysis Software

This Wireless Oxygen oximeter can record the data and transfer it to your computer, then you can analyze it.
Technical Parameters

* USB and Wireless Interface to Computer
* Synchronous dispaly on the oximeter and computer
* Inner flash memory for more than 30 hours data storage
* Free Advanced software for sleep study and monitoring ~

Uses

This accessory is suggested for the following:

- Elder care
- Home health
- Kids and family
- Public safety

Features

This gadget offers both patients and caregivers a really easy, cost-efficient way to do routine monitoring and accumulate a historical data record about a patient's condition. They also support the distance delivery of medical care giving and monitoring with consistently accumulated data.

Weather Measurement Tools

One of the greater ways netbook technology is being used is in the teaching and practice of field science. There is no better teacher of biology, ecology, oceanography, and geology than the natural world itself. Virtually any study that takes place outdoors either has data that is driven by weather or puts the researchers in a position of vulnerability to fluctuations in weather. Being able to precisely and continuously monitor and record weather data is a big advantage for field scientists.

Weathershack

www.weathershack.com

Price varies

Uses

This accessory is suggested for the following:

- Backpack journalism
- Field research
- Kids and family
- Public safety

Media Creation Tools and Accessories

Netbooks are an invaluable tool for backpack journalists. They are easy to carry, inconspicuous, durable, and versatile. They are perfectly suited to targeting new formats like micro-blogging and short video recording. While many come equipped with both microphone and camera, these are generally embedded in a way that is intended to make it easy for netbook owners to take advantage of VoIP (such as Skype) and videoconferencing. To really conduct an interview, film a video short, or capture the scene around you, it will help a lot to have an external camera or microphone that you can connect directly to your netbook.

USB Mini Web Cam with Sucker

usb.brando.com.hk

$19.00

Uses

This accessory is suggested for the following:

- Backpack journalism
- Business, mobilizing
- Elder care
- Home health
- Field research
- Jobsite management, builders
- Jobsite management, landscapers
- Jobsite management, architects
- Jobsite management, interior designers
- Kids and families
- Travelers
- Public safety

Features

This selection of inexpensive web cams provides a rich set of tools if you want to collaborate over the Internet, capture an interview, record small amounts of video directly to your netbook, or aim your web cam manually.

USB Spy Pocket Video Audio Recorder + Flash Drive + Writing Pen

usb.brando.com.hk

$59.00

Uses

This accessory is suggested for the following:

- Backpack journalism
- Field research
- Jobsite management, builders
- Jobsite management, architects
- Jobsite management, interior designers
- Travelers
- Public safety

Features

So I have to admit that this Spy Pen is included partly just because it is fun. However, as a multifunction peripheral, it really does pay its way. It can record both audio and video, has an embedded flash drive, and is also actually a pen. And for sneaky journalism, or ad hoc video/audio capture, it's a great, inexpensive, convenient little accessory.

Portable Podcast Recorder

www.rolandus.com

$450.00

Uses

This accessory is suggested for the following:

- Backpack journalism
- Business, mobilizing
- Field research
- Musicians
- Public safety

Features

This little Roland audio recorder is a professional quality device, and this is reflected in the price. It is an industry standard, and if you choose to invest in one of these, it is probably the last one you'll ever need to buy. Its distinguishing features include very high recording fidelity and the ability to capture recordings to a secure digital (SD) card. (Note you need to make sure that your netbook can read SD cards, or has a USB card reader.) If you use the device to capture private information such as medical histories or sensitive conversations, you can maintain absolute privacy of the recorded material.

Mobile Business Tools

Netbooks enable you to take your business on the road. You can keep all of your important data with you, and connect to the office intranet or cloud services when you need to. There are many tools available for the mobile business person that are lightweight and small enough to be carried in a briefcase. Don't head out for your next business trip without them!

Flatbed Scanner

www.usa.canon.com

$49.99

Uses

This accessory is suggested for the following:

- Business, lowest TCO
- Business, mobilizing

- Elder care
- Home health
- Jobsite management, builders
- Jobsite management, landscapers
- Jobsite management, architects
- Jobsite management, interior designers

Features

This about the lightest, slimmest scanner you'll find, and it's inexpensive as well. It is just over an inch thick, which makes it easy to slip into a standard briefcase. It is a key item of equipment for capturing high fidelity copies of paper documents, photos, and drawings, including documents that require signatures and handwritten notes.

Business Card Scanner

www.bizcardreader.com

$209.00

Uses

This accessory is suggested for the following:

- Backpack journalism: print, broadcast, and video
- Business, lowest TCO
- Business, mobilizing
- Jobsite management, builders
- Jobsite management, landscapers
- Jobsite management, architects
- Jobsite management, interior designers

Features

No one should ever go to a conference, trade show, or other large professional gathering without one of these. Using this gadget with a netbook creates an absolute minimum of fuss for everyone, and you don't have the inconvenience of keeping track of bits of paper.

The World's Smallest HD Camcorder

www.theflip.com

$229.99

Uses

This accessory is suggested for the following:

- Backpack journalism
- Business, mobilizing
- Field research
- Jobsite management, builders
- Jobsite management, landscapers
- Jobsite management, architects
- Jobsite management, interior designers
- Travelers
- Kids and safety
- Public safety

Features

This camcorder wins the category honors for portability and multifunction value. For mobile business processes, health and safety or journalism uses, you could end up lugging a lot of individual devices around, which means more weight, more batteries, and more chance of losing or damaging a key tool. Spending a little more on this item gives you very good recording performance, nice storage options, and ultra-low weight for your overall kit.

Pico Projectors

www.aaxatech.com

$239.00

Uses

This accessory is suggested for the following:

- Business, mobilizing
- Jobsite management, builders
- Jobsite management, landscapers
- Jobsite management, architects
- Jobsite management, interior designers
- Musicians
- Public safety

Features

This little ultra-portable projector is considered the best in its class, and this is reflected in the price. Using this relatively small object, you can do a presentation featuring projections of up to 6 feet, which easily serves small- to medium-sized groups. This is a great tool for mobilizing business conferences, but also for holding ad hoc meetings where it is important for a group to see and share image-based information.

RFID Reader

www.rfid-in-china.com

Price varies

Uses

This accessory is suggested for the following:

- Business, mobilizing
- RFID
- Field research
- Public safety

Features

Radio Frequency ID (RFID) tags are used to identify and secure everything from merchandise in brick and mortar stores to surgical instruments. (Think of anything people really want to keep track of and be able to locate easily.) RFID chain of custody applications has seen triple digit year-over-year growth over the last three years, and will probably continue to grow rapidly as software catches up and provides customized and niche solutions and prices of RFID tags continue to fall. This is the source for low-cost, easily portable RFID tag reader/writer units.

Tools For Phones and Calling

One of the most popular features of netbooks is the ability to use services such as Skype on the move to make low-cost, or free, calls wherever you are. Try and use your netbook's built in speaker microphone or webcam in a crowded café, though, and you'll soon realize why it makes sense to purchase some external equipment. A cheap USB headset will make a world of difference to your calls, giving you privacy and call quality that you wouldn't otherwise have.

Logitech USB headset

www.bhphotovideo.com

$34.95

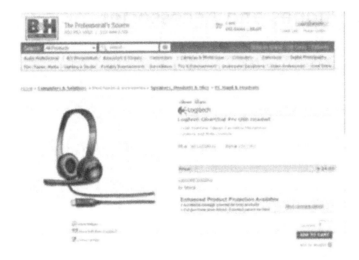

Uses

This accessory is suggested for the following:

- Backpack journalism
- Business, lowest TCO
- Business, mobilizing
- Elder care
- Home health
- Field research

- Jobsite management, builders
- Jobsite management, landscapers
- Jobsite management, architects
- Jobsite management, interior designers
- Travelers
- Kids and families
- Public safety

Features

This low-cost headset delivers good sound quality and noise control, which can dramatically improve VoIP quality, but is relatively inexpensive and durable. These headphones also include a noise-canceling feature, which cuts out background noise giving you much clearer sound reproduction in public spaces.

VoIP Phones and Accessories

www.echostore.com

Price varies

EchoStore.com

Skype Store

Our USB phones and adapters work with the following service providers:
Skype, Globe7, VoipBuster, VoipStunt, VoipDiscount, Internetcalls, X-Lite/X-Ten/EyeBeam, MSN Messenger, Yahoo Messenger, VoipCheap, FreeCall, NetAppel, SparVoip, Google Talk , Net2Phone, Gizmo, SJPhone, Stanaphone, Sipgate , DialPad, Firefly, Nortel IP i2050, Vonageswe, Vonage, Ubiphone, and so on Linux, MAC

USB Wireless Dual Phone
Regular price: $139.99
EchoStore Price: $88.99

USB Cordless Phone, USB-WIDL
Regular price: $119.99
EchoStore Price: $49.99

USB to RJ11 Adapter for linux and Windows(ECK)
Regular price: $79.99
EchoStore Price: $29.99

Skype Phone for windows/linux
Regular price: $79.99
EchoStore Price: $18.39

Au600 skype usb to rj11 adaptor with forwarding function
Regular price: $99.00
EchoStore Price: $35.99

USB SPEAKER PHONE P4K
Regular price: $89.99
EchoStore Price: $33.99

Uses

This accessory is suggested for the following:

- Backpack journalism
- Business, lowest TCO
- Business, mobilizing
- RFID
- Elder care
- Home health
- Field research
- Jobsite management, builders
- Jobsite management, landscapers
- Jobsite management, architects
- Jobsite management, interior designers
- Travelers
- Kids and families
- Entertainment
- Musicians
- Public safety

Features

This is a site for Skype convenience items and non-mobility tools. You can set up VoIP call stations that use phones that are virtually indistinguishable from wire line cordless handsets. This could be a great option if you need to set up an ad hoc office. (Think traveling response teams, collaborative sessions, temporary call centers, and workshops.)

Looking Ahead

In this chapter, you've seen that your netbook is actually more than a highly portable computer; it is a foundation upon which you can build a great variety of lifestyle, work, and entertainment experiences. The hardware accessories you choose can give it capabilities that were the stuff of science fiction not so long ago. They can also make you safer, save you money, and provide opportunities to creatively engage in connected mobile culture.

In the next chapter, I'll discuss another way to make your little netbook a productivity tool that belies its small size and ready portability: cloud-based services and software that give you access to heavy-lifting office applications, collaboration tools, and data management facilities.

Chapter 4

A Beginner's Guide to Cloud Lifestyles

In this chapter, you'll learn how to find, use, and share a variety of useful applications that will increase the amount of tasks you can perform with your netbook. One of the biggest benefits of netbooks is that they are your fastest ticket to an emergent lifestyle based on *cloud computing*. Making the most of the cloud and its power to provide you with flexibility, convenience, and resources that fit both the character and the scale of your needs requires two things: a bit more shopping and a little planning ahead. This chapter will help you accomplish both these things, or at least get pretty well along with the job. If you skim through the descriptions and advice on cloud tools given here, you can start to form a picture of exactly what you might want to have at the ready, when you unplug for a day of business, entertainment or generally mobile, connected life.

What Is the Cloud?

So what is cloud computing? In the language of computer engineering, your netbook is a *viewer,* and the external software and services you access with it are *"in the cloud"*. When engineers and software architects draw plans for networked applications that connect phones, computers, and other digital devices, they lump all of the technology that transfers information between senders and receivers in a single element, and refer to it as "the cloud." Take a moment to examine Figure 4-1.

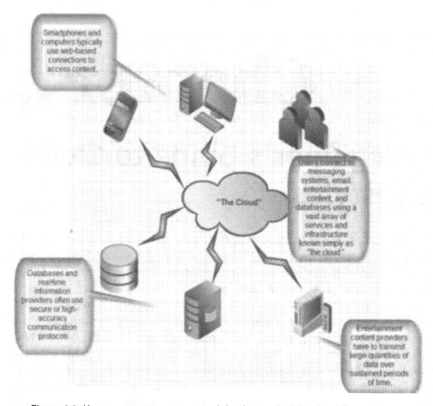

Figure 4-1. Users connect to content and databases via "the cloud."

If you have something electronic that you want to connect to *another* electronic something, somewhere else, and the two things actually have an agreement on how they plan to communicate, the cloud will take care of the rest.

It is almost impossible to overstate the practical benefits of this. The fact that cell phones have more or less been able to do this for voice communication and text messaging tends to erode the psychological impact of cloud computing, but think about this: the emergence of generally and cheaply available cloud computing services has already begun to exert a leveling influence on the global population greater than anything since the invention of the magnetic compass or chronograph. The cloud is effectively removing borders and barriers that have been in place for hundreds of years.

The cloud is a huge boon to the average information consumer for several reasons. First, the economics of cloud computing will have roughly the same effect that the massive advances of chip technology had throughout the 1980s and '90s. Every year will bring improvement in what your dollar can buy.

Here's why:

- **With cloud computing, you can pay as you go for tools, services and resources.** This lowers economic barriers and enables participation of previously excluded populations in the developing world and disadvantaged groups in the developed world. Growing the user pool makes everyone's costs decline over time, because pricing for cloud services is based on economies of scale, where costs are shared across huge pools of consumers.
- **Cloud services offer the best trade-off between power, flexibility, and cost:** Say you need to create diagrams from time to time. You can use a web-based drawing tool for a one-off (I used Gliffy, which is discussed in some detail later in this chapter). But what if you need to make sure the contents of the diagram remain private, or you need to collaborate with someone else? In that case, you might have to buy and install a software tool on your computer. There are three costs involved here: the initial purchase price, the local storage and other resources necessary to use the diagramming tool, and the ongoing requirement to maintain the currency of the application and manage the data associated with your use of it. *With cloud computing, you can choose your level of commitment and investment, which is a really big advantage.* You can get to know a tool before you spend a lot of time or money, and can walk away relatively easily if it doesn't work out or something better comes along. You can also afford to try more things, which tends to fuel innovation, because you have less at risk if you try something that doesn't work well.
- **You get to delegate non-productive tasks like system management to professionals:** Most people are really terrible about doing the routine tasks of computer maintenance, such as backing up important files, updating programs, and doing scheduled, systematic security audits. None of those things is fun. They are time-consuming, and unless you are pretty savvy and absolutely meticulous, they won't help in a crisis. By contrast, cloud-based storage, software tools, and services are (often) very professionally managed. It is someone's *job* to do scheduled backups of your data, store it in a secure fashion, and guarantee its availability, or you can decline payment for services. Many cloud technology providers have entry-level programs that are free (or free for a limited period of time), where fees step up with your level of usage and the rigorousness of your requirements. If you attach any value to your time or your stored data, cloud management services are a really cost-efficient investment.

There are several subtle differences between using a netbook and using any other means of running your digital life. Here are some of the key things to keep in mind, and they are the reasons that netbooks can be generally better partners for enjoying the cloud lifestyle than other options.

- **Low cost:** At roughly half the cost of a laptop, a lot more people can afford to participate in the cloud lifestyle.
- **Ultra-portability:** Given a small investment in wireless hardware and a data plan, you can literally connect to the Internet from anywhere there is mobile phone reception. In many areas of the world, you can enjoy wireless connectivity based on pervasive wireless Internet services, which eliminates the need for specialized hardware. This not only means that you can work or enjoy entertainment from most anywhere, it means that you can do things in new ways and new places that simply weren't possible or were cost-prohibitive before. Want to register voters on a street corner? Use a netbook and cloud-based voter registration support (www.moveon.org). Want to monitor the nocturnal activities of tomato hornworms? A netbook can hold a charge for up to eight hours, be made to take time-lapse photos using a web cam, and operate unattended in a relatively hostile environment. Want to do team Sudoku or play chess with someone in Poland while you're waiting in the minivan for soccer practice to end? Pull the netbook out of your purse, connect up, and play.
- **Sturdiness:** Because many netbooks have no moving parts, they are inherently more durable than laptops, which almost always include a hard disk. (Even ruggedized hard disks are subject to failure if they experience moderate impacts). Taken together, the combination of durability and low cost opens up a variety of uses to which laptops aren't well suited: harsh, demanding, or chaotic environments are all less likely to bring you to grief with a netbook.
- **Comparatively long battery life:** You'd have to look far and wide to find a netbook that wouldn't last through a feature length movie download. Most last considerably longer if you enjoy stored content (using a flashcard, USB stick, or the like). If you aren't watching movies or listening to music nonstop, you can expect a netbook to hold a charge through several days of intermittent use. The convenience of this is so terrific that it's hard to appreciate until you've taken a road trip or two with a netbook, using it to get maps, find restaurants, or do last-minute bookings of lodging and transportation. It is necessary to point out that there is a vast range of battery performance among netbooks, and these have chiefly to do with two factors: the size of the screen and the size of the battery. But if these things are equal (or nearly so), then only one other thing has a big impact, and that is the amount of time spent connected to a wireless network. The reason for this is that, next to backlighting the

screen, powering the wireless antenna is the most demanding task in terms of battery resources.

So what's the downside to the cloud? Security. The actual machines that your data is stored on as part of the cloud are actually very secure, but the problem comes with transferring your data to and from the cloud. Let's take a look at security in general and how you can protect your netbook.

Think Through Your Security

Even if you don't choose to buy a single add-on security product or service, there are some security and privacy techniques that can do a lot to protect you, if you take the time to investigate them and use them to your best advantage. First, you should find, understand, and appropriately set the protections your web browser affords. Later in this chapter, you'll read about some useful features of two of the best (and most popular) web browsers today: Microsoft Internet Explorer and Mozilla Firefox. Another thing that you can very easily and inexpensively do to protect yourself as you surf, shop, and socialize on the Web is to be smart about how you use passwords. Understand what makes a good password, vary your passwords across the sites you use, and keep them fresh.

NotED

There are effective ways to manage passwords that allow you to keep them from getting stale, but also to store them in a fashion that doesn't make them easy to steal or accidentally disclose.

Security Tuning Your Browser

Many netbooks ship with either Windows Vista or Windows XP. This is a great advantage if you have existing Windows-dependent files or programs that you want to transfer, if you want to set up file shares between your desktop (or laptop) and your netbook, or if you just feel more comfortable with Windows. If any of these is a major consideration for you, chances are you are pretty happy with Microsoft's Internet Explorer and plan to keep using it. If so, take the time to tune it appropriately for your netbook, using the integrated tools. One of the most important protections you can provide yourself as an Internet Explorer user is to apply any and all updates that Microsoft publishes. For Vista users, these are both free and transparent, and frequently address known security flaws and vulnerabilities. You can visit the Windows Update or Microsoft Update sites and look for updates and version upgrades. Upgrading preserves your current choice of home page, search settings, favorites, and compatible toolbars. If you have a second (or third) browser installed, upgrading will not change your default browser.

ExplainED

Special Note: It is widely considered a "Best Practice" to enable Microsoft's automatic updates to your Internet Explorer browser. Microsoft actively tracks and addresses known security threats, and makes every effort to keep you safe by supplying this service to all Internet Explorer users free of charge. If you choose not to use their service, you are vulnerable to a wide variety of threats and malware, and could experience serious consequences such as identity theft. The bottom line on automatic browser updates: just do it.

The reason it is especially important to stay on top of these free protections is that most hackers are two things: smart and opportunistic. The smart part means they devote hours, days, months, and in some cases even years to looking for arcane security vulnerabilities in Microsoft's browser products. And this is where the opportunistic part comes in. When hackers find an opening that can be exploited by malware or a clever hack, they automatically have a huge pool of potential victims upon which they can prey. They often do this is in a methodical way, using various lures and "web-crawling" programs to find systems they can compromise. So, if you stay connected for long periods of time, frequently go to download sites, or do a lot of financial transactions online, you can become a target of opportunity.

It is a simple matter to get set up to receive automatic updates. Use the Tools drop-down menu that appears on the right-hand side of the Internet Explorer screen (see Figure 4-2) to launch the Updates Dialog. (This is for Internet Explorer 7 and later.) You can also use the Windows Update facility, which allows you to get updates for other Microsoft products as well. If you use Vista or Windows XP, click the Windows Start button, choose All Programs, and from the list that appears, choose Windows Updates. Follow the instructions found at the update web site. These change with the availability of new update material and responses to specific threats.

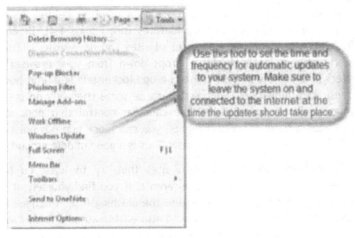

Figure 4-2. Use the standard Microsoft Internet Explorer tools to help protect yourself from known threats by applying Microsoft's updates to both Windows and Internet Explorer.

Occasionally the updates are large or numerous, so you'll probably want to set them to happen at a time when you won't be using the computer (see Figure 4-3). Make sure to be connected to the Internet and powered on at the time the updates are set to take place, but don't leave yourself signed in to any applications or web sites that contain valuable or sensitive information. Closing connections helps ensure that no one can gain access to your privileged information simply because you have an open, unattended connection to the Web.

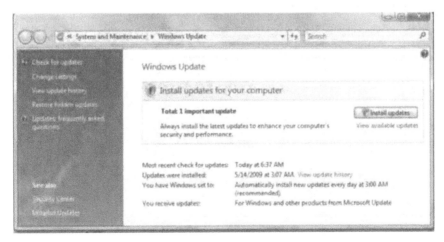

Figure 4-3. Installing updates with Windows Update.

The Internet Explorer Tools drop-down menu has a lot of other helpful items that let you fine-tune security and privacy features (see Figure 4-4). Delete Browsing History lets you clear web addresses of sites you have visited. This means they won't appear in the list that drops down from your browser's address bar after you close the browser. The pop-up blocker lets you limit how web sites you visit can launch new windows. Because some sites rely on pop-ups for legitimate reasons (for example, the calendar control that pops up when you try to book a hotel room or a flight), you can block pop-ups but be prompted to allow them on a case-by-case basis. This is a good middle ground.

The phishing filter helps protect you from sites that try to lure you by pretending to be someone or something they aren't. If you find yourself at a site that makes you uncomfortable, you can use the phishing filter to check it against a database of known scammers. You can also enable automatic checks. Automatic checks may slow you down or annoy you if you visit a lot of download sites, but they are a very good free protection.

Managing add-ons is not for the faint of heart, unless you are fairly sophisticated in your understanding of the architecture of web applications. However, once in a while malware alerts are issued for threats that are serious but don't have official patches or updates from the publisher of the products that contain the vulnerability. (This recently happened with Adobe's Acrobat reader.) A lot of the short-term fixes and defenses in these situations involve making small modifications to the way the browser treats add-on components, and if you have good instructions on how to implement such a defense, you shouldn't be afraid of doing so. The Manage Add-ons dialog has a button that will reset everything to the defaults if you make a mistake, get cold feet or the modification becomes unnecessary.

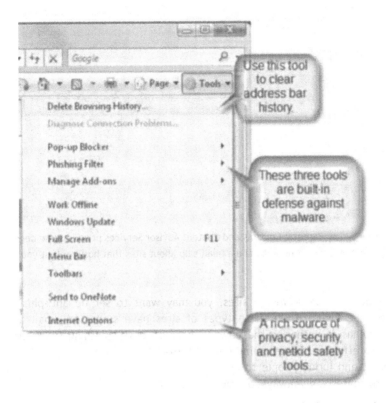

Figure 4-4. Internet Explorer has a lot of helpful built-in tools that are worth exploring and using if they suit your needs.

The Internet Options Dialog organizes a lot of security and customization capabilities in a single place, so it is easier to make several changes at once, especially if they impact one another. For example, you may want to exercise control over how your netkids use the computer and also make sure that they can't easily be snared by scammers. You can set up parental controls and content advisories using tools on the Content Tab, as shown in Figure 4-5.

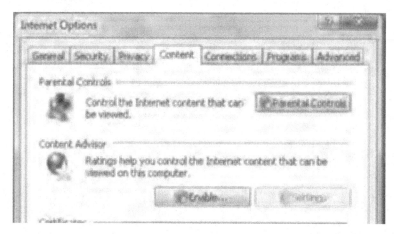

Figure 4-5. The Parental Controls and Content Advisor Services provide some degree of protection for your netkids, and a head's up about sites that host content you've agreed is off limits.

If you visit a lot of download sites, you may want to set up anti-phishing warnings (see Figure 4-6). These types of sites have surpassed email as a primary means of ensnaring the unwary, because email phishing filters have become so effective that scammers have turned to the use of pop-ups, free downloads, and luring people to click on links. Links are often presented as leading to contests, giveaways, or mildly lewd images.

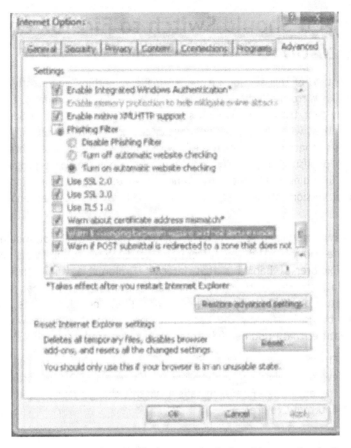

Figure 4-6. You can set Internet Explorer to check the addresses of web sites you visit against a database of known phishers. This might not be a bad idea if the netbook is being used by a young person or if you visit a lot of free download sites.

NotED

Special Note: Refrain from using "free" as a search word. Doing so will lead you to lots of dubious sites.

Why You Should Switch to Firefox and How to Do It

Given the title of this section I'd like to make something abundantly clear: I don't dislike Microsoft. I don't even dislike Internet Explorer. Really. I finished writing my first truly giant Windows program for version 1.03 in September 1986. I worked with the team that developed the Windows operating system extensions so that people could use CDs with Windows. I've written three books that were published in a lot of languages about how to write programs for Windows, including one specifically on how to write programs for Windows CE, which is a version intended especially for small devices such as phones and PDAs.

Windows, Microsoft, and I go way back. The true reason I think you should do as I have done and make the switch from Internet Explorer to Firefox is not that Internet Explorer is bad. It's that Internet Explorer is very popular. Too popular, in fact. Most of the hacks and malware in the world target it. It is a simple matter of arithmetic and nothing more. (Well, not that simple, I guess. That last bit isn't entirely the case, because Firefox has some wonderful, unique features that I find helpful, entertaining, and productive.)

Installing Firefox is fast, easy (see Figure 4-7), and low risk. If you don't like it after a few days, you can switch back to Internet Explorer without any problems, because when Firefox installs it doesn't change your default browser or disable Internet Explorer.

Figure 4-7. Go to the Firefox download site and get a copy of the self-installing package.

One of the things that makes Firefox the best non-Microsoft option out there is that it has a vibrant, global community of open source software developers at work improving it 24/7. If you aren't familiar with the open source philosophy, here's how it works. Open source developers openly share the source code they have written and take part in projects like Firefox of their own volition. Very few of them get paid directly for working on a specific product. Usually they have businesses or professional interests that benefit indirectly from their participation. As a result, basic versions of Firefox and other open source projects are available free to end users. If you want or need additional services, you can hire an open source consultant.

When an open source project is very successful (and Firefox is definitely in this category), a huge number of people worldwide work on it all the time, improving, hardening, and defending it against threats and fixing bugs. And by a huge number, I mean more people than even Microsoft can hire and manage. Here are a couple of the benefits of Firefox that make it a really compelling option:

- **Firefox is updated 48 times a day with information on web forgery sites.** If you get lured to a fake site that's masquerading as a trusted site, Firefox will stop you.
- **If you change your passwords as often as you should, use strong passwords, and don't use the same password everywhere, it is virtually impossible to keep track of them without records.**
  However, if you keep passwords in your netbook without encrypting the files, you run the very significant risk of having them stolen, either by someone who gains physical access to your netbook or by malicious software scanning for password files. Firefox integrates web password management in a way that is both secure and convenient.

Password "Best Practices"

By virtue of their portability and small size, it is an unpleasant but necessary thing to recognize that netbooks are also easier to steal, lose, or, perhaps most seriously, temporarily *lose control of*. (Say, for example, you leave it unattended and someone who has physical access to it has the opportunity to infect it with malware, install keyboard logging programs, or manipulate files without your knowledge.) In a practical sense, passwords are the one form of security and privacy defense over which you have almost complete control. A good password will stop all but the most well equipped and determined hacker.

The following are rules for what makes a password a "good" password:

- **It must be guess-proof.** You shouldn't use things like you name or the names of people close to you, birth dates, phone numbers, addresses, words that appear in any dictionary (in any language) or obvious misspellings of these. Remember that if your password comes under attack by a password-cracking program, the hack can do billions of search-and-compare operations in a reasonably short time. (This is why you shouldn't use legitimate words. All serious crackers have access to authoritative copies of dictionaries. In fact, many of them use the free ones that are available on the Web!)
- **It should be eight or more characters and contain a mix of all the types of symbols a given site allows.** What I mean by this is that if you can use letters and numbers, then "Dwe$Il22o" would be a pretty strong eight-character password. (This is also going to be incredibly difficult to remember unless it has some meaning only you know, or if it is used so frequently that you are unlikely to forget it. More on this in a bit.)
- **It should not be a password you created by substituting similar glyphs in a legitimate word (or name, birth date, phone number, and so on).** What I mean by this is that if you decide to use your phone number as a password, you can't make it strong by substituting uppercase "O"s for zeros or lowercase "l"s for ones. A smart cracking program will try these kinds of substitutions.

It's not hard to create a strong password if you follow these rules and experiment a little bit. To get the hang of it, and to test passwords for important online accounts (banking, email, shopping, and so forth), you can go to the Microsoft password strength checking site at `http://www.microsoft.com/protect/fraud/passwords/checker.aspx` and see how well you've done. If your attempt falls short of creating a good, safe password, you can try other combinations until you come up with one that measures at least "strong."

Of course, it doesn't matter how hard your passwords are to crack if you store them in a way that makes them easy to steal. Contrary to popular belief, there is nothing wrong with keeping written records of your passwords, as long as you store them in a safe place. (This applies to handwritten, paper records as well as digital records.) You have to take into account who can potentially access your passwords. Do you live in a college dorm or fraternity house? Do you have a lot of roommates? Casual visitors? Babysitters? Housekeepers? Offline storage may not be the most secure choice if many people have frequent access to your space.

On the other hand, you need to have convenient access to your records of strong passwords, or you'll quickly tire of the extra effort. If you don't have a secure place to store offline password records, a good middle ground might be keeping them on a USB key in an encrypted file. This way, they aren't actually on your computer until you need or want them and they are safe from prying eyes. If you should lose or demolish the USB key, you may be in for some inconvenience, but probably not at great risk for identity theft.

Get Set: Getting Mobile Productivity Services and Strategies in Place

Setting up to access services and tools you'll use extensively is a job to handle in some settled spot where you can safely store passwords and where you can easily pair your netbook with a wired computer or laptop if you need to do so. Here are a few points to keep in mind when you are setting up your netbook for max productivity, enjoyment, and ease of use:

- Netbooks really let you travel light, so it's best to keep the load slim and emphasize things you know will be personally important to you. Internet radio? Working collaboratively? Skype? Email? Watching your favorite television shows? Start with your known needs and choose a suite of applications and services that meets those. Make sure these work optimally before you add things that are interesting but 5not "mission critical".

- The cloud services from which you can choose present a stunning variety of opportunity, and some of it is admittedly esoteric. By all means, try things that appeal to you. If you don't like them or they are superseded by something better, move on. For things you try and decide to give a miss, if there are installable parts, make sure to wipe them off your netbook. Unlike computers with endless storage space, netbooks can become cluttered. Both performance and battery life will suffer.

- This is an exciting and rapidly evolving space, and chances are, for any common task there will be competing solutions. This is great for you as a consumer, and will drive innovation. It also means that you should evaluate your options, and not just once. For example, Google, Zoho, Adobe, and others all offer document-handling and collaboration tools. They have the predictable strengths of their creators' based on experience in their respective core businesses. Take the time to look at all of them before settling on one, and if you frequently work, play, or collaborate with others, find out what they like.

So with all these points in mind, here's a tour of some of the best-of-breed cloud tools and services.

Adobe Acrobat.com

Acrobat.com is a pretty terrific set of productivity tools that allows you to do typical home or school related work from wherever you are. It is a true cloud computing experience, and a really convenient, attractive, and well considered one. It also has the advantage of being a very complete solution. You get all of the online services you need from a single, consistent set of tools, including:

- Multi-person file sharing
- Cloud-based data storage
- Ability to convert files to Adobe's PDF format to prevent loss or unwanted changes
- Online word processor
- Web conferencing

The Acrobat.com usage terms state, "Adobe makes the Services available to you only for your individual use (including personal use and business use that directly benefits you individually)," so these services aren't meant for enterprise use.

You can use Acrobat.com to create, collaborate on, and share documents (see Figure 4-8). The key benefit to the average person is these tools allow you to hold meetings and share work in progress without the absolute requirement that everyone involved be physically present each time you need to conduct business. Anyone who has ever coached a soccer team, planned a group fundraiser, or participated in any sort of organization knows two things:

- Communication is key.
- With every person you add to a team, the difficulty of communication increases by a factor of 10.

Don't be intimidated by the fact that Adobe's tools are obviously the descendants of those designed for running global enterprise. This definitely *doesn't* mean they are "too big" for organizing a Boy Scout troop or a local petition drive. *It means they are tested, proven and effective.* So give them a look if you have something you want be able to organize and hand off to someone else in a reasonably coherent, seamless fashion.

If nothing else, you'll find that getting people to attend meetings and work on group projects is a whole lot easier if they can do it from anywhere, have a good idea of what parts of the workflow happened without them, and see where things are headed.

Maybe one of the most impressive things about Acrobat.com is that, unlike many other online toolsets that force you to exchange your privacy for the use of the cloud-based services, it respects and guards your privacy. Adobe employs some of the most effective technology available for Internet security, and uses it to protect you, your collaborators, and your data and information. When you access Acrobat.com, you use Secure Socket Layer (SSL) technology to connect to the Adobe servers. This is the same technology used by sites like banks and online shops. Both your login ID and your data are protected using really durable security measures, including personal authentication and data encryption. The bottom line is that you can rest assured that Adobe is not browsing your information for its own purposes, nor is it disclosing your information to third parties.

Another key advantage of Acrobat.com is that, although the versions described here are free, many of the key tools are subsets of chargeable Adobe products. The "for purchase" versions largely remove the limitations of scale inherent in the free versions. The big advantage of this is that if you outgrow the free version, you won't be faced with having to start from scratch with another solution.

Figure 4-8. Use Acrobat.com to create, collaborate on, and share documents.

Here is a summary of the Acrobat.com tools, including what they do and their best features:

Share

One of the attractive things about Acrobat.com online office suite is that it allows you to completely protect your personal privacy and the details of your communications in a way that other web-based solutions can't really duplicate. If you're a business user on the road and pressed to close the deal, but wary of transmitting sensitive information via insecure channels or using web mail, then your worries are over. You can easily and conveniently share information using Acrobat.com without ever losing control of its distribution. Share lets you embed a link to the information without ever passing it across open channels.

When you want to share a document, you simply upload it to your Acrobat.com online storage and enter email addresses for people with whom you want to share. You can create a message to go with the share notification if you like, but this isn't required. Your collaborators are notified by email. The message includes a link they can use to view or download the document. If you haven't set restrictions on access to the document, then the people who receive Share notifications can access it without being members of Acrobat.com. If you have placed restrictions on document access, then your readers must also be members. Access restrictions are applied on a document-by-document basis. Just to be clear about this, you don't have to do anything "special" to share a document.

- It can be in any common format (DOC, PDF, JPEG).
- It can be gigantic, because you aren't going to be providing access via email.
- Access is inherently controlled, because you are emailing a link.

This is all accomplished through the use of controls that are displayed at the time you upload the document.

When you store documents online using Acrobat.com, they are each given a unique web address, which makes it possible for you to access them via links embedded in other documents (see Figure 4-9). There is no limit to the number of people with whom you can share a document (see Figure 4-10), so you can use them to enrich web site content or to create on-demand content.

Figure 4-9. If you don't want to expose your document by sending it to recipients as an email attachment, you can use Share to offer them a link instead.

Figure 4-10. Share also gives you fine-grained control over who can see a particular document. You can allow or deny access to information on a person-by-person basis. It's easy to add, change, and delete authorized viewers using Share's privacy settings.

There are some restrictions on the types of files you can share using Acrobat.com, and these are worth noting. These restrictions are mainly aimed at preventing abuse of copyright laws and proliferation of objectionable content. Table 4-1 lists the types of files that you can't store on Acrobat.com.

Table 4-1: File types that cannot be stores on Acrobat.com

Type of file	File Extension
Audio	MP3, AAC, OGG
Video	MOV, WMV, FLV, XVID, DIVX, RETG
Font	TTF, DFONT, OTF
Archive	TGZ, RAR 7Z, SIT, JAR, WAR, CAB
System or executable files	EXE, DLL, JS, VB, BAT, CMD, COM, CPL, SH, CSH, TCSH, KSH, BASH, ZSH, INF, HTA, HLP, INS, ISP, VB, JSE, LNK, MS, PIF, SCR, SHS, WS
Web files	CHM, CRT
Databases	MDB
Raster images	PCD, SCT

ConnectNow

Adobe ConnectNow lets you conduct live meetings over the Web and use collaborative tools to facilitate communication, learning, and creativity. ConnectNow one-ups the traditional teleconference. It enables rich, full communication, and supports it with great tools for creating products such as documents and presentations. It provides a low-cost alternative to physical travel, which helps with reducing travel costs, saving time, and increasing productivity. Less expensive than special purpose facility-based telepresence solutions, it obviously has lower fidelity. It is also limited to three simultaneous meeting participants.

However, ConnectNow significantly lowers the barriers to entry for teleconferencing, being easy to access and simple to use. Because it web-based, it is singularly portable. You can use any web browser you like, and the only add-on you'll need is the Adobe Flash Player runtime, available for free download at www.adobe.com.

To start a meeting, just enter the unique URL of your meeting room in your browser's address bar. Meetings don't have to be scheduled in advance, and the meeting room URL is constant (like your address or phone number). The people who attend your meeting need not be Acrobat.com members.

ConnectNow uses ordinary web protocols, so meetings can take place across corporate firewalls, which can restrict other forms of Internet traffic if they are not specially configured to allow access.

ConnectNow is a rich product that offers web meeting participants a lot of tools and opportunities to interact (see Figure 4-11).

- **Screen sharing** lets other meeting attendees see what's happening on your screen, so you can share dynamic materials like spreadsheets and media. You can also control the degree to which you screen is shared. You can optionally show individual windows, applications, or your entire desktop.
- **Whiteboard** is really a shared, multiuser drawing program that lets collaborators make diagrams and mark up images together, using a familiar drawing toolset that supports the creation of fairly elaborate graphics. Files are exchanged in PNG format and can be reused by their creators.
- **Remote control** is a real gem for either teaching or remote troubleshooting. Given permission by the device owner, a meeting participant can take control of another's desktop. You can run applications, change settings, and modify open documents.

- **Multiple audio options** enhance your teleconferencing experience. If you use Skype to talk to friends and family, you know that the sound quality isn't always everything it ought to be. ConnectNow offers you the option of using web-based VoIP, or if high-fidelity sound is of importance, you can use one of the conference numbers provided by Adobe for traditional teleconferencing.
- **Unique meeting room URLs** enable you to meet at the same URL all of the time.

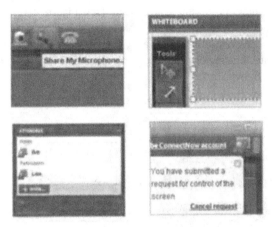

Figure 4-11. ConnectNow allows you to share almost all of the resources on your system among meeting participants, but exercise control over how much they see, hear, and can access.

Buzzword

Adobe's Buzzword is a surprisingly full feature toolset for word processing and collaborative document authoring. It has a lot of powerful features like flexible handling of lists and image insertions. Because it is an online service, your documents are safe from loss or corruption if something happens to your netbook. It acts like your word processor but lives in your browser, so it is conveniently accessible not only from your netbook, but from an Internet cafe, in a hotel, or at your desk. And how your document looks onscreen is how it will look if you print it out, or perhaps even more important today, how it will look no matter which browser a reader uses.

Like ConnectNow, Buzzword isn't just a mobility tool. It is also a collaboration and team-building tool. Any number of coauthors can write, edit, review, and comment on documents. Authors can control who sees documents and when. You can also track edits and make comments. One really sophisticated feature of Buzzword is its integrated tools for revision control. This is a really important task when several people are handling a single document. If you suddenly need to get a document back in the state it was two days ago, it's a simple matter. Roll back the changes, and presto! This comes up surprisingly often when people work on documents simultaneously, because they can accidentally overwrite one another's work. Buzzword's history feature lets you see and compare changes, and revert to previous versions of the document.

Coordination among authors is made much easier because the status and authorship of documents is very transparent (see Figure 4-12). You can sort Buzzword documents by author, date, file size, or access role. Buzzword's Change History preserves information about what each simultaneous author is doing (for example, editing or reading) or the date and time of the last version a particular author reviewed.

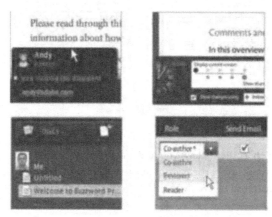

Figure 4-12. Adobe Acrobat.com Buzzword is a nice, lightweight word processor with really strong collaboration features. You can control ownership, access, and visibility of documents. You can also make sure that multiple authors' changes don't collide.

Create PDF

Adobe's PDF (Portable Document Format) file format is a key tool for working with documents that need to be portable to all types of computers, or need to be protected from changes as they are circulated among readers. You create a PDF by taking existing files and running them through the Create PDF tool (see Figure 4-13). Most common file types can be incorporated in PDF documents, as shown in Table 4-2.

Table 4-2. File types that can be incorporated in PDFs

Source of file	File Extension
Generic Text	TXT, PS, RTF
Image files	BMP, GIF, JPEG, TIFF, PNG
Microsoft Office	DOC, XLS, PPT, PRJ
Open Office	ODT, ODP, ODS, ODG, ODF
Star Office	SWX, SXI, SXC, SXD, STW
Word Perfect	WPD

The ability to make PDF files is built into the Acrobat.com suite. You get up to five freebies, but if you need to do this frequently, you'll have to purchase Adobe Acrobat (not to be confused with Acrobat.com) Also, a single PDF can't be more than 200MB in size, but it would be rare to approach this size. Note that you need to download the Adobe PDF Reader to open and use PDF files. The reader is free, but can take considerable time to download and install. Also, it may want to reboot your computer after it installs.

Figure 4-13. Create PDF lets you protect the integrity of documents and make them easily portable to any computer. You can do the conversion either by browsing to the filename or by "dragging and dropping."

My Files

MyFiles is an online storage system that makes Acrobat.com the quintessential cloud computing productivity suite. You can keep up to 5GB online, and access files from anywhere, using any computer or browser. This turns out to be a lot of storage space, so keeping your online content organized could become an issue. MyFiles includes a searching interface that lets you browse stored content by author, file type, alphabetical order, date created, last updated, or a combination of these (see Figure 4-14).

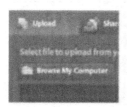

Figure 4-14. You can use MyFiles to browse your computer, locate files you want to upload, and quickly move copies to your online storage area. Once they are there, you can access them from any browser. Find specific uploaded files fast with MyFiles storage searching tools.

Google Tools and Applications

If you could use a special, satellite-based remote sensing instrument that measured brainwaves, its meter would pretty likely be pegged when it passed over Google headquarters. No question, those folks are seriously a brain trust, and the tools they make for us mobile computing lifestyle types are great. And of course, what's even more amazing is that we are always describing them as free tools. They are not free. At least not in the sense that Google isn't receiving something of value in exchange for your use of them. Before you settle on the use of Google apps for significant business or personal use, take the time to learn what it is you are providing. What follows is an excerpted version, drawn from Google's Privacy policy, which can be found in full here: www.google.com/privacypolicy.html.

In these excerpts, emphasis has been added to draw your attention to things every Google apps user should know.

Google stores the following kinds of information about its users. There is no "sunset," no chance for you to view, challenge, or correct it if it is mistaken; and no accountability or transparency about the way and the sources to whom they distribute it:

- **Information you provide:** When you sign up for a Google Account or other Google service or promotion that requires registration, you are asked for personal information (such as your name, email address, and an account password).

- **Cookies:** When you visit Google, one or more "cookies" is sent to your computer or device. (Cookies are small files containing a sequence of letters and numbers.) Cookies uniquely identify your browser. Google uses cookies to target you for advertising and to tailor content served to your browser.
- **Log information:** When you access Google services, servers automatically record information that your browser sends *whenever you visit a web site.* These server logs may include information such as *your web request, Internet Protocol address, browser type, browser language, the date and time of your request, and one or more cookies that may uniquely identify your browser.*
- **User communications:** When you send email or other communications to Google, they are retained in order to process your inquiries, respond to your requests, and improve Google services.
- **Affiliated Google Services on other sites:** Google offers some services on or through other web sites. Personal information that you provide to those sites may be sent to Google, which applies its Privacy Policy. *The affiliated sites may have different privacy practices.*
- **Gadgets:** The information collected by Google when you enable a gadget or other application is processed under Google's Privacy Policy. Information collected by the application or gadget provider is governed by their privacy policies.
- **Location data:** Google offers location-enabled services, such as Google Maps for mobile. If you use those services, Google may receive information about your actual location (such as GPS signals sent by a mobile device) or information that can be used to approximate a location (such as a cell ID).
- **Links:** Google may present links in a format that enables them to keep track of whether these links have been followed.
- **Where your information goes**: Google processes personal information on servers in the United States of America and in other countries. In some cases, they process personal information on a server outside your own country.
- **Who Might Have Your Information**: Google may process personal information to provide its own services. In some cases, Google processes personal information on behalf of and according to the instructions of a third party.

That's not to say that you shouldn't use Google's tools, just that you should be careful when using them, and that you are aware of how your information is being stored. With that in mind, let's take a look at some of the tools available from Google.

Google Calendar

Google Calendar is a cloud-based shared calendar tool that lets you track your own appointments, keep your friends and family informed about your plans, and selectively distribute information about your schedule (see Figure 4-15).

Figure 4-15. Getting Started with Google's shared calendaring app.

Once you've entered a few personal details, you're free to use the service. To illustrate this, I'll go to my calendar page and set up a few important appointments and events I don't want to forget (see Figure 4-16). Notice the Settings link in the My Calendars drop-down menu. You can use this feature to tell Google Calendars who should be allowed to have access to a particular calendar. This link prompts a dialog box that lets you enter the email address of the person with whom you'd like to share calendar information. You can enter as many of these as you like, and they apply to that specific calendar only.

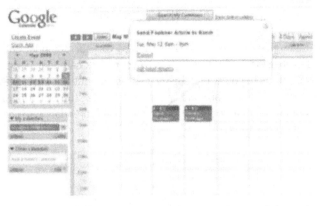

Figure 4-16. Using Google Calendar to record appointments and share plans with friends, family, and collaborators.

What's even better is that you can set up the Google Calendar to text message your mobile phone and remind you of events and appointments (see Figure 4-17). This is great if you tend to be forgetful, but even better, it means that if someone else can make appointments on your calendar, you can be immediately notified.

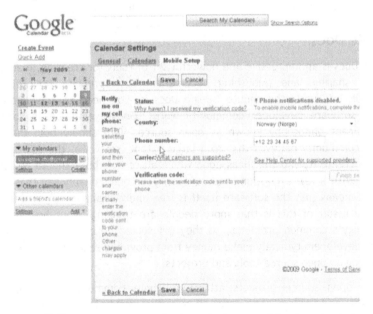

Figure 4-17. You can set up your calendar to text your mobile phone to alert you when appointments are added, updated, or cancelled.

You can also keep more than one calendar (see Figure 4-18). This is useful if you want to track your business and personal activities separately. Using this feature, you can give family and friends access to your personal calendar and business and professional contacts access to your work calendar. Of course, this has the potential to become hopelessly confusing, but for one great Google Calendar feature: while you provide separate calendars for others, you can see all of your appointments and obligations on a single calendar, with dates color-coded by appointment type.

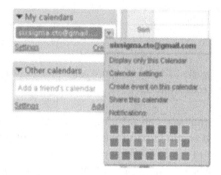

Figure 4-18. Google Calendar lets you keep multiple calendars to maintain privacy, but you can also see a single consolidated view of all your appointments.

Google Docs

Google Docs is an impressive and powerful set of tools for creating, managing, storing, sharing, and publishing documents. To appreciate how elegant, powerful, and up-to-the-minute Google Docs is, you need to know how the Google software developer community works. Google embraces a software development philosophy known as open source. Very simply put, the open source community believes that to a large extent, software, the source code used to create it, and the ideas upon which all of it is built should be openly shared. With a few exceptions and caveats, you could reliably say that "open source" means that the software itself is free and is maintained for free. The ultimate result of this is that more people are thinking about how to solve technology's common problems, so they get solved better and sooner. Open source developers typically make money from providing extensions, support, or consulting on open source tools and projects.

Vibrant open source projects attract a whole community of developers, designers, and implementers from all over the world. This means that when you choose to use open source products, it is very likely you will have the opportunity to benefit from all of this creativity, at little or no cost to yourself.

Google Doc's Template Gallery is a perfect example of open source at work (see Figure 4-19). Templates are basic designs for documents, and are typically used to standardize document presentation and format. A nice looking template can make an ordinary document look very professional (or amusing or creative). Google Docs offers hundreds of these templates that you can use at will when starting a Google Docs project.

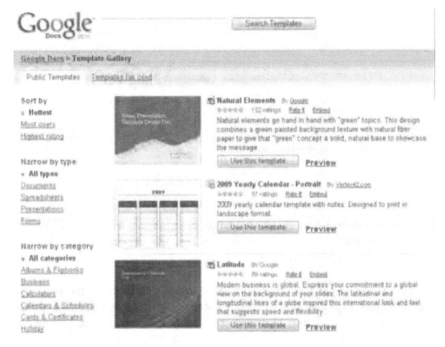

Figure 4-19. Google Docs' Template Gallery lets you start a project using open source document templates that will jumpstart development, provide great aesthetics, and work well in web browsers, offline word processors, and in print.

One of the tremendous advantages of Google Docs is that it has an offline mode. This means that when you are stuck somewhere without an Internet connection, you can keep working productively. This is going to be a fairly frequent occurrence for netbook users, for two reasons. First, there still are a lot of places without wireless access. And second, you'll get about half as much time out of a single battery charge in connected mode as you do working offline. This is because it takes a lot of juice to power the antenna. If you are doing something that is basically non-collaborative (such as editing a document), you may as well disconnect and conserve power.

If you click on the Offline link in the upper right-hand corner of any of the Google Apps (this includes Google Calendar, Spreadsheet and Presentation), you can set up the app to work using locally stored tools and information when you are not connected. The setup is simple, but will probably prompt you to download a component called Gears if you don't already have a Google Offline App installed (see Figure 4-20).

Figure 4-20. Google Docs lets you work on documents without an active Internet connection if you do a minor amount of setup. (You need to be connected to install offline access to Google Docs work.)

The next time you connect to your online Google Docs account, the files get "synched" (see Figure 4-21). This simply means the changes you made while working offline are written back into the document stored online. Because Google considers its online version of the document authoritative (or in other words, the one that really counts), it synchs your documents before it will allow you to begin working. Depending on the extent of your changes and additions, this can take a while. You'll see a progress box to let you know how this operation is going.

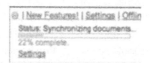

Figure 4-21. Google Docs makes you wait to begin working on a document until the online and offline versions are updated with the most recent content.

Google Docs documents are sharable and can be authored collaboratively. You set access controls on documents by assigning roles like Owner, Collaborator, and Viewer. Each of these roles grants a certain degree of access to the document. If documents are designated Published, anyone can view them. It is not necessary that they have a Google account.

Google Spreadsheets

Google Spreadsheets offers a lot of the same features as Google Docs (after all, a spreadsheet is just a special class of document), but it has one feature that is so unique it would be giving you less than your money's worth not to mention it: The GoogleLookup function. Pretty much any spreadsheet has all sorts of functions (think SUM, SINE, AVERAGE, and so on), but GoogleLookup is unique because it is a function that isn't strictly mathematical or strictly a database operation. Using the formidable power of Google searching and data caching technology, GoogleLookup allows you to insert something a lot like a really tightly targeted web search as the contents of a spreadsheet cell.

It works like this:

```
=GoogleLookup( "entity"; "attribute")
```

Where

- *entity is the name of a person place or thing you want information about; and*
- *attribute* is something that describes or defines entity.

So, for example, *=GoogleLookup("Denali"; "height meters")* would return 6,194 as the contents of the spreadsheet cell; but *=GoogleLookup("Denali"; "height feet")* would return 20,320 as the contents of the spreadsheet cell. This is an incredibly powerful feature, especially if the lookup data is something that can change frequently. (Think stock prices, airfares and population numbers.) That said, not every combination you try is going to produce reasonable results, because there are things to which even Google doesn't pay much attention. Make sure you try a lookup a few times before counting on it or distributing a spreadsheet that uses it.

Google Presentations

Google Presentations is a fully featured tool for creating, editing, and dynamically presenting a series of slides. Like Google Docs and Google Spreadsheets, Google Presentations benefits from hundreds of free templates for various types of presentations. It offers a robust set of tools for creating and organizing slide sets (see Figure 4-22).

Figure 4-22. Google Presentations gives collaborators a solid set of tools for creating and organizing presentations.

By accessing slide sets over the Web, any number of people in various locations can view a presentation simultaneously. Each attendee has to sign in to the presentation, and then initiate the slide show using a Start presentation control. Viewers have the option of following along with the presenter or navigating through the slides at their own pace and in their own order.

Skype

Skype is *double* free software for making phone calls over the Internet. The software costs nothing and the calls are free as well (if both callers use Skype). You can download the Skype telephony software here: www.skype.com/download.

There are versions for every imaginable variety of Windows and Linux, but pay attention and make sure you get the one that matches whatever you have, because it matters (see Figure 4-23).

Figure 4-23. Make sure to download the correct version of Skype for your operating system. Usually, the download site will correctly determine which version you need. If not, use the list of versions at the right of the screen.

To place and receive voice-only calls from your computer, you'll need a headset that includes both headphones and a microphone. Your computer may come with built-in speakers and a microphone, but for privacy (and improved performance) you may want to use a separate headset. Many netbooks include these accessories at no extra charge, so check every corner and cranny of the box before you pitch the packaging your netbook came in.) If you plan to make video calls, you'll need a web cam as well, but a lot of netbooks have those integrated.

Skype voice and video calls are free because they use exactly the same infrastructure to connect you to your conversation partners as the larger web. A Skype-to-Skype call (one that is conducted between two people using computers) isn't going through the regular phone system at all, so no minutes or long distance charges apply, no matter how long or often you talk. The exact technology involved is called VoIP, which stands for Voice over Internet Protocol. Calls to wire line phones and mobile phones are chargeable, but typically at a small fraction of what you'd pay for telephone system calls.

International calls currently start at 2.1 cents per minute. For between $3.00 to $13.00 per month, you can set yourself up for unlimited calling to any country in the world.

Setting up Skype involves a few steps, though the process is not difficult and the Skype web site has about the best step-by-step instructions you'll ever see. Setup differs a little, depending on which operating system you use, so it's best to just visit this URL and get the exact procedure for your netbook device and your needs: www.skype.com/help/guides.

Skype is very popular with families and friends who just want to keep in touch (video calling is especially nice for this) and for people who travel a lot to places where access to traditional phone systems is difficult or costly. In general, the audio quality of calls is good, but perhaps not always quite as good as it would be using the traditional phone infrastructure. This generally isn't a problem for personal calls, but could be more of a consideration for business callers. Also note, Skype works for toll-free numbers.

ExplainED

Special Note: Because Skype doesn't use dedicated communication networks; it should never be used to make emergency calls (911 in the U.S. or 112 in the EU). Use a wire line phone or a mobile phone for emergency calls, because the phone systems have infrastructure in place to help emergency services providers find you even if you aren't able to make yourself understood.

Gliffy

Gliffy is a versatile, high-octane diagram-making application. You can create flowcharts, network diagrams, floor plans, organization charts, SWOT diagrams (strengths, weaknesses, opportunities, and tests), wireframes, UML diagrams, business process modeling, and so on. You can use it to create just about anything you can think of that can be represented with 2D graphics. Find it here: www.gliffy.com (Figure 4-24).

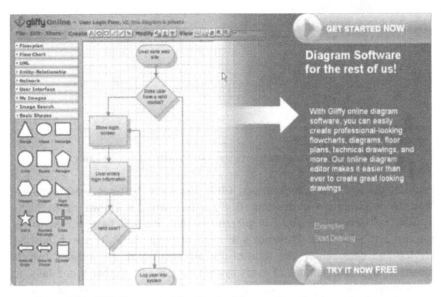

Figure 4-24. Gliffy is a powerful online tool for creating drawings, charts, and diagrams.

Gliffy is a browser-based, fully online application. This means there is no local mode of operation, so your files are not available when you aren't connected to the Internet. Of course, this means you can't just use it anywhere. But it offers good support for team projects. You have fine control over the access you grant people who collaborate in the creation of diagrams, and Gliffy also provides integrated document version control. This means every time you save a file, a record is made of the whole file and of the differences between the current and previous version. So if requirements change or someone makes a mistake, you can roll back to a prior version of the drawing very easily.

Gliffy also has great security features, so you can be sure that sensitive information going into your drawings is never within view of prying eyes. If you use Gliffy with the Secure Login option, all of your work is encrypted employing the latest in Secure Socket Layer (SSL) technology (see Figure 4-25). SSL is a method of coding data before it is sent over the Internet, so that no one can get access to it while it is being transferred to the server. One downside of working in the fully private mode is that data transfers are generally slower.

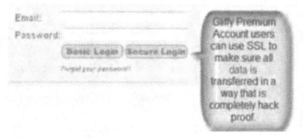

Figure 4-25. Gliffy Premium Account users can transfer all data securely.

For business and professional users, Gliffy has some features that would be hard to duplicate on a desktop. Gliffy offers what is known as a "high-availability" service, meaning it guarantees that you will have access to its systems and your data whenever you need or want it. Gliffy's web hosting service and data center use state-of-the art equipment, redundancy (which means it has more than one of every system component, so that if one fails, it can immediately switch to a backup), and 24/7 monitoring to offer near 100% uptime.

Zumodrive

ZumoDrive is a cloud-based storage service that lets you have one big (even giant) library of digital assets (documents, music, video, photos, programs, and so on) that you can access from any device you own (Figure 4-26). Think of it as super-sized data storage. ZumoDrive has a free plan that gives you 1GB, and plans for 20 to 500GB starting at $2.99 per month. Find it here: http://zumodrive.com.

Figure 4-26. ZumoDrive gives you the flexibility to access large collections of personal content without using local storage.

By using ZumoDrive to keep everything in one conveniently accessible place, you can access your digital content from your netbook, iPhone, laptop, or desktop computer, without having to manually transfer files between devices. You never have to be concerned about how much storage space you use or about backing up data. All of the ordinary considerations of file management disappear.

This means that you'll be able to play any tune from your entire music library, regardless of its size, from your netbook (or laptop or iPhone). ZumoDrive lets your music follow you from device to device, because songs aren't physically confined to any of them. You can also do this with photos and photo albums. If you save your pictures in ZumoDrive when you upload them from a camera, they will be automatically preserved and organized into photo albums. To share pictures in ZumoDrive, just right-click their folder to get a link. You can email these links or embed them in a web site or blog. Sharing folders allows you to collaborate with other people. Once you have a shared folder with collaborators, any modifications to files are immediately and automatically visible to all of them. You can restrict access to your shared files using ZumoDrive's Shared Files Options.

You can store any sort of file on ZumoDrive (Figure 4-27). It looks and acts just as it would if stored on any other drive on your computer. To add a file or folder to ZumoDrive, simply drag-and-drop the file or folder into your ZumoDrive from its current location. When you add files to your ZumoDrive, they are uploaded to a secure server in the background. You check the status of your uploads by right-clicking the ZumoDrive tray icon. ZumoDrive content is immediately available from all your devices. You can also access content offline, by flagging particular content as Keep Local when you are connected to the Internet. This can be a good option if, for example, you want to watch a movie. Your netbook doesn't have to power the antenna and the screen at the same time if the movie is stored locally, so you could download while attached to wall current, and then watch it later using the battery. No worrying about whether you'll get to see the whole thing before the screen goes dark.

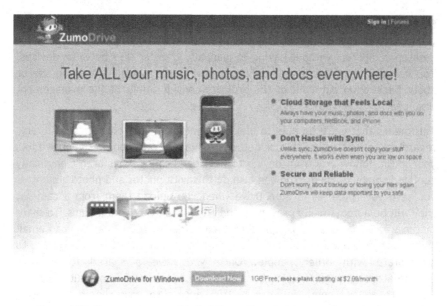

Figure 4-27. You can store any kind of file on ZumoDrive, regardless of size or format.

Go! Fun and Entertainment "Must Haves"

As you will no doubt know by now, you can have a lot of fun with your netbook. When you add the Internet into the equation, enabling you to stream music and movies and play games with friends, that fun goes to another level. To get the most out of the Internet, though, you may need a few extra small applications or plug-ins for your web browser, that enable it to run things like Flash, or the QuickTime video player.

Flash Player

The Adobe Flash Player is software that enables you to watch animation and movies in your web browser. Flash content is very popular with web designers, because it allows them to create sophisticated animation, graphics, and sound that work on most operating systems and browsers and a great variety of devices. You've probably seen hundreds of examples of Flash-based content all over the Web. In fact, if you have watched media in your browser and it involved glitzy video with a soundtrack, odds are it was Adobe Flash content. The most compelling reason to have Flash Player installed on your computer is that a lot of gaming, entertainment, and learning opportunities out there that depend on it.

Flash Player is installed on 99% of Internet-enabled desktops worldwide, and on a wide range of popular devices like mobile phones and netbooks (Figure 4-28). It is a standard component of some web browsers, and is available as an add-on component for most others, including recent versions of Mozilla Firefox, Opera, Safari, and Internet Explorer.

So, basically, no matter where you are, how you connect to the Internet, or what language you speak, there is a version of Flash Player that will meet your needs. Flash Player, while it is proprietary software, it is 100% free to end users. Adobe has a big incentive to get lots of people to download it, because that drives sales of the development tools they sell to people who produce content. In all likelihood, Flash Player was on your netbook when it left the factory. If not, you can download it here: www.adobe.com/products/flashplayer. Accept the license terms, run the install, and start enjoying great Flash Content right away. There are always some fun Flash sites at Adobe's Site of the Day page: www.adobe.com/cfusion/showcase

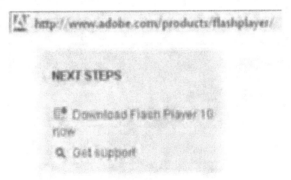

Figure 4-28. You can download the Flash Player here if your netbook didn't come with it installed.

You should evaluate how Flash Player's default security settings align with your needs and expectations, whether it came preinstalled or you installed it yourself. Using a strategy not unlike that of your web browser, items executing in the Flash Player can leave small files on your hard disk that allow content to playback more smoothly and to resume a playback from a previous stopping point instead of having to start all over each time you quit the player. This has the potential to compromise the security of your netbook, and to allow web sites to track your travels around the Internet. If you want to see what the current Flash Player security and privacy settings are, you can right-click inside any Flash Player window that appears on your browser. The easiest way to get a Flash Player window for the purpose of this investigation is to point your browser to Adobe's Flash web site (www.adobe.com/products/flashplayer), where there is always a snazzy Flash Demo on the home page. A right-click brings up the floating menu. Choose Settings, as shown in the Figure 4-29.

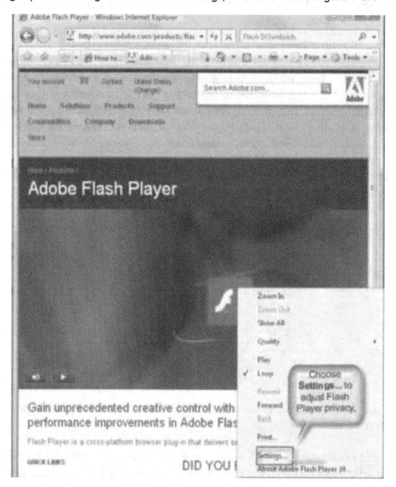

Figure 4-29. You may want to change the Flash Player's privacy settings to keep it from allowing personal information and web surfing histories to be shared across Flash applications.

You'll probably want to leave the settings you see in the basic Settings dialog as they are, because they are necessary to view much of the Flash content you'll encounter on the Web. However, you can extensively customize the degree to which your data, personal information, and computer are exposed by Flash Player using the Advanced options for Flash Player settings (see Figure 4-30). Fine-tuning advanced privacy and security settings allows you to control several things, but at a minimum, there are three that are worth a look before you begin using your netbook for sending and receiving Flash content. I discuss these shortly.

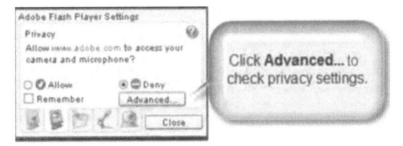

Figure 4-30. Fine tune Flash Player security and privacy settings with this dialog box.

Clicking the Advanced button takes you to Adobe's Flash Player web page, where you can learn more about the ways you can customize the behaviors and privacy aspects of the player (see Figure 4-31).

ExplainED

Special Note: You make changes to the security and privacy behaviors of Flash Player using Adobe's web site, not using local tools on your own netbook. This means that to adjust settings, you must be connected to the Internet.

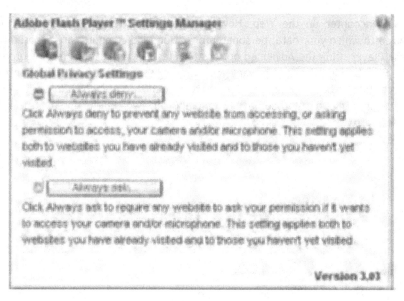

Figure 4-31. Use Adobe's Tools to establish appropriate security and privacy cntrols on the Flash Player, and take the time to read warnings and instructions carefully.

The three "must visit" security and privacy control panels are the Global Privacy Panel, the Global Security Panel, and the Web Site Privacy Settings Panel. Use the links displayed in the menu at the left side of the Settings Manager page to access each of them (see Figure 4-32). After you have visited a page, its link in the Settings Manager Table of Contents will remain highlighted. This is a helpful reminder of which pages you have visited and which you still need to review.

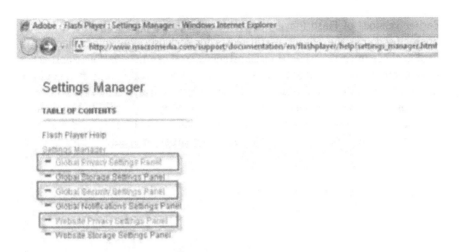

Figure 4-32. Use the Settings Manager links to review, at minimum, the Global Privacy, the Global Security, and the Web Site Privacy Settings panels.

You can control a web site's access to your local camera and microphone (see Figure 4-33). Remember that whatever is captured by these devices can very easily be sent out over the Internet to the site controlling the player.

Figure 4-33. You can set limits on which Flash Applications can take control of your local web cam and microphone.

Earlier versions of Flash Player had some security loopholes that have largely been closed, but the potential still exists for seriously determined hackers to exploit these in certain special circumstances. You can take various approaches to this threat. Do nothing and chances are you won't have a problem unless you happen to be in the wrong place at the wrong time. Always deny these methods of access, as shown in Figure 4-34, and you'll be fully protected, but some apps may not run properly or not run at all. The middle ground is simply to ask to be prompted to allow or disallow the access if the situation arises.

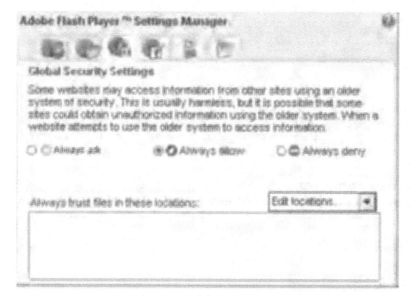

Figure 4-34. Choose which level of access you allow for older (and possibly insecure) Flash apps.

The Web Site Privacy Panel is sort of like a firewall for Flash Player, with respect to the camera and the microphone. If there are sites you always want to deny or sites you always want to allow, you can record them here as Always Deny or Always Allow. This saves you the trouble of seeing and answering the allow/deny prompt over and over and can make the content viewing experience more enjoyable for safe sites. It also means that you'll never accidentally allow access to a site you don't trust.

QuickTime

Available for both Windows and Mac, Apple's QuickTime Player is free to end users, and the newest release, Version 7, is a solid platform for netbook video playback that hosts thousands of high-quality content experiences.

QuickTime 7 uses the H.264 codec (short for COder/DECoder, the software that decompresses the video), which is one of the newest and best-performing video compression technologies. The H.264 codec compresses video very tightly without sacrificing either picture or sound quality, and you can play files back using the full screen of your device. The QuickTime 7 Player is also smart enough to automatically discover your netbook's connection speed and pick the best quality data stream that its bandwidth can support. This means that your video downloads won't stop and start because playback uses data faster than you can download it.

QuickTime also provides superlative multichannel audio and can even render "surround sound" for movies that include this effect. If your netbook doesn't come with it preinstalled, get the free download from the Apple site (www.apple.com/quicktime/download) shown in Figure 4-35.

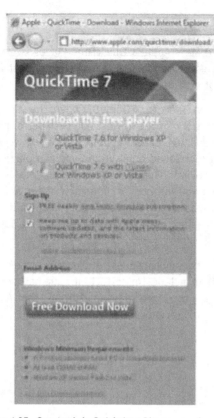

Figure 4-35. Get Apple's Quicktime Player as a free download from Apple's main site.

Connected Mobile Life Support

There are certainly things you *need* to do and have before you get out there with your netbook, but there is a whole additional category of things that, while not necessary, are so entertaining, fun, or convenient that you'll want them anyway.

Pandora

Pandora is a free Internet radio station that is designed to play only the music that you, specifically and personally, will enjoy. Its playlist is customized for everyone who listens to it, and it is free (Figure 4-36). You can download it here: www.pandora.com. (Every five minutes, you have to listen to a brief ad, which is how Pandora makes money.)

Figure 4-36. Pandora Internet Radio creates a personalized playlist based on a few simple instructions from you. The service is free and it is a great way to discover artists and music you might like.

Pandora picks music for you in an extraordinarily clever way, based on the Music Genome Project, founded in 2000 by Tim Westergren. Here's how it works: A group of musicians and music-loving technologists decided to undertake the most comprehensive analysis of music and musical elements ever, and patterned it after the Human Genome Project, which was in progress at the time.

What they wanted to do was create a scheme by which they could define relationships between musical works at the most basic level. In order to do this, they developed a vast database of musical characteristics, which they called musical genes. The musical genes of a given piece record qualities including melody, harmony, rhythm, instrumentation, orchestration, arrangement, lyrics, and elements of vocalization.

What this means in practice is that when I tell Pandora that I enjoy a particular artist, it finds music of similar musical genetics and plays it for me quasi randomly. In most cases, this has the effect not of filling your playlist with all the works of the particular artist you chose, but of others who have something in common with the one you already like. In this way you discover new music that you are likely to enjoy, with virtually no time or effort spent searching for it. You get to rate the songs it picks for you, and if you strongly dislike one, it avoids music that heavily shares the song's genetics. Conversely, if you give something a big thumbs up, it takes that into account when matching for your playlist.

ExplainED

Pandora is available in the U.S. only. International readers might want to try Last.fm or Spotify.

Hulu

Hulu is an online video site that provides free access to hit television shows, movies, and clips (Figure 4-37). The Hulu partners (NBC Universal, News Corp., and Providence Equity Partners) offer content from well over 100 leading providers including NBC Universal, Comedy Central, Lionsgate, MGM, MTV Networks, National Geographic, Paramount, PBS, Sony Pictures Television and Warner Bros. You can download it here: www.hulu.com.

Figure 4-37. Watch your favorite television shows online, at your convenience.

You'll find current, popular, primetime television shows such as *The Simpsons, 30 Rock, The Daily Show with Jon Stewart* and *The Office*. Episodes become available the morning after they air on their regular channels. There is also a rich selection of classic material like *Buffy the Vampire Slayer, The A-Team, Airwolf* and *Married...with Children*. Hulu offers feature-length movies as well.

In contrast to some other Internet video and movie sharing sites, Hulu acquires the rights to distribute content, making it available to users legally. You'll need to install Adobe Flash Player version 9 to watch, and you may legally share full-length episodes or clips by email or by embedding them on a Web site, blog, or social networking page.

ExplainED

Hulu is currently available in the U.S. only, though they are working to broaden their coverage throughout the globe.

ESPN

Though some of the individual leagues and sporting associations have their own dedicated sites, it's hard to beat ESPN Online for the breadth of its coverage. The ESPN Corporate group aggregates more than 60 sports media properties, and covers a global variety of sports at their online site, ESPN360.com (Figure 4-38).

ESPN360.com is available at no charge if you use an ESPN360.com-affiliated Internet service provider to connect. You can download it at www.espn360.com. It is typically available as a free service from U.S. college campuses and U.S. military bases, but can be pricey for other consumers. So far, there are no big general moves to give away sports content, but it doesn't hurt to keep your eyes open.

Figure 4-38. You can watch live sports on ESPN360, but there are some strings attached.

Google News: Mainstream News Feeds

Google News is basically a do-it-yourself newspaper that is built on the fly every time you open it (Figure 4-39). The front page allows you to choose the categories of stories that are displayed and what rank they get on the page. It can optionally pick stories it thinks you'll like based on what it knows about your search history (and that is probably a lot). You can set Google News to send you alerts when your favorite feeds have new items available. Tell it your ZIP code and you'll get a mix of local stories with national and global ones. And best of all, you can read it at any time of day and it will be "fresh off the presses." You can download it here: http://news.google.com.

Figure 4-39. Create a custom news page using Google's news feed aggregator.

Alexa: Where the Surf's Up

Alexa's traffic rankings are based on a secret formula (Figure 4-40). Basically, it uses a mix of its own traffic data and data collected from other, diverse sources. Ranks are based on a moving three-month window. A site's ranking reflects its reach and the number of page views generated for the domain. (A domain is a full web site name that ends in ".com," ".org," and so on.) Using this measure, a site gets credit for being viewed by people who don't necessarily enter at the home page. This is key, because a very large proportion of page visits are generated by search engine results, which don't necessarily lead users to home pages and portals. Reach is determined by the number of unique Alexa users who visit a site on a given day. Page views are the total number of Alexa unique user URL requests for a site. (It doesn't count if the same person visits a single page more than once in a day.) You can download it at: http://alexa.com.

Figure 4-40. Alexa.com is a web metrics site that tracks the relative popularity of sites and of particular pages.

Alexa uses various technologies to crawl and categorize sites in order to identify relationships among sites, which can be both interesting and useful for aspiring web buzz experts. The service is free, and a great tool for doing basic research. It is also entertaining to see what the hottest URLs are at any given moment, because these usually include not a little scandal and gossip.

Addictinggames.com

AddictingGames is the largest online games site in the US (Figure 4-41). It reaches over 10 million unique users per month, and offers a great variety of games, puzzles, and other entertainment. You play these games online, so you need a connection to enjoy them. Games at the site are free, supported by ad revenue, so expect to see a few commercial messages. Also, not every game at this site is appropriate for the very young or extremely sensitive. For older kids and adults, there are lots of games on Facebook, but bear in mind that there may be little if any privacy protection around participation there. Use common sense, and don't participate in online games at social media sites if it would be embarrassing if your boss, your neighbor, or your grandma found out about it. You can download it at: www.addictinggames.com/index.html.

Figure 4-41. Access free games, puzzles, and other entertainment at AddictingGames.com.

Urbanspoon

Urbanspoon is an online restaurant review and locator site that has it all: every imaginable type of restaurant, in most all North American cities, including reviews, pictures, directions, contact information, and so on. Most recently (see Figure 4-42), Urbanspoon's web site has been updated with a version of the delightful Urbanspoon iPhone app. Here's how this works: let's say you're out on a Friday night with your pals and you can't think of (or agree on) a place to eat. Use the Urbanspoon Restaurant Slot Machine to pick a place for you, by giving it some (or a lot, or no) information. You can constrain its choices by type of food, price, and location. So for example, if you play the Restaurant Slot and tell it you want something mid-priced, Italian, and within a mile of you, it will find a moderately upscale Italian place pretty close by. If there are ten of them, it randomly picks one. You just keep doing this until it finds something for you that strikes the right note. Download it at www.urbanspoon.com.

Figure 4-42. Urbanspoon will help you find a restaurant that suits your whims, budget, and geography, in virtually any city.

Looking Ahead

This chapter wraps the first section of this exploration of getting started with netbooks and cloud computing. You learned about the cloud, what lives there, and how it can broaden and enrich your life. You've seen what a netbook really is and isn't, and how to find one that fits your needs and your budget. You know where to find the add-ons and extra services that make you a power cloud dweller. And in this chapter, you've gotten the essentials for being immediately productive, for getting the best of live and on-demand entertainment and content, and how to make your netbook a portable lifestyle accessory that will rapidly become indispensible. In the next part of this book, we'll run through some projects showing you how to get started with some of the great software found in this chapter.

Chapter 5

Hot Tickets for Netbook Software, Media, and Content Experiences

In the mid 1980s, having a command of computing technology became key for people entering the job market, but there was a significant lag in response by educational institutions. First, it took time for the public to recognize that teaching technology skills was not only an appropriate task for public education, it was a vital one in terms of keeping businesses competitive. Second, considerable funding and resources were required for schools to gear up to teach the skills necessary for students to function productively and effectively in a rapidly transforming workplace. And finally, teachers were tackling an entirely new subject area on the fly. Through these challenges, we've learned a lot about how to teach, use, and benefit from technology. It is time to put those lessons to use, because the transition to cloud culture and ultra-mobile computing represents almost as significant a change as did the first wave of the technology revolution. Here's why:

- **Ubiquity**: Netbooks really *are* going to be everywhere, and almost everyone will own and use them for personal communication, entertainment, access to cloud-based data and software, and to receive services. This changes both what is possible, and what will come to be expected in terms of personal access to the cloud.

- **Changing habits regarding resource consumption**: A variety of trends are converging to create a "forcing function" that will modify the way people use energy and raw materials. As we shift away from reliance on oil, preferences will shift to smaller homes; more efficient transportation; more centralized, engaged communities; and more energy-efficient life styles. Netbooks fit right in with this scenario, because they are more energy-efficient than other computers.

- **Aging populations**: A recently published study by The National Center for Policy Analysis projects that, in addition to Medicare and Medicaid, the average 65 year old is going to spend $240,000 to pay out-of-pocket health care costs to cover the remainder of their life. *Average* in this context means a lot of people will pay *more*. Clearly, distance delivery of health care services and increased automation of care giving for people with chronic illnesses will be necessary. And here's how that equation has to work: netbooks + cloud-based services = cost containment + health care access.

- **Virtual workplaces**: As the technologies underlying the Internet continue to progress, some really important things are going to happen that will collectively change the way we "go to work":

  - You'll be able to pay for and get a specific quality of Internet service.

  - New technologies will close many of the loopholes cyber criminals use today and make it much easier to detect the physical source of malware, reveal identity of perpetrators, and rapidly interdict attacks and attackers.

  - Online collaboration tools will make geography increasingly irrelevant.

The combination of netbooks and cloud services is going to change the workplace and day-to-day life as much as any tech phenomenon yet, so it's worth learning about its tools, techniques, and possibilities. This chapter contains six projects for you to work through. They provide hands-on experience to help you learn basic skills and concepts, as well as to use some of the fun and interesting peripherals from Chapter 2. Each project takes from one hour to several days to complete, so pick one that interests you and dive in.

Project 1: Making a Pandora Radio Station

This project is a "soft" introduction to several aspects of cloud computing and netbooks. It gives you the opportunity to use simple USB peripherals if you have them, such as a wireless mouse and stereo speakers, but these are not necessary. With this project, you will explore cloud-based entertainment services, cloud-based data storage, and social media.

This is a relatively easy project that should take between 15 and 45 minutes to complete. It is suitable for users aged 12 and older. It will show you how simple USB accessories work, and familiarize you with the basic concepts and functionality of cloud-based services. You will see how, using the cloud, you can have access to large amounts of content on demand, without having to store the content locally on your netbook. You'll also see how cloud services are readily customized, personalized, and shared among the contacts you select, and that you can access free, high-quality entertainment content easily from anywhere on the Internet.

Pandora is an excellent music tool. It is powered by a musical "inference engine" that categorizes music based on its underlying structure, instrumentation, and cultural qualities. You can train Pandora to suggest new music that you might like by telling it artists and genres that you enjoy (see Chapter 3 for more on Pandora). It will then create a radio station based on your personal tastes. You can use Spotify, Last.fm, or a similar service if Pandora is not available in your country.

Required Equipment, Support, and Services

- Netbook
- Broadband connection
- Headphones or integrated speakers

Optional Equipment, Support, and Services

- Integrated wireless capabilities and a wireless mouse
- JBL Creature II Speakers for high-quality sound in a fixed setting (Figure 5-1)

CREATURE II - WHITE
3-Piece Desktop Speaker System

JBL's Creature II three piece speaker system
produces high-quality stereo sound for movies, MP3's,
movies and gaming experiences.
Featuring cutting-edge sci-fi design and superior
sound performance, JBL Creature II is a unique "plug
and play" solution, compatible with all Macs and PCs
– both desktops and portables – as well as MP3
players and Walkmans. JBL Creature II offers
consumers cool design and exceptional sound
proving that excellence does not have to come in an
expensive package.

The JBL CREATURE speaker system includes a
touch volume control.

The CREATURE II audio system utilizes a straight
forward interconnect technology.

The powerful subwoofer provides clean low bass.

The mini-stereo jack connection allows enjoyment of
high quality audio from a variety of devices such as
digital music players, computers, stereos and portable
listening devices.

Figure 5-1. Use USB speakers to experience how cloud-based services can provide
entertainment for groups or in social settings like dances or exercise classes.

Scenario

Depending on the amount of time you are able to invest, your degree of
interest, and your plans for using your netbook for entertainment, you can take
a variety of approaches to hands-on learning, such as the following:

- Set up a station based on your favorite musician or band.
- Refine Pandora's choices by rating the songs it plays and trying three
  more.
- Share a playlist with someone. Be sure that your playlist is exposed to
  them after you share it. Unshare the playlist and have them try to
  view it. What has happened?
- Set up a playlist for a school or community party.

You can also use Pandora to learn about music, because it has very
sophisticated musical pattern matching capability that it uses to define
relationships among songs. To learn more about this, do the following:

- Choose two or more Pandora pre-defined stations.
- Identify the features of the music that make each song or work part of
  that station (tempos, rhythms, instrumentation, and other musical
  characteristics).
- Compare and contrast the two stations.

Pandora is a nice "lifestyle accessory" in that it can provide a soundtrack that befits a particular activity and implicitly keeps track of time. For example, you can set up Pandora playlists for the following activities:

- A half-hour exercise routine (Pandora plays a commercial about every half hour, so you'll have an implicit timer).
- Light household chores.
- Relaxation and de-stressing.

Project Procedure

1. Go to http://pandora.com/. Note that if you live outside the United States, there are licensing issues that may prevent you from using Pandora. If so, try www.spotify.com or www.last.fm.

Pandora will prompt you to enter your username and password or to create a new account (see Figure 5-2). In this exercise, you will create a new account so you can familiarize yourself with the site and discover amazing new music.

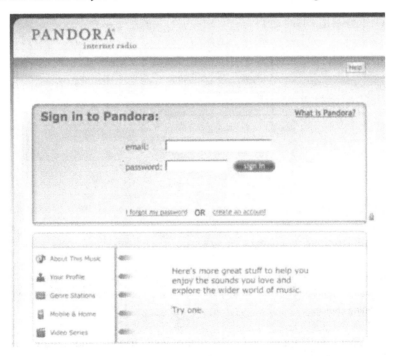

Figure 5-2. Pandora invites you to sign in or create a new account if you are visiting the site for the first time.

2. Enter your email address and birth year, then create a password, indicate your sex, and read through the terms of use.

Your personal profile and preferences will be sent back to Pandora headquarters in San Francisco to map the Music Genome Project (see Chapter 3 for more on that). As always, there is some risk that your personal information can be disclosed when you provide it in response to any solicitation on line. In this case, it is used to run an inference engine that continuously refines its understanding about what people like based on their fundamental demographics and their subsequent choices of music. This seems to me to be a relatively benign kind of nosiness, in return for hours of entertainment tailored to your tastes.

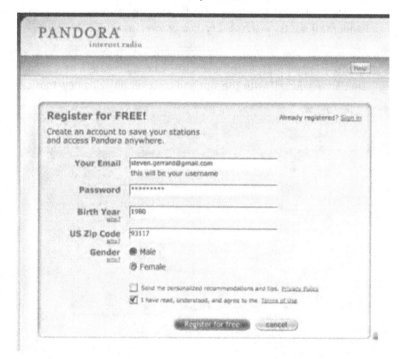

Figure 5-3. Pandora uses your demographics as a starting point for its musical inference engine. It guesses what you might like based on your age, gender and listening choices.

3. Upon registering, you may invite your friends and family to use Pandora. This step is optional.

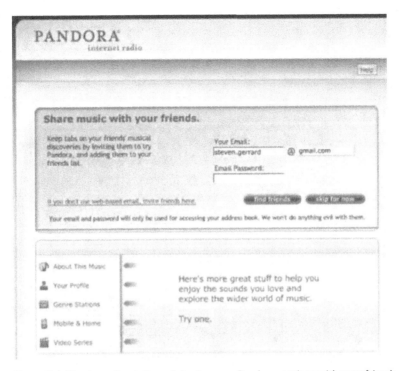

Figure 5-4. You have the option of sharing your Pandora stations with your friends and family.

4. Now for the good part. Enter the name of a musical artist whose work you particularly enjoy. You will find that as you type in the name, many artists who collaborated with that artist appear as well. Select your artist and Pandora will create a station that plays their music as well as music with similar traits and qualities. For this example, I picked the Jazz Liberatorz, a group comprised of three French DJs that draws heavily from jazz and meshes it seamlessly with late-90s hip-hop beats.

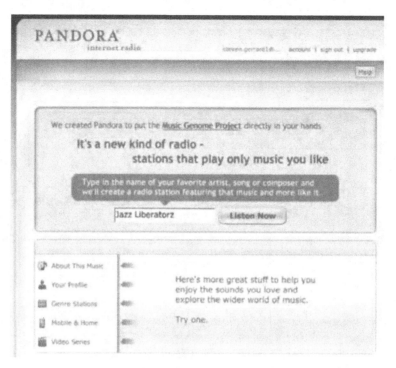

Figure 5-5. Supply an initial choice for your station and Pandora will take it from there, guessing what you might enjoy for about half an hour before interrupting play for a commercial. (You can stop a song if you don't like it, and Pandora will use this information to inform other suggestions.)

5. Pandora will begin to play music for you, with commercials playing about once every half hour. This is an excellent way to find new artists you enjoy. You can influence the playlist by giving the "thumbs up" to the best music and clicking the "thumbs down" for music you don't care for. This trains Pandora so it plays more of what you enjoy in future. You can rename or otherwise edit your stations in the Pandora Options drop-down menu, shown in Figure 5-.

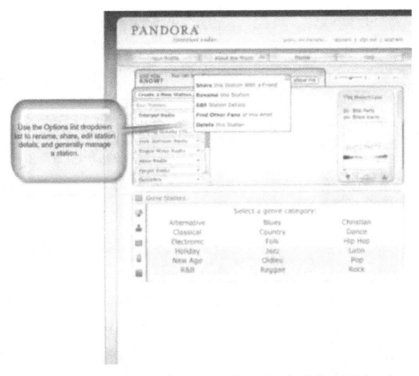

Figure 5-6. You manage the details of your stations using the Options List drop-down menu. It appears when you click the downward pointing triangle to the right of the station's name.

6. Under your station's Edit tab, it is possible to rename your station. You may also seed other artists and songs to your "like" and "dislike" lists, and give your station a truly distinct sound. When you click on the link for you station, its page includes list controls to which you can add artists and songs that you like. This helps Pandora refine its guesses about new music you might enjoy. See Figure 5-7.

Figure 5-7: Seed stations with artists and songs you already know you like. Pandora will look for similar music to suggest.

Pandora is a great way to enjoy the music you love and broaden your tastes and preferences. The web site is integrated with both the iTunes store and Amazon.com. This means you can directly purchase the mp3 or actual CD the song is on. It is possible to have as many stations as you like, meaning you have access to virtually anything you can describe. Data management is completely transparent. Put another way, you don't have to do anything but enjoy the music. Storage of your playlists is handled by the service.

With this project you learned:

- Netbooks are excellent "viewers" and "consumers" of cloud-based educational and entertainment content.
- Much cloud-based entertainment is free, if you don't mind listening to some occasional advertizing.
- USB-connected speakers can turn your netbook into an entertainment source for a group or gathering: think exercise classes, dances, sing-alongs, or music for parties.
- Pandora exposes listeners to new music by introducing them to music they are likely to enjoy, based on their stated preferences and personal profile information.

Project 2: Downloading and Using Skype

One of the best reasons to own a netbook is that it can replace a variety of existing devices at a much lower cost. If you live in a place that has good wireless coverage, chances are you can dramatically downsize your mobile phone plan by relying on your netbook and the Internet calling service Skype. In addition, you can use Skype for video calls, which provide a rich, connected experience that can be almost as good talking face to face.

Installing and using Skype is a simple process, and should take you between 15 and 45 minutes. In this section you will install and run Skype, learn how to find friends and family on the Skype system, and practice using the video chat feature.

Inexpensive video conferencing has many uses in addition to the pleasures of being able to easily and cheaply converse with friends and family. Small businesses and distance educators increasingly rely on it as a communication tool. Experience using Skype (or similar services) will make you a better candidate in the job market and provide access to services and opportunities to do personal business.

Required Equipment, Support, and Services

- Netbook
- Headset (if the netbook doesn't have an integrated speakers and microphone)
- Logitech Quickcam Orbit AF web cam or Logitech Quickcam Deluxe (if the netbook doesn't have an integrated camera)
- Internet access (call quality will improve with speed and bandwidth increases)

Optional Equipment, Support, and Services

Visit www.skype.com to see a wide selection of Skype capable accessories.

Scenario

Imagine that your closest college chum has been selected to work as a teacher for an international school in Belgium. She will be there for an entire year, and while you are excited that she was able to secure a very competitive job, you also are disappointed because she'll be so far away. However, you can both stay in touch by downloading and using Skype.

Project Procedure

1. Go to http://skype.com/ and click Download Skype Now (see Figure 5-8).

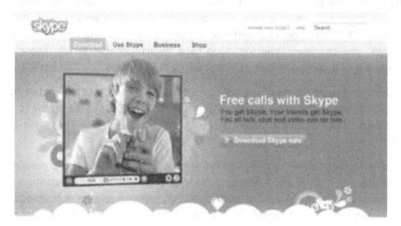

Figure 5-8. To get started with Skype, you first have to sign up and download some client software.

2. Follow the instructions on the next page and save the Skype file to your computer. You will see the status page shown in Figure 5-9.

Figure 5-9. If you already have Skype on your desktop or laptop, you still need to download the client components to your netbook.

3. Once the file has downloaded, run SkypeSetup.exe and follow the Setup Wizard, shown in Figure 5-10.

Figure 5-10. Follow the the setup instructions that appear after you have downloaded the Skype files.

4. To create a new Skype account, you must give your full name, create a username, create a password, and look over the Terms of Service and Privacy agreement. Then enter your email (for confirmation), country, and city. See Figure 5-11

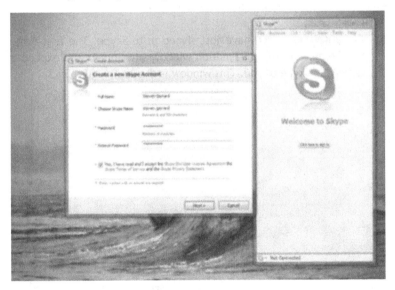

Figure 5-11. Create a new account by providing the necessary information.

Now create your new account and supply an email address so you can retrieve or reset a forgotten password. See Figure 5-12.

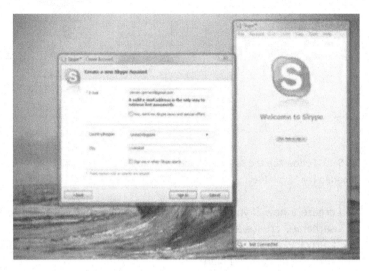

Figure 5-12. Set your profile information and sign in.

5. Congratulations, you have just signed in to Skype. The first time you run Skype, a useful information window will appear and explain basic actions in Skype to you. This window is shown in Figure 5-13.

Figure 5-13. After you sign in, Skype welcomes you and walks you through some basic Skype settings.

6. You can make a test call in Skype to make sure the program has downloaded correctly and that your microphone and speakers or

headset are working correctly (see Figure 5-14). This process also familiarizes you with how to make actual.

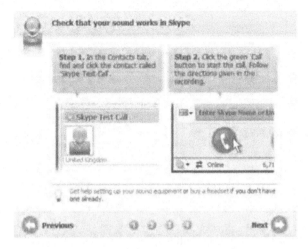

Figure 5-14. Be sure your sound is working to your liking by doing a Skype test call.

7. In the Contacts tab, you will see a single contact called Skype Test Call. Highlight that contact and click the circular green call button near the bottom of the Skype window to initiate a test call to the Skype Test Call Robot. It is a simple exercise that allows you to make sure your headset and microphone are working properly.

8. Adding a contact is very simple in Skype. Just click the Add Contact button and a search bar will appear. Enter a friend's username and hit the search button (see Figure 5-15. Their name should appear, and you can add it to your friends list. (Note that your contact should also have a Skype account.)

Figure 5-15. Add contacts to your Skype phonebook for easier dialing.

9. Your friends have to be online to contact them. When they are offline, there will be a grey Skype icon next to their name. When they are online, the icon will be a bright, neon green (unless they've set their status to Away or Do Not Disturb). See Figure 5-16.

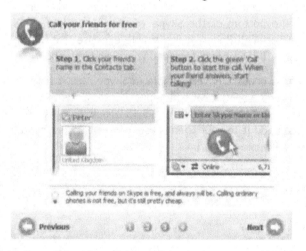

Figure 5-16. If your friend is available to chat, the icon next to his or her name will be neon green.

10. It is also possible to call phones from Skype, though except for toll free numbers in the United States, this is not a free service. You can use PayPal or a credit card for chargeable calls.

Simply click the link that says "Call cheaply to mobile phones and landlines." Follow the steps to make the call. See Figure 5-17.

Figure 5-17. You can also use Skype to call ordinary phones rather than just other Skype users.

11. With the aid of a web cam, you can use the video chat option. To do so, call one of your contacts. When he or she answers, you have the option to enable video chat. This way the person you are talking to will be able to see you, and you can also see yourself in a smaller box. You can continue doing this until you wish to end the conversation.

ExplainED

You will need to have installed your web cam first if it is not built in. Also, even if you have built-in speakers and microphone, you may sometimes want to use an external headset (say you are in a noisy environment or it's a situation where privacy and discretion are important). If you choose to use external devices, you have to let Skype know by correctly installing hardware and setting appropriate Skype options. You can get Skype accessories from a variety of locations, including Skype's own web store.

You can now in touch with your friends and family, even when they are trekking across the globe! Your contacts will appear in your Contacts lists, as shown in Figure 5-18.

Figure 5-18. Use Skype to keep in touch with friends and family (and coworkers) all over the globe.

Skype is a very popular and powerful communication tool. If Skype becomes a primary communication tool for you, and particularly if you use it for business, make a point of backing up your contact list from time to time. My low-tech method for doing this is simple. Just highlight the contacts list in your browser, copy it to the clipboard, and paste it into a text editor. From there you can print it and file it somewhere handy.

But as wonderful a tool as it is, Skype should never be used to make emergency services call. Use a wire line phone if possible or use a mobile phone. Also, if you need an absolutely inflexible, high-level of quality of service, Skype might not always be able to provide this. Use wire line phones for critical business or personal communications.

With this project, you learned:

- Skype is a convenient, flexible way to keep in touch with friends and family.
- Skype is free or inexpensive, depending on how you use it.
- Skype is reasonably reliable and delivers a good quality of service, assuming you have uninterrupted Internet access.
- Skype video calling can be used to conduct remote business meetings and deliver educational content.

Project 3: Upload a YouTube Video

In this project, you will develop the skills necessary to produce short video segments and post them on YouTube. You will also see how to ensure that your video is available to a specific audience. Once your video is online, you will be able to observe how social media rapidly grows communities and communicates humor, ideas, and innovation. This is a medium-difficulty project that will take you between 45 and 90 minutes to complete.

This project will help you learn the basics of capturing good quality video material for short segments. Netbooks are great for capturing and uploading relatively small amounts of material, but they aren't suited to editing because of their small amounts of RAM and video memory. This means that the original capture that you create needs to conform closely to what the end product will look like.

To achieve this, try and get tight shots, taken close up, with little panning or zooming. Simplicity is key to a good YouTube production, and getting the most out of limited time space and tools takes a little practice. If you're a budding videographer, you can experiment with various versions of a production until you discover what works best for your script or idea. Learning how the audience reacts to your post will help refine your production techniques and give you feedback on whether or not you are accomplishing your objective.

Required Equipment, Support, and Services

- Netbook
- Broadband connection
- Integrated web camera or hand-held camcorder with USB download capability

Optional Equipment, Support, and Services

- Wireless router, hotspot, or modem, and access to a mobile provider's data network
- Networked storage devices containing multimedia
- USB memory storage device or a USB-interfaced multicard reader to transfer videos from your phone, hand-held camera, or digital video recorder to your netbook

Scenario

You are a journalist. You and your team have captured a time-sensitive news story that you want to publish immediately in several forums. However, you are traveling in a place that does not have easily accessible Internet. One member of your team has a video clip, another has written commentary, and one has still photos. Using the portable Verizon router, you provide your team access to the Internet and make simultaneous posts. (You can use Flickr, MySpace, or other social media sites to post the non-video content). You can also link videos to your Facebook account.

Project Procedure

1. Capture between 30 and 90 seconds of video using either a hand-held digital video camera or a web cam attached to your netbook. Follow these guidelines for the video shots:

   - Shoot tight, close-up shots, and try to fill the frame as much as possible.

   - Avoid panning, because it defeats the compression algorithms used by digital video formats.

   - To depict motion, try to capture the subject coming directly toward you or going directly away from you.

   - You won't be able to do any editing, so keep trying until you get the sequence you want.

2. Connect wirelessly to the Internet using your wireless modem, router, or hotspot. See Figure 5-19.

Figure 5-19. Connecting to the Internet using a Verizon wireless modem.

3. Go to www.youtube.com. This brings you to YouTube's homepage, shown in Figure 5-20.

Figure 5-20. The YouTube web site.

4. You must have a YouTube account to upload videos. An account is free and takes only a few moments to create. You can get full, up to the

moment instructions on how to do this by looking here: www.youtube.com/signup

Once your account is activated and you wish to upload a video, click the upload button in the upper right-hand corner of the screen. You then have the option of uploading a file from your netbook or uploading directly from a web cam. For this exercise, you will be uploading a file from your netbook. See Figure 5-21.

Figure 5-21. Upload your video to YouTube here. It's pretty simple and the instructions are easy to follow.

5. You have multiple options for uploading your desired file to YouTube. Cameras and camcorders, such as the models featured later in this chapter, can store video files that you can upload directly if the device is connected via USB. For this exercise, you will upload files directly from your computer.

6. After clicking Upload Video and selecting a video file from your netbook, you will be prompted to fill out information about your video file, as shown in Figure 5-22. This information includes title, description, tags, video type, and privacy level. When finished, click the Save Changes box, which is just below the privacy settings.

Figure 5-22. Provide details for the video clips you upload so that you and others can find them using keyword searches.

7. It is possible to view all previously uploaded videos to your account by clicking the My Videos tab, shown in Figure 5-23.

Figure 5-23. See the details about the clips and its viewership.

Congratulations on getting your first video online for the world to see! All uploaded videos can by managed in the "My Videos" section. When you upload videos, you need to be aware of issues regarding your own and other's personal privacy. Regardless of what privacy controls you create on these sites, remember that they are essentially public places that can be accessed by schools, parents, prospective employers and others. Deleting an unfortunate video doesn't guarantee its demise. People can and do download and share content among themselves.

Also, familiarize yourself with what is and isn't legal to capture and share. Pirating content from concerts and performances can land you in trouble, and displaying any form of sexual content that includes someone under 18 is a federal offense, which carries serious penalties. In many cases you must acquire a model's release to use identifiable images of people.

With this project you learned:

- Small screen videography requires different production values than large formats: shoot close, take tight shots, and use a minimum of camera motion.
- Netbooks are great for capturing and transferring "on-scene" coverage of events, but you can't expect to edit them much. Develop a style that is concise and gets your point across simply.
- To get good short content, you have to start with a plan or a script.
- If you use a wireless router or modem, you can upload from anywhere there is mobile phone service. This means you can cover unfolding natural events, work outdoors, or capture events taking place in crowded public spaces.
- If you use a wireless router, you can work with a team and share your Internet access to provide everyone upload capability.

Project 4: Zoho Document, Productivity, and Collaboration Tools

With this project, you will learn how Zoho.com's cloud services can support a small business or nonprofit organization, reducing total cost of ownership of technology tools and infrastructure. Zoho is a service that offers software similar to productivity suites that you have used in the past to create text documents, spreadsheets, presentations, and the like. Using these tools and a netbook, small businesses and nonprofits have the ultimate flexibility. You can work from anywhere, have access to very comprehensive toolsets and resources, and yet only pay for what you need, when you actually need it. Once proficient with the Zoho application suite, you can share information and work collaboratively, using a solution that can gracefully scale up as rapidly as you needs require.

This is a medium-difficulty project that will take you between one and three hours to complete. You will become familiar with the productivity and collaboration applications that Zoho offers to create documents, spreadsheets, and presentations alone or with the help of others. This is an immensely powerful business tool, but you can also use it for personal document creation or for collaborating with friends and family to create and share files and documents online.

Unlike many low-cost solutions, Zoho can scale-up to meet the needs of a growing business or organization, at a known cost and without delay as your needs grow. Zoho is ideal for situations where collaborating team members are geographically dispersed, where holding IT costs down is a very significant objective, and where the business process is highly mobile.

Required Equipment, Support, and Services

- Netbook
- Internet access

Optional Equipment, Support, and Services

- None

Scenario

Small business: You are starting a small Community Supported Agriculture business, in which local farmers grow produce that is sold in advance to members. For a fixed fee, members receive a half-bushel of locally grown, seasonal produce each week. You have to keep track of what farmers are producing, what produce will be ready for distribution in a given week, and of member payment status. You also need to alert members about when and where their produce will be available for pickup each week, and provide a projected harvest schedule so they'll know what to what they can expect in their baskets.

Nonprofit groups and service organizations: You need to provide your members easily accessible information about the organizations' calendar of events, governance documents, and ways to contribute and participate. You also need to keep track of contributions and expenditures in a completely transparent way. Also, assume your group does advocacy and education work. For these functions you want to make a library of pre-assembled presentation material available as well.

Job skills training: You need to demonstrate proficiency in the use of document creation and management tools, a spreadsheet program, and a shared calendaring system to apply for an upcoming position as an office manager.

Project Procedure

1. Go to www.zoho.com and observe the comprehensive list of applications provided by this site. There are three types of applications available on Zoho: Productivity & Collaboration Apps, Business Apps, and Utilities. See Figure 5-24.

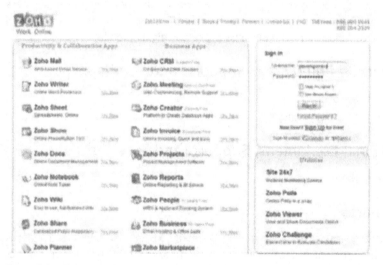

Figure 5-24. Zoho provides a really comprehensive suite of cloud-based productivity apps.

2. To have access to the online suite of programs, you must register. You can do so for free by clicking the Sign Up link in the top right-hand box.

3. Once you have registered for Zoho and verified your account (done by reading the confirmation email sent to your regular email account), you can use the featured programs.

4. There are two typical 'home bases' to work from. One is Zoho Personal and the other is Zoho Accounts. Zoho Personal is a site where you can check and read your email (see Figure 5-25). You also have instant access to the online suite of programs. Zoho Accounts still gives you access to the online applications, but its primary function is to enable you to easily monitor and manage accounts that are connected to yours (for example, an employee's account).

Figure 5-25. Here's how your Zoho workspace looks initially.

Zohos Services provides the tools and resources necessary to manage most small businesses and organizations (see Figure 5-26). The beauty of this solution accessed from your netbook is that you can have cloud access to all of your organizational and business intelligence while traveling or working away from your office, but without the security and privacy concerns you'd have if you were storing the information on your computer.

Figure 5-26. Click the appropriate link to get to the tool you want to use.

5. From either one of these sites, click the Writer tab to access the word processing application.

6. Writer is the sleek, elegant word processor provided by Zoho. You can quickly learn everything you need to know to get started by visiting http://writer.zoho.com/home.

Upon using it for the first time, a brief document explaining how to use the program and its special features will be present (see Figure 5-27). This document will explain the tab-based interface of writer, how the sidebar works, and basic editing procedures. It will also walk you through how to share your document with coworkers and post it to an audience on a blog. It is possible to remotely comment on others' work as well, in order to suggest changes and improvements to a document.

Figure 5-27. Zoho has great support for beginning users. You can't miss the tips, because they are part of the startup screen.

One area where Zoho Writer really shines is the ability to work on up to 25 documents offline. There is a Go Offline link near the top of the page. When you click this, you will be prompted to download a program called Google Gears (see Figure 5-28). After installing this, you no longer have to worry about whether you will be in an area with Internet access. You can modify your documents offline, and Zoho will automatically sync them next time you log in.

Figure 5-28. **You can use Zoho and you files offline if you need to .**

7. Zoho Writer, shown in Figure 5-29, is an application you and your employees can count on to get the job done. Any other questions you may have about Writer can be answered in the list of options under the Help button.

Figure 5-29. Zoho contains abundant options for getting help and advice, and each tool has its own area in the forums where you can ask questions to other users.

8. From Writer, click on the Switch To button and select Sheet. This will take you to the spreadsheet application on Zoho, shown in Figure 5-30. This application is ideal for storing data and accounting. It is possible run programs using macros as well.

Figure 5-30. Zoho has full featured charting and spreadsheeting capability.

9. Click on the Product Links button and you will immediately have access to countless examples of other users' sheets on Zoho (see Figure 5-31). You can check forums and blogs for know-how and ideas, learn the keyboard shortcuts to work more efficiently, and use public sheets and templates to hit the ground running.

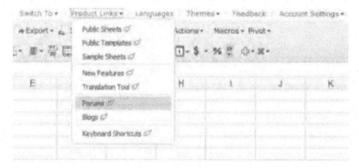

Figure 5-31. One of the best things about Zoho is that you can learn and grow as part of an active community of users. Check out the forums to learn tips, tricks, and trends.

10. Sample sheets are available to solve typical problems, form pivot reports, and give you examples of functional macros. See Figure 5-31.

Figure 5-32. You rarely have to start from scratch, because there is a rich set of templates.

11. Forums are there for you to ask and answer any relevant question that comes up in your work. You can start a new thread by clicking on the New Topic button and sending useful feedback to other Zoho users from here (see Figure 5-33).

Figure 5-33. Find "your people" in the Zoho forums.

12. Writer can function in over twenty languages. To change the language to your desired setting, simply click the Languages button and make your preferred selection (see Figure 5-34).

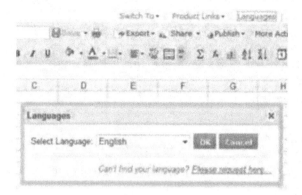

Figure 5-34. Zoho supports more than 20 languages.

13. When your sheet is completed and you wish to export it, Zoho gives you eight possible file types to choose from. See Figure 5-35

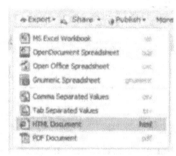

Figure 5-35. Zoho supports diverse document formats.

14. When your document is completed or ready for others to review, you may share it. Do this by clicking the Share button. A box will appear clarifying whether you want to share the entire document or just a few select sheets. You will be prompted to distinguish between the Read Only members and the Read/Write members. You may also select whether you would like to be informed whenever a change is made to the document. Finally, you can select the invitation email language, depending who will be reading this document. See Figure 5-36.

Figure 5-36. You get fine-grained control over document access and visibility using the Zoho tools.

15. It is possible to publish your file by embedding it in a web site or blog by clicking the Publish button (see Figure 5-37 for the Publish drop-down list). You also can make the whole or part of it public to Zoho with this feature.

Figure 5-37. Click Publish to determine how much of your document you want to publish and who you want to be able to see it.

16. It is possible to program using VBA in Zoho Sheet. You can create Macros from scratch, record Macros via the Record Macro selection, or create them in the VBA editor. These can accomplish any number of tasks, if you are willing to devote time to them. It is also possible to

179

view your Macros by selecting the View Macro selection (see Figure 5-38).

Figure 5-38. If you like programability in your spreadsheet tools, Zoho can do some sophisticated things.

17. Zoho can also create pivot tables to count, sort, and sum data from a particular sheet. The pivot can then display this new information on an entirely new sheet.

18. Zoho has commonly used functions built into its interface for easy access (see Figure 5-39).

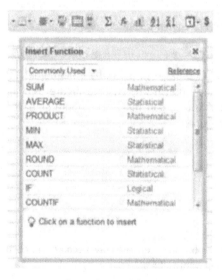

Figure 5-39. The most commonly used spreadsheet functions are built in to Zoho .

19. Zoho also contains a chart wizard for rapid conversion of numerical data into a visual representation, shown in Figure 5-40.

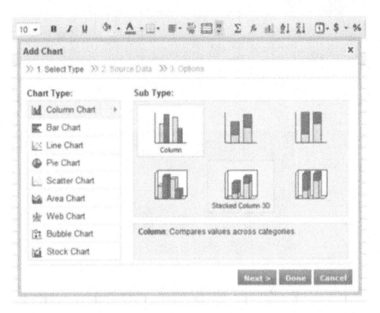

Figure 5-40. Zoho has a nice charting "wizard" which can automate the graphical display of your data.

20. Zoho Sheet has all the components necessary to stand alone as a spreadsheet editor. From Sheet, click on the Show button under Switch To to navigate to the presentation program.

21. Zoho Show, shown in Figure 5-41, is ideal for making presentations to the board during a meeting or to an audience on the other side of the planet. You can create your own presentation using Show, or you can take a look at others posted by current Zoho users. When you have your presentation, you can make it private for yourself and your employees, or you can broadcast it to all of Zoho.

Figure 5-41. You can remotely show presentations using Zoho's sharing tools.

If you decide to remotely show your presentation to an audience in Kyoto, Japan, for example, you have the ability to receive immediate feedback from them (see Figure 5-42). While displaying your presentation, Zoho enables a live chat with your participants. This feedback will help you better understand what your audience thinks and, in turn, help you sell your service more efficiently.

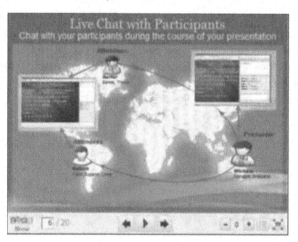

Figure 5-42. You can also share out your desktop, which gives participant hands-on access to examples and information.

22. Zoho also allows you to share your desktop with the participants in your presentation, shown in Figure 5-43. Thus, everyone can participate in interactive examples, even though they are separated by thousands of miles!

Figure 5-43. You can share your desktop with other presentation participants.

23. Now that you have seen the workhorses of Zoho's repertoire, let's take a look at some of Zoho's more useful applications available on the site. You can navigate out of Show to Docs by clicking the Switch To button. Inside Zoho Docs, you will be able to manage every single document you saved in Zoho. You can put them in groups and add tags to them to make them easier to organize. It also lets you monitor which documents are shared by you and to you. This application is essential to keeping large amounts of information under your control.

24. The Zoho Wiki (see Figure 5-45) is an ever-expanding bank of knowledge available to all Zoho users. Wiki is a name for an encyclopedic collection of information that is jointly produced and maintained by a community of contributors. The most popular of these is Wikipedia. You can make your entries public or private, depending on the nature of the information. It is also possible to categorize the type of information you upload and change the appearance to your liking.

Figure 5-45. Here is the beginning of a user created Wiki using the Zoho tools.

25. The Zoho Planner (see Figure 5-46) is very convenient and easy to use. It lets you enter a description of your goals every day. It also features a to-do list, appointment times, and notes that will help you stay on top of your busy schedule. You can also attach documents and put tags on future dates using the Create Event button in the toolbar at the left of the main Calendar page to make sure you don't forget anything important.

Figure 5-46. Create Events to remind yourself of important stuff and store them in your Zoho Calendar. Unlike your phone, which you can lose, forget, or let go dead, your schedule will always be safe and accessible on the cloud

26. Zoho features a built-in chat service for you to keep in touch with friends, family, and employees. See Figure 5-47.

Figure 5-47. Chatting is useful, so it is integrated into the other Zoho tools.

27. Zoho Meeting allows people to remotely meet and discuss issues of importance (see Figure 5-48). You must subscribe to Zoho Meeting to have the full benefits of the application, such as if you want to meet with more than one person at once. You can get full cost information at www.zoho.com/crm/comparison.html.

Figure 5-48. Zoho has online meeting tools.

28. Now you will create a meeting with one presenter and one participant. After clicking the Create Meeting button, you will be sent to a page where you set the date, time, and subject of the meeting (see Figure 5-49). An optional agenda can be added, and then you supply your and your participant's email ID. It is also convenient to add their Skype ID if available for the meeting. If the Auto button is pushed, the participant will automatically be able to control your desktop. If the Prompt button is pushed, your permission will be asked for this to happen.

Figure 5-49. Set up your meetings by setting date, time, attendees, and topic, then have everyone notified by email.

29. After continuing, a summary of your meeting details will appear. Now, simply login to Zoho Meeting at the specified time, and you will be able to communicate with your participants. See Figure 5-50.

Figure 5-50. You have a bird's-eye view of meeting status on the Meeting Details page.

You now have a taste of what you can do with Zoho. Many other Zoho applications exist, but you will almost certainly use the ones discussed here most frequently. However, definitely make the effort to find out more about Zoho and all it has to offer. It provides a massive amount of useful products and services, and because it is a cloud service provider, the products are continuously kept up to date without any need for you to pay extra money for a new version. One of the great things about using Zoho is that you can largely delegate the responsibility for the security, availability, and integrity of your data to the service. Unless you store local copies that you can work on offline, you can behave strictly as the user of a managed service. If you store critical or private data locally, then you must take steps to ensure that it is properly backed up and secured.

With this project you learned:

- Zoho provides a relatively comprehensive suite of office productivity tools and collaboration options.
- Because all resources are cloud based, you can scale your usage up and down at will and pay only for what you actually need.

- Storing your data in the cloud means that data backup and system integrity work is effectively outsourced. You don't have to worry about making backups, enforcing security policies, or ensuring the integrity or availability of a specific device.
- Using Zoho's cloud-based tools allows you to create highly mobile business processes, because you can access your tools, data, and business intelligence from anywhere you have Internet access.

Project 5: Deep-Traveling in Barcelona

In this project you will see how you can make the most of your netbook while traveling. We will look at the skills needed to become a "deep traveler," or someone who travels for a purpose rather than just as a tourist. You will develop the skills and routines necessary to create a rich, well-organized record of travel and experiences, and to be able to share those accounts of adventures and learning with others. I'll also give you some tips on how to develop an eye for good visual content, and how to hone your writing skills. You will learn how to use travel in a purposeful, thoughtful way to expand your knowledge and understanding of the world, and create cloud communities around your interests and experiences.

This is a medium to advanced-difficulty project, and will probably take between 15 and 30 minutes after the initial equipment setup. You will learn how to use a minimalist setup capture images and video from multiple perspectives that would be impossible with bulkier technology. You will also see how to capture interviews, conversations, and the sounds of a city with a portable podcast recorder, and how to upload audio to iTunes as a podcast. You will also get a closer look at the spy pen gadget from (discussed in Chapter 2), and see how you can use it to capture candid vignettes of city life on video and experiences unobtrusively.

Required Equipment, Support, and Services

- Netbook
- Intermittent Internet access
- Intermittent access to a full-sized PC with lightweight video editing capabilities
- Brando USB Mini web cam with sucker
- Roland Edirol R-09
- Brando USB Spy Pen

- Inconspicuous luggage for carrying and storing your netbook and peripherals
- Anti-theft device (Kensington lock slot or similar physical securing device)

Optional Equipment, Support, and Services

- Offline storage media (USB sticks, flash cards, secure digital card). Note that most netbooks support USB devices at a minimum, but other storage media might require external support in the form of a multi function card reader.
- Secure logon device (biometric logon or USB key).

Scenario

As a deep traveler, you have your work cut out for you. There is so much to see and do, so much great food to try, and so much to learn and enjoy. As a deep-travel writer, your task is to capture the essence of the places you visit and share how your point of view is transformed by the experience of having been there. This sort of content development is more reflective than that of the last project, both because it is ongoing and because you have more time and more variety of media with which you can record your experiences. Some of the things you want to shoot for in documenting your deep-travelling experience are:

Have authenticity and immediacy in the voice in which you describe your experiences. Develop complete content as you go rather than taking lots of pictures or videos and trying to write down your reactions, thoughts, and experiences later

Capture the spontaneity and excitement of the experience. Sometimes less is more. A still photo can better and more economically capture the moment than 60 seconds of narrated video.

Suggest, don't describe. For your readers, your deep-traveling accounts are sort of a "magic carpet". You want to intrigue and awaken imagination with a bit of rich description, as opposed to providing a minute-by-minute account of events

Project Procedure

1. The flexible USB suction web cam (see Figure 5-51) liberates its user from the constraints of a typical web cam imbedded in a laptop. You

will take advantage of its suction and swivel neck in this project. Sometime during the day, if you are, say, taking a long metro ride, try to find a seat near the back. Stick the web cam on the window, and point it down the metro car. Hit record, and let it document your entire trip.

Figure 5-51. The flexible USB Suction web cam.

2. With video editing software, shrink the duration of your video from 10 to 12 minutes to 10 to 20 seconds. This will make an excellent transition piece for any video you might post, or as a simple stand-alone video.

3. The combination of a netbook and the USB flexible web cam makes using Skype very simple. This combo's compactness makes it easier and more convenient than ever before to stay in touch with loved ones while traveling. So, log into Skype, call your mother, and show her the view as soon as you get a connection with sufficient bandwidth.

4. The Roland Edirol R-09, shown in Figure 5-52, is great for picking up both interview conversation and ambient city noise. Take this device to a place where there will be very distinctive sounds, such as cathedral bells, foghorns, fireworks, or birds. Basically, anything other than the roar of traffic offers a sense of place and a few seconds of relaxing and enjoyable listening. The R-09 has a low-cut filter to kill background noise and yields high-quality audio. It gives you the choice

of saving files in MP3 or WAV format. It also comes with a 64 MB SD card for storing audio files. The R-09 can record in either 44.1 or 48 kHz. 48 kHz is better for personal interviews, because it has slightly higher perceived quality, but you must be careful because it also takes up more memory.

Figure 5-52. The Roland Edirol, one of the favorite and most used interview recording devices of professional journalists.

5. The Brando USB spy pen has many functions (see Figure 5-53). It works as a 2GB USB drive, audio, and video recorder. (And it's really a pen, too, as you can see in Figure 5-54.) This is a great tool for capturing short, candid takes.

Figure 5-53. Good quality night photography, using the spy pen.

6. There is a small, round button at the top of the spy pen. When pushed, it turns the video recorder on. The lens is located directly above the pocket clip, and it is quite difficult to see. The microphone is inside the clip. Note: Use common sense when traveling with this fun item and when using it. And it probably needs to be in checked luggage when you fly.

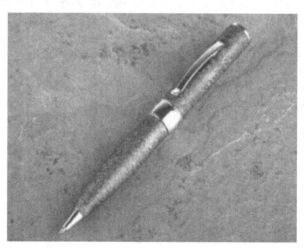

Figure 5-54. The spy pen: inconspicuous video recorder, and workable writing tool.

7. A small LED, directly opposite the camera, will come on once the button is pushed. While warming up, it will be orange, but once it shines blue it is recording video.

8. To stop recording, push the button again. Now the device is warmed up, you can resume recording with a quick press of the top button. Video is recorded in 352×288 resolution in AVI format.

9. To turn off the spy pen, press down the top button for a few seconds. The LED will turn off. Your videos can be uploaded to your netbook via the built in flash drive.

Figure 5-55. The spy pen in its packaging.

This project has shown how you can use your netbook and its peripherals as the primary recording devices for detailing your travels, but you'll probably want to download the multimedia content to a desktop computer at a later date in order to organize, edit, and format the final products. For a long trip (more than a couple of weeks), spending a couple of hours in an Internet café to handle these jobs will probably be a welcome change of pace.

All video and audio recorded in this project can be uploaded from the capture devices onto your netbook for easy access.

Use the free Windows Movie Maker to edit video clips on a Windows machine or Apple's iMovie if you are using a Mac. (Most Internet cafes offer Windows hardware only.) When your content is clean and sleek, you can upload it to the portal of your choice: a blog, social media site, or personal web site.

With this project you learned:

- To effectively communicate travel experiences, you'll need to be savvy enough in the use of your peripherals to be able to quickly setup and capture sound, images, or video. This takes practice and organization. Know how your devices work well enough that you can activate them and capture material while you are being distracted and jostled.
- Know how much data a capture will produce, and try not to collect vastly more than you can use. It ties up storage, is difficult and time-consuming to edit down, and your ideas will get lost if you are bogged down with too much material.
- Develop a compact working style. Netbooks are vulnerable to theft because they are small, relatively valuable and easy to resell. Keep an eye on your gear when you are collecting content.
- Be spontaneous and curious, but respect the privacy and cultural values of others.

Project 6: Setting Up A Portable Vital Signs Monitoring Station

This project is designed to prepare people with minimal training to set up a highly portable, low-cost facility for quickly, easily, and non-invasively reading blood pressure, heart rate, temperature, and blood oxygen saturation. This netbook-based station can be used at health fairs and health education events, at large gatherings to support onsite first aid, as a preventative tool at sports practices and competitions to monitor athletes for overheating or physical stress, and for home monitoring of health status indicators.

This project is quite simple, but it requires the use of some of the specialist equipment that I covered in Chapter 2. It will take you between 45 and 90 minutes to set up the equipment, then about 10 minutes to take the readings. You'll see how to operate the Wireless Blood Pressure Monitor and the Wireless Pulse Oximeter, and how to download data from these instruments to the netbook before using cloud-based services to record patient histories.

In this project, you will learn how to set up a netbook-based workstation that lets you monitor basic but important health status information virtually anywhere, and at a minimum expense. Almost anyone can set up and reliably run the most basic vital signs monitoring configuration described here. With a modest extra effort, this project can be adjusted to allow users to track statistics such as blood pressure and heart rate over time, to set up for multiple users who save readings to cloud-based archives to create personal histories, be deployed in emergency response situations, and be used in health education events.

Required Equipment, Support, and Services

- Netbook with two or more USB connectors
- Wireless Pulse Oximeter CMS-50E
- USB wrist blood pressure monitor

Optional Equipment, Support, and Services

- Internet connectivity.
- Cloud-based storage for users to store vital sign histories.
- For outdoor use or in areas of heavy ambient glare, a painter's umbrella or shade canopy make screens more readable.
- USB hub, to provide additional connectivity for peripherals like wireless modems and printers.
- Volunteers or teachers operating the station would benefit from a Red Cross-approved first aid course, including training in how to administer CPR.

Scenario

Health education curricula: Service and education groups can use a netbook equipped with a blood pressure cuff and heart rate monitor to provide mostly unattended access to users who are curious about the state of their heart rate and vital signs. This station can be part of a broader health education effort that links circulatory health to eating and exercise habits or promotes early diagnosis of "silent" diseases like high blood pressure.

Athletic health monitoring: By nature, sports practices require athletes to operate at the high end of their cardio-vascular performance range. When athletes train under adverse environmental conditions like extreme high or low temperatures or altitudes, they can experience adverse health consequences that aren't adequately predicted by sports physicals. Investing in a netbook-based vital signs tracking station can give coaches and trainers a way to accumulate and track histories for individual players, and do early remediation for athletes that might be at risk. For example, overheating is often a problem for late summer football practices. Having trainers do temperature, heart rate, and blood pressure readings on players at 20-minute intervals could allow coaches to identify players who are having problems and target them for rehydration and cooling. Rotating players through the test station as they come off the field wouldn't interrupt play, could do a lot to prevent the incidence of heat exhaustion and heat stroke, and, as a bonus, would give coaches a way to measure their player's improvements in cardiac fitness.

Independent elders: An elderly parent is opposed to entering an assisted living community, but his health is in a state of decline. He can look after himself, but must be cautious and monitor his health to protect himself from a serious complication. He can use these devices every day to observe the nature of his pulse, the frequency of his pulse (pulse ratio), and the amount of oxygen carried in his blood stream (SpO2). This data can be uploaded onto a netbook and analyzed to maintain his health more easily.

Project Procedure

1. First, practice with the blood pressure monitor, shown in Figure 5-56, as a stand-alone device. With simple, one-touch operation, the USB wrist blood pressure monitor can accurately monitor and store the height and width of a patient's pulse. Operate the device and see the systolic and diastolic pressure (in mmHg) and the pulse rate on the LCD screen. This device can also detect an irregular heartbeat and notify the user.

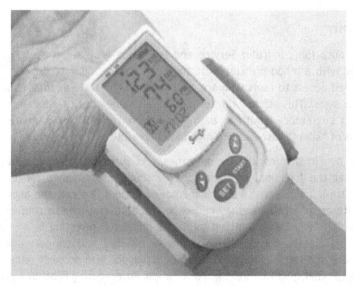

Figure 5-56. Blood pressure and heart rate are displayed in large type for easy visibility.

2. The blood pressure monitor has a built-in alarm system that can go off as many as three times a day to remind any user to take a rest or any medication.

3. Now experiment with the Wireless Pulse Oximeter, shown in Figure 5-57. Slip it onto a finger, and see that it displays the blood oxygen saturation level (SpO2), pulse rate, and a waveform and bar graph of the pulse rate are displayed in color on the OLED display. Set alarms for both high and low levels to ensure a patient is notified if he leaves a healthy zone. Observe how the device saves power by going into sleep mode when no signal is received for four seconds. Advanced software comes with the device to monitor SpO2 and PR while the patient is asleep.

4. When attached to a netbook, output can be viewed simultaneously on the device and the netbook screen.

Figure 5-57. Fingertip pulse oximeter is very easy to transport and deploy. Pairing it with a netbook allows you a good way to store and manage the data you collect.

5. The device can store up to 30 hours of data using built in flash memory. Data may be stored in two ways on your netbook. There is a text summary of a patient's SpO2 levels and pulse ratio, and there is also a graphical representation of the data. The text summary is best for observing the exact oxygenation levels a patient experienced. The graphical representations of the data show trends and depict general health: you can see how his pulse and SpO2 levels changed or remained constant over a given interval of time. See Figures 5-58 and 5-59.

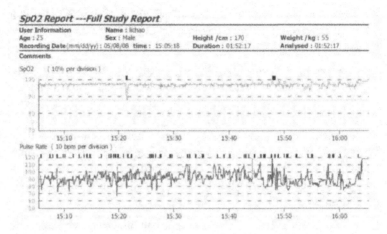

Figure 5-58. Preserving a precise record of observations over time is key to sound evaluations of health status.

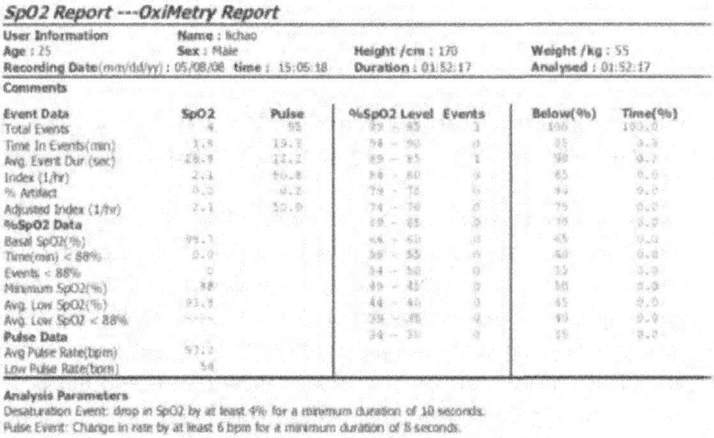

Figure 5-59. You can download reports from the device and store them on the netbook or transmit them to a repository if you are connected to the Internet.

This project assumed that you aren't necessarily operating while connected to the Internet for two reasons: first, it allows you to provide health status monitoring services literally everywhere. If you happen to be in Topeka, Kansas, when a tornado blows through, or in Anchorage, Alaska, when an earthquake rocks the world, you can flip open your netbook, get out your small set of peripherals, and start helping people then and there. Second, by operating in mostly unconnected mode, you double your battery life.

This said, one of the most useful things about this is that you can accumulate a record of data for an individual over an extended period of time. This is very useful, both because it will make apparent the effects of stress on their vital signs and because it can help to identify their particular version of "normal." For doing this sort of longitudinal measurement, you'll want to upload accumulated data to a repository to ensure that it's safely preserved and completely accessible. See the project on Zoho earlier in this chapter for approaches to cloud based recordkeeping and data management.

With this project you learned:

- The combination of a netbook and USB devices for measuring vital signs allow you to record basic vital signs information quickly and reliably, from just about everywhere.
- Your observations are easy to preserve and create individual histories for patients. If you choose to store them in a cloud based repository (either an ad hoc repository like Zoho, or a special purpose medical database, you can ensure they are preserved and easily accessible.

Chapter 6

Best of the Web Part 1: Business and Reference

Okay, so the Web has always been there, at least for the purposes of popular consciousness, which has the historical attention span of a mayfly. But once you embark on a connected mobile lifestyle, netbook tucked neatly into your messenger bag, the Internet looks a little different than it did when you were tethered to the wall socket. Nuances matter, not just because of the size of a netbook or the fact that it's powered by batteries. Rather it is a matter of our fundamental perceptions about connectedness. You are now a de facto part of global thought culture, and you can join up with your posse of likeminded peers at will.

Depending on what netbook you choose, how you set it up, and what accessories you're packing, *you can essentially tailor the Web to meet your needs and reflect your personality*. Think of it this way: Web 2.0 was characterized by the ability of individual web sites to mesh and provide additional value through technical collaboration. With your netbook, it's a new day on a post Web 2.0 planet: netbooks = the Web unplugged. It's a totally different experience, even though the basics are the same.

This collection of "Best-Of" web sites and content portals reflect that reality. Netbooks as a tech and social phenomenon mean a whole lot more than just being able to find information or do email tasks from anywhere. They effectively decouple your life from the demands of geography, on a 24/7 basis. Personally, I find a lot of resonance in the Patrick Henry credo: "Give me liberty or give me death." But in my particular case, the liberty I really want is from working in a cubicle or spending my time behind the wheel enmeshed in freeway gridlock. Even being self-employed and working mostly from home hasn't really freed me from confinement, because until now I was largely dependent on nonportable resources that were concentrated in my labs and office.

No more. Properly personalized, a netbook allows you to store resources and tools in the cloud. I only have to pack my netbook and a toothbrush, and I can set sail knowing I'll be fully functional anywhere I dock. For this reason, as a netbook user, I see the Web very differently than I did before. If I am traveling, it can be my anchor, because online communities of friends and colleagues are only a wireless connection away. Business gets handled, work gets done, and I know what the family is up to. The sites in this chapter provide a spectrum of tools for the connected mobile life, and no matter who you are, how you live, or where you go, you'll find a lot of this stuff to be essential in a brand-new way.

News, Politics, and Opinion

The Internet is an instantly updatable medium, so it is perfect for breaking news. Most TV news stations and print newspapers have an Internet equivalent page covering the big stories and a whole lot of minor stories that didn't make the main news. They're also a handy archive tool, allowing you to scan back through old news for research or to catch up on stories that you missed.

CNN

www.cnn.com

CNN.com (see Figure 6-1) is probably the premier news source for national and world news. CNN requires little introduction as a reliable news source. CNN.com is the place for travelers to find world and national news about politics, entertainment, technology, business, and sports. The site keeps latest news and lead photos "above the fold" so readers can browse to subjects of interest. Navigation hierarchy does not use mouse-over drop-down menus, instead taking readers to the page selected for consistent article browsing.

CNN.com features

- clean and fast navigation;
- consistent format throughout for easy navigation;
- reliable news; and
- global focus.

Figure 6-1. CNN.com is the best comprehensive mainstream news web site.

Fox News

www.foxnews.com

Fox News present national and international news and commentary that speaks to a politically and socially conservative American demographic. Fox News boasts of its "fair and balanced" perspective. Better known for its television presence, Fox News picks up the online slack with news about the United States, world, business, politics, and leisure on foxnews.com, shown in Figure 6-2. Foxnews.com features over 60 contributors, including such luminaries as Bill O'Reilly, Karl Rove, and Geraldine Ferraro. The web site is easy to navigate, and provides pop-ups with latest news and breaking stories. Foxnews.com is a good site for accessing spin and no-spin to stay current while on the go.

Foxnews.com features

- current news and commentary;
- news and photos of latest stories above the fold; and
- content that displays well on small screens.

Figure 6-2. Fox News is the premier outlet for news with a conservative viewpoint, and is known for provocative commentary and opinion.

Huffington Post

www.huffingtonpost.com

The Huffington Post (Figure 6-3) is the pulpit of Arianna Huffington, an incisive, gloves-off author and syndicated columnist. The aggregated news site and blog spares no one from the bright glare of accountability, but particularly scourges the military industrial complex, ultra-conservative political and religious interests, and anything that has the slightest whiff of racism or sexism.

Huffingtonpost.com is

- unapologetically liberal;
- as combative as Rush Limbaugh, but smarter and without the substance abuse problem; and
- a source of global coverage and analysis.

Figure 6-3. The Huffington Post is a news aggregate and source of liberal commentary, founded by author and columnist Arianna Huffington.

Slate

www.slate.com

Slate (see Figure 6-4) is a daily online magazine bringing a unique editorial slant to national news on politics, business, arts, and science.

Slate.com has a solid reputation for news reporting with a wry editorial twist. The award-winning Slate.com was among the first Internet magazines, and is free to readers. It presents news and commentary mostly on issues in the United States. The site's time-tested Web presentation is clean and to the point: mouse-over drop-down menus provide easy and fast access to stories of interest. Slate.com displays well on small screens and makes it easy to keep up with spin and buzz while on the move.

Slate.com

- constantly updates its lead story;
- displays comfortably on small screen; and
- includes no gimmicks or pop-ups.

Figure 6-4. Slate.com pioneered the Web e-zine niche and has a reputation for being a "clean site" with no annoying pop-up ad windows.

The Daily KOS

www.dailykos.com

The Daily Kos (Figure 6-5) is a political blog site founded by Markos Moulitsas. It is a collaborative and community oriented, and the parent company, Kos Media LLC, funds a fellowship program to help launch a new generation of liberal activists. There are a dozen or so regular contributors, with three or four new ones introduced each year. Kos readership gets between 2 and 4 million visits each weekday, which makes it a fairly significant influence in the alternative news niche. The standard edition is free, but readers can opt to pay for an ad-free subscription. (Ads are mostly related to activist causes and political candidacies.)

The Daily Kos is known for

- liberal "netroots" activism;
- dKosopedia, a collaborative political encyclopedia along the lines of Wikipedia;
- election trends data tracking; and
- political opinion polling results.

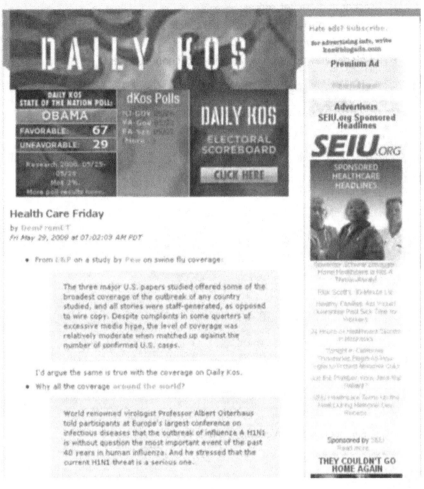

Figure 6-5. The Daily Kos is a liberal political opinion blogsite and news aggregator that features a collaborative, community-building emphasis.

BBC

www.bbc.co.uk

The BBC website (Figure 6-6) provides news, sports, cultural, and political coverage to the entire English-speaking world. If you want an authentic glimpse of the daily lives of the other inhabitants of this global village, you'll find it here.

bbc.co.uk provides

- soccer and cricket scores;
- coverage of politics from the perspective of people on the ground, around the world; and
- a global viewpoint on economic interconnectedness.

Figure 6-6. bbc.co.uk is an excellent source of global news.

Weather

Just like with the news, weather reports have also made the transition to the Internet. Again, the Internet's ability to be frequently updated with the latest information means that you can find much more up-to-date and detailed information than you can in other formats. The other great thing about weather on the Internet is that it's incredibly easy to find weather reports for any other location in the world, so you can check accurate forecasts before making a trip, or just see if it's snowing on Uncle Jim!

National Oceanic and Atmospheric Administration

www.noaa.gov

The NOAA website (Figure 6-7) is maintained by the U.S. Department of Commerce. It is the "big daddy" of weather sites because the government can provide so many technical services. NOAA is where most other weather forecasting sites and stations get their information, so here you are getting information straight from the horse's mouth. You can learn about fisheries and oceans, satellite technology, climate change, and coastlines. There is more at NOAA than simply weather. The most useful weather information is found by typing a city and state or ZIP code into the search box provided. That will display weather information for specific locations throughout the United States.

NOAA.gov

- displays in-depth science and research information; and
- provides data and weather information for specific locations.

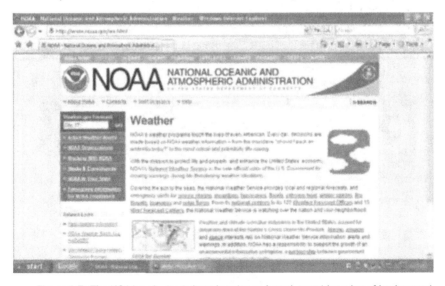

Figure 6-7. The NOAA web site is largely science-based, provides a lot of background information and research, and also provides accurate local current conditions and forecasts.

The Weather Channel

www.weather.com

Weather.com (Figure 6-8) is the online source for The Weather Channel's insight into current weather conditions and news. The site provides numerous video links to keep you up to date on local and national forecasts, severe weather and storms, and to provide information on, for example, tornado safety. You can follow links to travel tips, including road conditions; health tips, including pollen counts; home and family pointers, including weather safety tips; and information on how weather will affect sports and outdoor activities.

Weather.com is a news-oriented web site and provides text and video news stories. Its user interface is clean and easy to navigate, and displays well on small screens. Presentation is customizable and offers information on your desktop via RSS feeds.

Weather.com provides

- the latest weather news;
- video links; and
- safety and travel tips

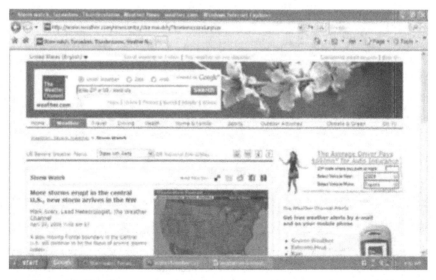

Figure 6-8. Weather.com provides access to The Weather Channel's insight into current weather conditions and weather news.

Weather Underground

www.wunderground.com

Weather Underground (Figure 6-9) is a free, global Internet weather service that provides real-time and up- to-date weather summaries and predictions for anywhere in the world. You can discover where hurricanes and tornados are brewing, where it is snowing and if the skiing is good, or you can easily search for and find information about marine weather. You can view radar and satellite photos, and read the latest science about climate change. Weather Underground will even help you set up your own private and automated weather station to contribute local conditions to Weather Underground. Weather Underground's user interface is easy to navigate, intuitive, and offers tons of features. There is advertising on every page, but because the site and its content is free, advertising can be expected and overlooked. The site fits well on a small screen, and can be optimized for several mobile uses.

Wunderground.com

- provideds local and global weather coverage, and
- is asily optimized for mobile devices.
- Photos and maps, radar and satellite images

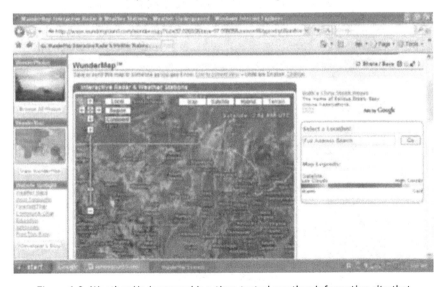

Figure 6-9. Weather Underground is a time-tested weather information site that provides real-time conditions, forecasts, and weather news and information worldwide.

Aviation Weather

http://aviationweather.gov

NOAA's Aviation weather center (Figure 6-10) is the prime resource for general aviation pilots, balloonists, hang gliders, base jumpers, and just about anyone that takes to the air on purpose. It can also be a good source of information for people who engage in other outdoor activates, because it provides information about weather conditions and forecasts that might matter if you are to be beyond the reach and comforts of civilization for a while.

Aviationweather.gov provides

- good forecasts on thunderstorms, their severity and duration;
- key information for pilots and airstrip operators; and
- community-generated pilot reports that give locale-specific, firsthand accounts of weather activities.

Figure 6-10. Use the Aviation Weather Center to inform travel plans and to find out about potentially severe weather.

National Weather Service Marine Forecasts

www.weather.gov/marine

Marine Weather (Figure 6-11) is critical to any offshore activity, whether it be sailing, kayaking, or power boating. Netbooks can provide great access to information about upcoming weather events when used with a wireless modem. Since a charge can last for several days, even a kayak trip in open water could be a lot safer and more carefree if you have the ability to check the weather and monitor the tides en route.

- Know what kind of weather is coming
- Get locale specific observations

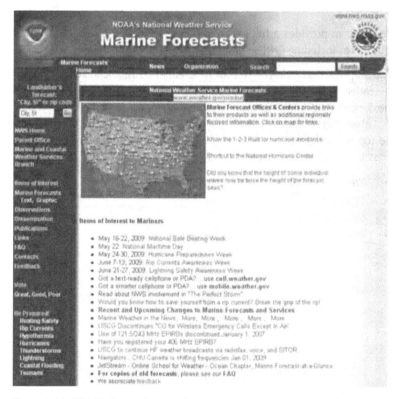

Figure 6-11. NOAA's Marine Forecasting servce uses extensive networks of human and remotely sensed measurements to anticipate severe marine weather conditions.

Finance

The money markets thrive on up to the minute information, and that's something that the Internet's perfect for. There are dedicated sites following all of the major markets and reporting on share prices and trading. Many sites also enable you to subscribe to alerts so you can instantly know when certain share prices change.

CNNMoney.com

http://money.cnn.com

Overview

CNNMoney.com provides a full range of financial news and services with access to a lot more, including CNN's comprehensive online world news.

It is no surprise that CNNMoney.com is a leader in financial news since it is a news leader in so many other sectors. CNNMoney.com opens with links to business news and markets, wealth planning, news for small businesses and more. Latest market indexes: DJIA, NASDAQ, S&P and treasury bonds all display at the top of the homepage before delving into news and analysis of the latest business information and market trends.

- Well-organized and clean on small screens
- Prominent access on the web
- Solid media fundamentals
- Worldwide presence and name recognition

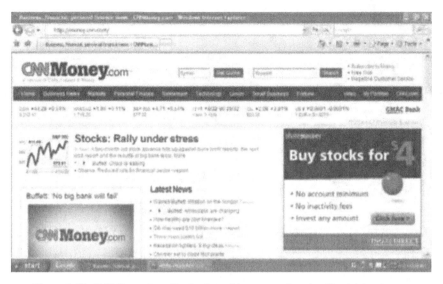

Figure 6-12. CNN Money is a site that provides comprehensive financial news oriented toward the more casual reader. It is consumer oriented and emphasizes person wealth management information.

SmartMoney

www.smartmoney.com

Overview

SmartMoney is the investor's friend with news and analysis to help make the right choices. Smartmoney.com is a member of The Wall Street Journal's Digital Network, and concentrates almost exclusively on investment news and advice instead of on more generic news. Smartmoney.com provides tools to help investors and small businesses analyze spending, arrange finances and build a portfolio. The site features timely news, money and investing always at the front of the desk, and shows top financial headlines and market charts at the top of its homepage.

- Easy to view and use on small screens
- Build and track your own portfolio
- Create your own watch list
- Personal wealth management tools and community

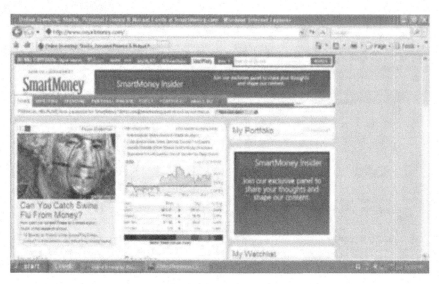

Figure 6-13. Smart Money is a trendy financial management site aimed at those with an entrepreneurial, hands-on attitude to managing their assets.

Forbes

http://forbes.com

Overview

In the competitive field of financial news, *Forbes* successfully made the transition from print media to the Internet, and stands among the giants of finance journalism. Forbes.com (Figure 6-14) provides Internet users with a wide range of hard news and commentary about everything financial. Forbes.com reports news from the United States, Europe, and Asia, and offers perspectives on world businesses and markets. The site's respected commentators provide opinions on diverse economic topics and review books of interest to investors and those in the business sector. Forbes.com fits a huge amount of information, including a video feed, on their homepage. Just scroll and click.

Forbes.com provides

- information that displays well on small screens;
- up-to-date market news;
- investment advice; and
- well-organized, clealy presented information.

Figure 6-14. Forbes is known for financial analysis and commentary, and takes on a wide variety of subject matter.

The Wall Street Journal

www.online.wsj.com

The Wall Street Journal may be more familiar as print media, but makes the transition to online news provider with grace and ease.

WSJ.com (Figure 6-15) delivers business news you would expect. But although the principle focus of WSJ.com is definitely finance, economics, and business, the web site delivers diverse news of interest to investors and non-investors alike. WSJ.com provides world and national news via links, stories, opinion, and video. As it has always been, and the online version is no different, WSJ.com delivers a good read.

WSJ.com provides

- a wealth of information that displays well on small screens;
- one-stop information gathering; and
- the financial links to other high-profile financial sites.

Figure 6-15. The Wall Street Journal is the premium financially-oriented news publication in the United States. WSJ.com pioneered the web-based financial reporting niche.

Bloomberg.com

www.bloomberg.com

Bloomberg.com (Figure 6-16) presents news focused on economics, commerce, and the mechanisms that make the business world go 'round.

Bloomberg.com starts right at the top with news links and market data, including charts from North America, Asia, and Europe. The site reinforces its journalistic intent by posting constantly updated breaking news stories and bloomberg.com exclusives. It displays top stories from the Web on the national economy, politics, personal finance, science, smart spending, opinion, sports and more. Video feeds complement links to diverse news topics.

Bloomberg.com provides

- content that displays well on small screens and is fun to browse;
- constantly updated news coverage;
- limited whistles and bells; and
- easy-to-access equities index reportage.

Figure 6-16. Bloomberg Financial News is one of the best sources for extremely current, sophisticated, empirical analysis of global financial markets.

Financial Times

www.ft.com/home/us

The *Financial Times* of London is a global news source focused on business and the economy. Ft.com (Figure 6-17) reports on many of the same events and phenomena as leading newspapers in the United States, but from a distinctly British/European perspective. This is an interesting read when world affairs pit one region against another, because it gives you the opportunity to see another perspective and to have a feeling for what the rest of the developed world is feeling and thinking about.

Ft.com lets you

- access a global perspective;
- see which advertisers are strongly positioned in the English-speaking global market; and
- monitor emerging economic trends that might be evident outside North America first.

Figure 6-17. The *Financial Times* is more or less the UK equivalent of the *Wall Street Journal*.

Students and Teachers

At its most basic level, the Internet is just a massive repository of information, and that information covers every topic under the sun. For students, this is a massive boon, as it enables them to search a variety of reference services to find the answer that they're looking for. Of course, this also has its bad side, as plagiarism is rife, but at heart the Internet is still a great resource.

Reference and Information

`http://dictionary.reference.com`

Dictionary.com (Figure 6-18) is an online spelling and grammatical reference. You can look up words (even if you can't spell them exactly). You can even use this site to cheat at crossword puzzles, using its puzzle solver. It has a thesaurus, and a really useful reverse dictionary (you supply the meaning and it supplies the word). Most of the services at this site are free, though if you need to look up medical or legal terms, you'll have to pay.

This site includes

- a dictionary;
- a thesaurus; and
- a translation tool.

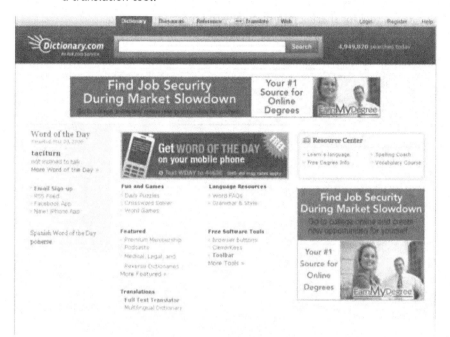

Figure 6-18. Find the right word, verify its spelling, access a thesaurus or get help translating at Dictionary.com.

Wikipedia

http://en.wikipedia.org

Wikipedia (Figure 6-19) a free database of reference material patterned after an encyclopedia. It is constantly being updated and expanded by volunteers from all around the world. Anyone with Internet access can participate in writing, editing, and expanding Wikipedia articles. Wikipedia receives around 65 million visitors per month, and there are better than 75,000 active contributors working on over 13,000,000 articles written in more than 260 languages. There were 2,898,040 articles in English on the day this was written. You can't take Wikipedia as entirely authoritative, especially where content is extremely controversial or where there are product descriptions involved, but as a general reference or a quick way to find background information on almost any subject, Wikipedia is a great tool.

Wikipedia provides

- free information on a variety of topics;
- a tool for sharing information with other readers; and
- content in more than 260 languages.

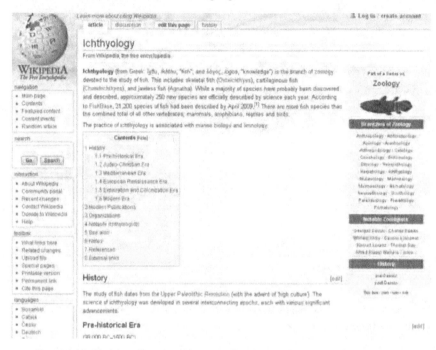

Figure 6-19. Find out about just about anything, in just about any language, using Wikipedia.

Google News

http://news.google.com

Google News (Figure 6-20) is a customizable news source, which obviously makes it handy for following specific current events or gathering details of an ongoing story. However, it won its place in this lineup of tools for students and teaches because it is available in dozens of languages. This is a unique resource for a student of any foreign language, because it allows you to build vocabulary and grammar skills while immersing yourself in the current events and culture of the subject country.

Google News provides

- a news source that is customizable; and
- news is multiple languages.

Figure 6-20: Google News is a customizable news source that provides content in multiple languages.

National Geographic

www.nationalgeographic.com

National Geographic supports exploration, research, and conservation efforts around the globe. Through research grants, the magazine, video, and IMAX productions, the National Geographic Foundation has educated people worldwide on the values of conservationism and environmental stewardship. The web site (Figure 6-21) provides rich multimedia content that examines our world and all of its sundry inhabitants, as well as the universe beyond.

NationalGeographic.com provides material and information on

- history and archaeology;

- green practices and lifestyles;
- science and space; and
- cultures and ethnography.

Figure 6-21. The web site of the National Geographic Foundation features some of the best nature photography available anywhere.

National Science Foundation

www.nsf.gov

The National Science Foundation (NSF) (Figure 6-22) is an independent federal agency that was created by Congress in 1950 "to promote the progress of science; to advance the national health, prosperity, and welfare; to secure the national defense...." With an annual budget of about $6 billion, NSF funds about 20% of all federally supported basic research conducted by America's colleges and universities. For math, computer science, and the social sciences, NSF is the number one source of research funding. NSF is the only federal agency whose mission mandates support for all fields of fundamental science and engineering, with the exception of medical research. It supports "high-risk, high pay-off" ideas, including many projects that sound like science fiction, but will be the stuff of everyday life in the near to midterm future. NSF's philosophy is that research should be tightly integrated with education, so that today's scientists are actively mentoring the next generation of top scientists and engineers.

This site provides

- discoveries from NSF funded research;
- classroom resources;
- transcripts of speeches and lectures; and
- science and engineering statistics.

Figure 6-22. The NSF site is a public portal that provides information about their research programs and results.

Union of Concerned Scientists

www.ucsusa.org

One of the unfortunate things about science and popular culture is that the nuances get lost. Because real science relies on the observation of subtleties over long periods of time, it doesn't lend itself to soundbites. Unfortunate casualties of the last 10 years are public understanding and appreciation of the facts and implications of global climate change. This complex issue faces every living thing on the planet, and humans are going to be called upon to change behaviors and lifestyles in order to mitigate its effects on our own and other species. Unfortunately, how, when, and where we do this has not been well communicated to the public. The Union of Concerned Scientists (Figure 6-23) is a group that has tasked itself with explaining these issues in a compelling, accurate, and pragmatic fashion. Many of its charter members are Nobel Laureates. This web site is a premier resource for students and teachers who want accurate, scientifically defensible information about some of the largest problems of our time.

This site provides information on

- global Warming;
- clean energy;
- food supplies and sustainability;
- nuclear technologies (power generation and weaponry); and
- scientific integrity.

Figure 6-23. The Union of Concerned Scientists provides leadership and information resources for public education about the key scientific issues of our time.

Tools for Self-Teaching

While the previous reference tools are useful for anybody, there are also sites on the Internet that are specifically meant for students. This includes sites like Cramster, an online study community providing help and support for all students, and tools like PlagiarismDetect that can help students keep their work free from plagiarism.

Cramster

www.cramster.com

Quite frankly, this is the largest collection of answer keys and solution manuals to every university that exists. Odds are, if you need it, it's here. It's not free though. Cramster is an online study/tutoring group that provides homework assistance for high school and college math, science, engineering, and business curriculum (see Figure 6-24). The Cramster community includes students, teachers, parents, and subject experts. Math, science, and engineering study guides develop students' problem-solving skills using practice tests, practice problems, and customized quizzes.

The site provides

- study guides and practice tests;
- lecture notes; and
- math problems and step-by-step answers.

Figure 6-24. **Hone your math, science, and engineering skills with Cramster.com.**

PlagiarismDetect.com

www.plagiarismdetect.com

Internet plagiarism is rampant, and both teachers and students need to confront this issue. More schools are adopting a zero-tolerance policy with respect to demonstrable incidents of copy-and-paste research. The trouble with this is that, while some plagiarism is simply a full cloth lift, many students do use copy and paste to take notes as they research. These cases are more difficult to manage both for students and teachers. PlagiarismDetect.com (Figure 6-26) will continuously check for plagiarism as you write a document. You'll know if you are using your research to synthesize ideas, or just restating someone else's work. This tool comes in both free and paid versions with different levels of performance and features. If you use Windows and Word, though, this is worth the $30 as a plugin. Continuous plagiarism checking will keep you honest and make you a better student and a better thinker. You need fast Internet to use the continuous checker.

The site provides

- very fast, background checking; and
- detailed reporting on plagiarism issues.

Figure 6-26. You might as well know first. It can save you a great deal of embarrassment, or worse.

Mostly for Teachers

Just like some sites on the Internet are aimed at students, there are also that are specifically aimed at educators. Using these sites, you can get support from a community of teachers with things such as lesson plans and resources.

The Educator's Reference Desk

www.eduref.org/Virtual/Lessons

Eduref.org (Figure 6-27) is a collection of more than 2,000 unique lesson plans that were written and submitted by teachers from all over the world. They are available for free reuse and distribution, and cover K-12, vocational education programs, higher education, and adult and continuing education. These lesson plans are also included in Gateway to Educational Materials (GEM), which links to over 40,000 online education resources. The Educator's Reference Desk is a service provided by the University of Syracuse, which pioneered Internet access to curriculum development resources.

The site provides

- lesson plans by subject;
- sample tests and quizzes; and
- curriculum-enrichment resources.

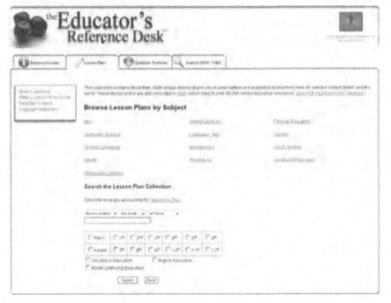

Figure 6-27. The Educator's Reference Desk is a rich source for teachers of any subject.

The Lesson Plans Page

www.lessonplanspage.com

LessonPlansPage.com (Figure 6-28) is another lesson plan resource, but this one is focused entirely on precollege curriculum. The site offers a Teacher Discussion forum, which is a good place to get the input and mentorship of people who may have taught the curriculum you are considering. It also has a library of math worksheets, which can be very handy if you have one or two students that need or want extra support or enrichment.

Here you can find

- seasonal lesson plans;
- science experiments; and
- a big library of printable math worksheets.

Figure 6-28. This site offers a teacher community as well as curriculum and teaching resources.

Information and Support for Acute or Chronic Medical Issues

One of the great features of the Internet is that it enables communities to thrive, especially for those that would otherwise find it difficult to meet up or find other like-minded individuals. This is especially true of healthcare, where individuals can find others with similar illnesses or problems and have an open forum to discuss issues. The web also contains a lot of general reference information on health problems.

WebMD

www.webmd.com

WebMD.com (Figure 6-29) is a site where you can get fairly comprehensive information on just about any kind of health concern. It is a great resource for first aid procedures and guidelines on how to handle sub-critical illnesses. It is a really nice thing to have easy access to while away from home, either for the day or on a much longer trip. In addition to information about minor illnesses and injuries, you can use it to learn more about chronic illnesses and complicated diagnostic procedures.

You can use it to

- find a hospital near you;
- identify unknown pills; and
- investigate your symptoms to know when to seek medical care and advice.

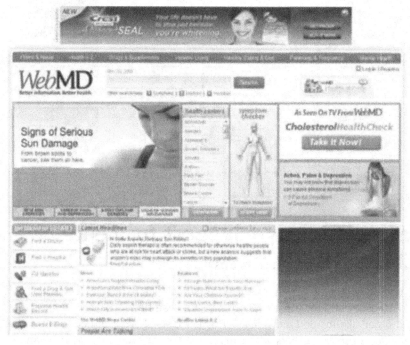

Figure 6-29. WebMD.com is a great source for medical information, at home and on the road.

American Diabetes Association

www.diabetes.org

Until we cure diabetes, we simply have to manage it, and this is a huge job. Meal planning means choosing the proper foods, in the proper amounts and combinations. It means maintaining a schedule for eating, exercising, and taking medications. Families of children with diabetes have an especially difficult job, because they have to teach youngsters to manage the effects of the disease before they have the maturity or skills to appreciate the long-term implications of their choices and behaviors. Diabetes.org (Figure 6-30) is a great resource and a port to other resources.

It provides

- tips on how to cope better with the effects of diabetes, at any age;
- support and education for caregivers; and
- the latest news about research and health management for diabetics.

Figure 6-30. This site focuses on diabetic support, education, and ways to lead a full, healthy life with the disease.

Alzheimer's Association

www.alz.org

A diagnosis of Alzheimer's is often as difficult for family members as it is for the patient. Support, information, and access to external resources are key for all involved with this disease. Those affected by the disease have a far better prognosis if they receive effective therapy and treatment; however, this can be a highly individual challenge. One of the key benefits of alz.org (Figure 6-31) is that it tracks the latest research and developments in caregiving.

This site can help

- teach you how to cope better with the effects of Alzheimer's;
- provide support and education for caregivers; and
- keep you informed on the latest news about research and health management for Alzheimer's patients.

Figure 6-31. This site is a resource for Alzheimer's patients and their families, and a portal to other resources.

Breast Cancer Support

http://bcsupport.org

Bcsupport.org (Figure 6-32) provides a breast cancer support group for survivors. It connects an active and compassionate community that is ready to offer support, information, and understanding. Newbies are welcome and encouraged to take part in discussions, and there is no registration process for this site. You can ask any question you want and probably get an answer from someone who has experienced exactly what you are facing.

There are special forums that discuss

- surgery and reconstruction;
- chemo and other treatments; and
- incidents of recurrence.

Figure 6-32. This breast cancer survivor site exists solely to provide support, engagement, and inspiration to those fighting breast cancer.

The Food Allergy and Anaphylaxis Network

www.foodallergy.org

Food allergies happen when the body's natural defenses mistakenly attack proteins in food that would be harmless for most people. For people with food allergies, eating the wrong food can trigger the release of strong metabolic chemicals, resulting in an allergic reaction. For some, the symptoms are mostly just annoying: rashes, hives, itching, or swelling. However, for others, the reaction can run wildly out of control and even become life threatening. Scientists estimate that about 12 million Americans suffer from food allergies, and living with these can be difficult. One reason that this can be a problem on a day-to-day basis is that many processed foods contain soy and peanut products that can trigger the most severe allergic responses. FoodAllergy.org (Figure 6-33) offers education and information about how to manage these conditions, ongoing research and advocacy efforts.

Find resources the help you

- teach kids how to avoid food that pose a risk;
- learn about anaphylaxis and what to do in case of anaphylactic shock; and
- keep up with emergent research and new therapies.

Figure 6-33. The Anaphylaxis Network is a site for people with allergies, but is also a must-see for anyone who has responsibility for supervising kids: parents, teachers, coaches, camp counselors, and caregivers should give this a look.

Mended Hearts

www.mendedhearts.org

MendedHearts.org (Figure 6-34) is a site for people who have beaten heart disease and want to do something to mentor others through the recovery process. This group has wonderful programs that benefit the mentors as much as the people who receive hope, encouragement, and inspiration from their mentors. The outreach programs include

- visiting programs that provide outreach with the support of local hospitals;
- group meetings in which patients and families get help coping with the strong emotions that diagnosis, treatment, or surgery can trigger;
- Internet-visiting programs; and
- Mended Little Hearts Programs that support parents of children born with congenital heart defects and heart disease.

237

Figure 6-34. Mended Hearts is an activist outreach group that supports people confronting heart disease and its treatment.

"Us Too" Prostate Cancer Education and Support

www.ustoo.com

UsToo.com (Figure 6-35) is the site of a grassroots organization started in 1990 by prostate cancer survivors who wanted to provide help and support to other patients, their partners, and their families. Us Too strives to enhance the quality of life for all those affected by a diagnosis of prostate cancer. No one should face prostate cancer alone, and Us Too offers resources for sharing, caring, and learning.

Its programs include

- patient education resources;
- local support groups; and
- web-based communities.

Figure 6-35. Us Too is a nonprofit support group for prostate cancer patients, their friends, and loved ones.

Utilities

There are a lot of applications and tools that you can download onto your netbook to add extra productivity and features. Some of these can be difficult to find, especially if your netbook uses a non-Windows operating system, but as always the Internet provides, and you'll find sites containing all kinds of usefula nd fun tools listed below.

Linux App Finder

http://linuxappfinder.com

If you have a Linux netbook, you already know that they work just as well as Windows machines when you are using cloud-based apps like the ones explored in Chapter 3. What can be a little more challenging is finding apps to do local jobs. The reason it's more challenging isn't that the apps don't exis; it's that most of them are free or very low cost, so they don't get the same kind of marketing that Windows apps do. The Linux app finder site (Figure 6-36) can help you locate tools to do just about any job. You need to be a bit vigilant about checking them out before you use them. Most of the time, if you search the name of particular app, you'll get a host of unfiltered feedback that will give you a good idea of how serviceable and current a particular tool is.

The site helps you

- search for apps you need; and
- download and install free or low-cost apps.

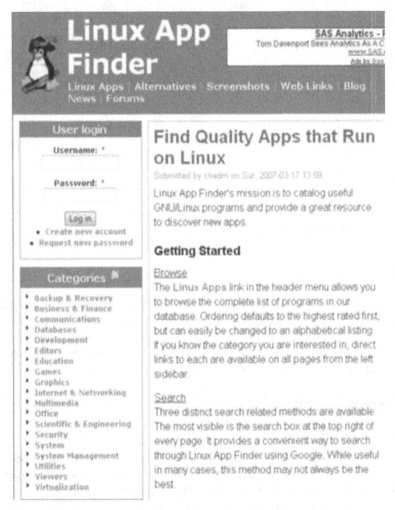

Figure 6-36. Find the local apps you need for a Linux Netbook using this service.

iGoogle

http://igoogle.com

iGoogle (Figure 6-37) is about the best and most entertaining customizable personal Internet desktop imaginable. Naturally, it's from Google, and there are always privacy tradeoffs there. However, if you are already using web mail, this is going to be a step up. It offers quick access to all of the Google cloud-based entertainment and productivity tools, loads of fun time-wasters (who doesn't need a little PacMan therapy now and then?), and an unending stream of add-on gadgets from third-party developers, some of which are extremely useful.

Use this site to

- customize your desktop; and
- access Google's cloud-based tools.

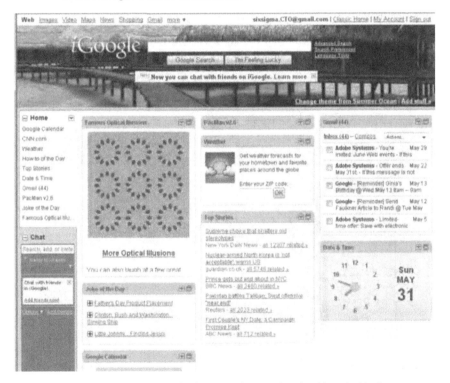

Figure 6-37. iGoogle is about the best interface to the cloud imaginable for a netbook user, because it provides convenient access to so many cloud-based tools and resources.

Portable Apps.com

http://portableapps.com

One reality you have to confront when you embrace a connected mobile lifestyle and an ultra mobile computer is that, ipso facto, you have relinquished a key security protection that was always there before, though you may never have given it any thought. Using a computer in public places and routinely carrying your netbook with you exposes you to the risk of unauthorized access, tampering, theft, or loss. And if any of these things happen, every scrap of personal information about finances, passwords, Internet surfing habits, business intelligence, and the like could end up exposed. This little tool, available at PortableApps.com (Figure 6-38) gives you a way to limit the amount of damage that can occur if your privacy is compromised, and to a certain extent, if your netbook is damaged or corrupted.

This tool helps you

- protect the information you store on your netbook;
- feel safer traveling with your netbook and living a mobile lifestyle.

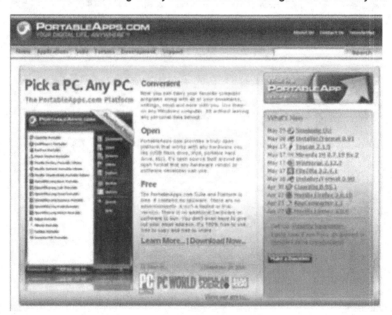

Figure 6-38. Carrying apps and data separately from the netbook is a good way to limit your exposure if the netbook is lost, compromised or damaged.

Summary

I've covered a broad selection of sites here. The Internet is a fantastic reference repository, and once you become familiar with its ways, you can find virtually any information you could want. In the next chapter I'll continue with this tour of the highlights of the Internet, but focusing on the more fun and friendly aspects. Prepare to be seriously entertained.

Chapter 7

Best of the Web Part 2: Entertainment and Lifestyle

Of course, the Internet can be used for much more than work. While the last chapter focused on the business opportunities opened up by netbook computing, here we'll look at the things you can do for fun. Your netbook is a powerful tool that can easily stream music or video for your entertainment. If you're a sports fan, you can use your netbook to keep track of your favorite team and discuss results with like-minded fans. If you're at home and stuck for something to cook for dinner, you can find recipes no matter what the dietary requirements. If you're planning a vacation, you'll find the best deals with the least hassle online. There is so much available out there on the Internet. I've cherry-picked the best here to get you started. Enjoy!

Sports

Sports fans rejoice! The Internet is buzzing with pages covering every sport imaginable. Whether you're a stats nut checking the latest scores and tables, or a grassroots fan looking for some lively chatter with friends and rivals alike before the next big game, the Internet has it all. It is also a great archive of footage from old and new games, so you can catch up on the key plays from a match you missed.

Bleacher Report

www.bleacherreport.com

The Bleacher Report is a great online space for keeping up with the latest news about sports while traveling. Bleacherreport.com (Figure 7-1) offers everything sports to those who don't have the time or the inclination to get their sports information from other sources. The site provides easy-to-find information on the NFL and NFL draft, the NHL, NCAA football and baseball, NASCAR, soccer, tennis, and your fantasy favorites. The Bleacher Report highlights analysis, videos, interviews, and even allows fans to write articles and express their own take on sports events.

You will find

- a site that is clean and easy to enjoy on small screens;
- constantly updated content; and
- tons of sports information in diverse formats.

Figure 7-1. The Bleacher Report is a handy place to find current information about all kinds of pro and semi-pro sports.

ESPN

http://espn.go.com

Even those who don't follow sports recognize the primacy of ESPN for the best sports and sports news coverage in the world. Espn.com (Figure 7-2) provides current sports scores right at the top of its homepage. You can read about ESPN's offerings on radio, television, and in print media. Enjoy sports headlines (customize them as you wish) and top stories in several sports categories. As you might expect, material on ESPN's web page is full of sports news and information, as well as clips and commentary on current sports events.

The site provides

- a wealth of information that displays well on small screens;
- sports journalism of the highest order; and
- knowledgeable comments and editorials.

Figure 7-2. ESPN is the place to find live sports, high-quality production, and extensive coverage of contests that might not make it onto broadcast TV.

FanNation

www.fannation.com

FanNation (Figure 7-3) is "the Republic of Sport." Partnered with CNN and *Sports Illustrated*, FanNation provides Internet users with a wealth of sports information and ways to interact.

One of the coolest features of FanNation.com is a constantly updated ticker that displays scores for ongoing games in Major League baseball, the NBA playoffs, the Stanley Cup playoffs, and whatever others games are ongoing. FanNation's homepage is extensive, and if you want to read the whole thing it takes some scrolling. It's worth it, though, because the wealth of news and information will satisfy any sports fan. FanNation's community is held together by blogs and message boards, "throwdowns," and comments where community users interact.

The site

- includes extensive content that looks good on small screens;
- provides lots to do, places to go, people to see; and
- allows freedom of expression with a strong information base.

Figure 7-3. FanNation is a community site for fans of American sports that takes a more interactive and engaged approach than the pure "news" sports sites.

Fanspot

www.fanspot.com

Fanspot.com (Figure 7-4) is a little different than some sports social networks because it makes no bones about getting sports lovers to exercise their fervor. The community is encouraged to wax outrageous, and practice for the craziness they will enjoy when cheering in the stands for their favorite sports teams. Fanspot encourages its members to blog their attitude, and presents users with "challenges" to weigh in on sports debates.

The site is

- clean and easy to read on small screens;
- free and easy to register on;
- a place for a sports community that is on the cutting-edge of sport craziness; and
- a little light on news.

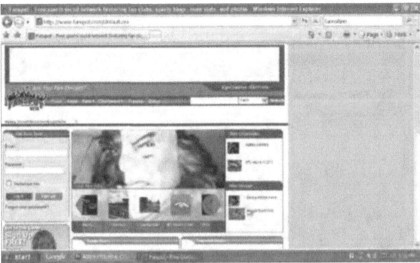

Figure 7-4. Fanspot is a web site for passionate sports fans who want to share opinions and interact with other fans whose life is also all about sports.

FreeTheFan

www.freethefan.com

Browsing freethefans.com (Figure 7-5) is a sport all by itself. Oh, you will scroll down to see the slideshow, videos, most recent headlines, and user-uploaded videos and links. You can join FreeTheFans' forum and earn points for posts. You can find out what other fans are watching at any given moment, and watch craziness broadcast from user sports bars. FreeTheFan also provides the latest scoop on all the major sports franchises.

The site

- is busy, but after all, it's sports;
- displays well on small screens, despite its bells and whistles;
- treats sport as infotainment; and
- treats sport as community.

Figure 7-5. FreeTheFan provides sports fans with numerous, interactive ways to explore sports facts and figures.

OnTheSnow

www.onthesnow.com

OnTheSnow.com (Figure 7-6) is the place skiers, snowboarders, and ski industry folks go to get the latest information on their sport. OnTheSnow provides information and snow reports from resorts, industry news, and ski equipment gear reviews and advice. The site provides ski and weather information from North America, South America, Australia, New Zealand, and Europe. OnTheSnow provides family guides, lift ticket and season pass deals, and tours you through user-rated resorts worldwide.

The site

- shines perfectly from small screens;
- includes great information for spontaneous skiers on the go; and
- provides up-to-date and timely news and information, including snow reports.

Figure 7-6. OnTheSnow.com is a tried and true source for skiing and snowboarding information anywhere in the world. It's the site skiers watch.

PlayGolfAmerica

www.playgolfamerica.com

If you want to learn about golf, PlayGolfAmerica.com (Figure 7-7) is the place to get started. If you're a seasoned duffer, read up on latest equipment, rules and etiquette, and golf fitness at PlayGolfAmerica.com. The web site includes search capability to find a golf course near you and answers golf questions from the obvious to the obscure. PlayGolfAmerica.com features programs including help for getting your family into the game, and provides program highlights and news from the PGA.

The site is

- clean, easy-to-use, and displays well on small screens;
- perfect for the travelling golfer looking for a golf course;
- a source for participation programs for golfers everywhere; and
- has something for golfers at all levels.

Figure 7-7 PlayGolfAmerica.com aims to link you up on golf courses all across the country.

SportsFanLive

http://sportsfanlive.com

SportFanLive.com (Figure 7-8) has features you would expect from a top-flight sports information site combined with a social networking site dedicated to the common interests of its users. Sports news is featured prominently and constantly updated. Additionally, the site offers what it calls "Athletetweets," where athletes post comments, or you can place and take bets with "Buxbets." If you register with SportFanLive.com, you can track your "Fanfeed," set up your own sports page, and make picks on everything, including the NFL, NBA, MLB, NCAA, and the Olympics.

The site

- is attractive and functional and displays easily on small screens;
- lets users search headlines for favorite teams;
- allows users to submit opinions and post blogs; and
- has a search tool for finding local sports bars where fellow fans gather to watch the game.

Figure 7-8. SportsFanLive.com is one of a growing number of sports social networking sites.

SI.com

sportsillustrated.cnn.com

It is no surprise that SI.com, a CNN network site, brings the widest variety of sports news to the Internet (Figure 7-9). Current sports scores in a variety of ongoing games displays at the top of the page. Additionally, you can navigate to every sport you can think of, including high school sports. SI.com is the starting point for finding dozens of photos and the latest news from dozens of teams in dozens of sports.

You can

- find lots of information that displays well on small screens;
- personalize SI.com with your favorite teams;
- read expert commentary from specialized sports experts; and
- check out the swimsuit pages!

Figure 7-9. *Sports Illustrated* is a leader in sports journalism, and teaming up with CNN to enhance its web presence brings sports coverage excellence to internet users worldwide.

Sports Monster

www.sportsmonster.net

Sportsmonster.net (Figure 7-10) is a little like a matchmaker for sports participants. If you are travelling and want to get in on a soccer game, for example, sportsmonster.net is the place to find recreational leagues, teams, and games. If you are an individual, join a team. If you have a team, join a league. Choose from over a dozen sports in a dozen cities; choose your skill level, a preferred sports facility, and choose when you want to play.

The site

- displays clean and colorful on small screens;
- offers team and individual sports and instruction;
- allows you to participate in the community that surrounds your sport; and
- allows you to track friends, teams, and your own participation.

Figure 7-10. Sports Monster links players with teams and teams with players. Sports participants can enjoy their favorite sports activity in a variety of American cities as individuals or as an entire team.

Travel

If you're looking for a great deal on a vacation, then look no further than the Net. There are hundreds of sites offering special deals on all kinds of trips from short-haul flights to Caribbean cruises to camel-trekking across the Sahara. You'll also find many of the big-name travel companies have sites on the Net that offer Internet-only bargains that you won't find in your local travel agent.

BookIt

www.bookit.com

Bookit.com (Figure 7-11) will make a happy traveler even happier. The web site features what it calls "short sales," special prices on package deals, offers that last only a day or two. Bookit.com helps travelers find what they are looking for, even if they don't know what that is. It organizes by region and theme and offers wonderful vacation packages from nearby airline hubs to vacation spots sure to please.

The site

- is busy, but displays well on small screens;

- includes good deals for travel all over the place;
- lists its best deals in the sections, "The Best of Bookit.com;" and
- suggests lots of places to go, and with good deals!

Figure 7-11. Bookit.com is a regular travel site, but it works and works well. It is easy to find what you are looking for, and even easier to find what you want even if you don't know what it is.

Hotwire

www.hotwire.com

Hotwire.com (Figure 7-12) offers a distinct service in helping people find 4-star hotels at bargain prices. Hotels with open rooms register with Hotwire to fill those rooms at discount prices. This allows a traveler to designate where he wants to stay. Hotwire finds open rooms in 4-star hotels and passes the savings along to the traveler. Hotwire shows where to find discounted flight and hotel information, and helps build travel packages including cruises, flights, hotels and ground transportation.

The site

- has no whistles and bells;
- provides clean and easy access to information;
- presents lots of special deals; and
- features great deals on domestic destinations.

Figure 7-12. Hotwire.com is a premier travel site for finding money-saving air fare, hotels, and all-inclusive travel packages.

IgoUgo

www.igougo.com

IgoUgo.com (Figure 7-13) is an Internet travel site designed to make your trip anywhere in the world easy to arrange, and fun and memorable.

IgoUgo.com is quickly growing into a premier travel site. It allows the traveler to make whatever arrangements she needs, anywhere in the world. Igougo.com provides destination suggestions right up front and provides a navigation map that features destinations around the world. Clicking on a destination brings up hotels, flight deals, and tour packages. IgoUgo.com's online community provides blogs and commentary giving traveler tips and photos for any number of world destinations.

The site is

- clean, with a fast and easy user interface;
- a source of information and suggestions on hotels, things to do, restaurants, and nightlife; and
- includes quick navigation to all the features that make igougo.com easy to use on the go.

Figure 7-13. IgoUgo.com is an Internet travel site designed to make your trip anywhere in the world easy to accomplish, and fun and memorable while you are away.

Kayak

www.kayak.com

Surprisingly, kayak.com (Figure 7-14) is free and doesn't sell anything. The site helps you look for what you need, searching over 200 sites at one time, and then sends you directly to the seller. Kayak.com's homepage is not fancy at all. Instead it is spare and clean, and doesn't host advertising and distracting flash banners. Kayak will hook you up with flights, hotels, and ground transportation, and can help you find deals on vacations and cruises. Kayak.com finds what you're looking for and sends you there to complete your business.

The site

- is clean and easy to use on small and mobile screens; and
- has no whistles and bells, just product for the traveler.

Figure 7-14. Kayak is perhaps the closest to one-stop shopping a mobile, on-the-go traveler can find. Kayak is a "travel search engine," able to search worldwide for travel information.

Lastminute.com

http://us.lastminute.com

If you are looking for a great deal on overseas travel, us.lastminute.com is for you (Figure 7-15). These are deals you'll have a hard time beating, and you don't have to plan ahead to get them. The site lets you pick departures from most major cities in the United States to most major cities anywhere outside North America. They also have specific sites for searching from different location in the world. As a test, I tried finding a reservation from Denver to Bratislava. (These cities have nothing in common except that they are hard to get to from one another.) I found a round trip for $664.94, which would usually be hard to beat with several weeks advance purchase.

The site

- has screamin' deals from the United States to anywhere outside North America; and
- spares you having to plan far in advance to get a good deal.

Figure 7-15. Lastminute.com is an internet travel site that provides deals for those who live and travel in the moment. Impulse travelers visit here to find the best deal on a last minute trip.

ASAP Tickets

www.asaptickets.com

No matter where you want to fly, asaptickets.com (Figure 7-16) will get you there, cheaply. They have deals with all of the major carriers and can offer you some fantastically low prices. They also make sure that the prices that they quote include all taxes, fees, and other surcharges so you can guarantee that the price you see on the page is the price you pay.

The site

- displays well on small screens;
- is perfect for "spontaneous" travelers; and
- offers a full gamut of vacation services.

Figure 7-16. ASAP Tickets is the great site for picking up deals on international air travel.

CIA: The World Factbook

www.cia.gov/library/publications/the-world-factbook/index.html

Sometimes our travel agendas take us to places where we don't know all the facts. While the CIA gets a bad rap on a lot of fronts, information on The World Factbook (Figure 7-17) provides travelers with great background information. The World Factbook describes physical geography, geopolitical information, demographic, governmental and economic findings, as well as all manner of other information. Information is valuable to both business and casual travelers. Especially helpful for those on the move, the CIA provides up-to-date warning and alerts, helpful in negotiating unknown countries.

The site is

- a wealth of comprehensive information about all countries;
- easily navigable;

- a good place to look for warnings and alerts; and
- constantly updated.

Figure 7-17. The CIA isn't all cloak-and-dagger. The agency's World Factbook page is a great place to find up-to-date information on practically any country in the world.

Lonely Planet Travel Guides and Travel Information

www.lonelyplanet.com

Lonelyplanet.com (Figure 7-18) provides information for the mobile connected traveler, from around the world, domestic to vastly foreign, from Houston to Antarctica. Long recognized as a standard in travel information, the Lonely Planet web site has information that is easy to access and view on mobile devices. Lonely Planet Travel Guides are available in hardcopy, but who wants to carry a bunch of books around when you can get the same information anywhere in the world online? While the standard information provided on the site is not as in-depth as that in the guidebooks, you can purchase the guidebooks, or single chapters from them, as PDF files (viewable in the free Adobe Reader software) that you can take with you on your travels at no extra weight. Lonelyplanet.com features an attractive user interface that allows users to discover whatever they need to know. Learn about travel services, shopping, and tips from a community of travelers that has visited the destination.

The site is

- Attractive and easy to use;
- includes information for the savvy and not so savvy traveler;
- Informs you on numerous destination offerings; and
- something for everyone.

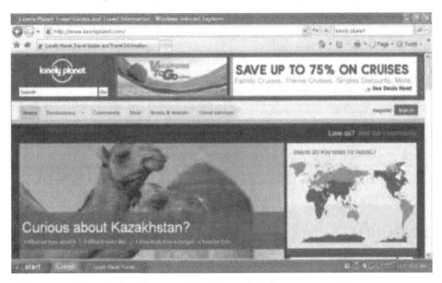

Figure 7-18. Everything the CIA didn't tell you! Travelers on the go rely on lonelyplanet.com guides for information about any destination.

Mobissimo Travel

www.mobissimo.com

Mobissimo.com (Figure 7-18) is a great example of a site that displays easily accessible information from its user community. MobiFriends contribute tips on flight bargains, hotels, restaurants, and destination experiences. The web site is fast and easy to use and could become a staple for a community of travelers constantly on the move.

The site is

- perfect for small screens and easy to navigate;
- has a search box located prominently on the homepage; and
- enables you to learn from experiences of fellow travelers.

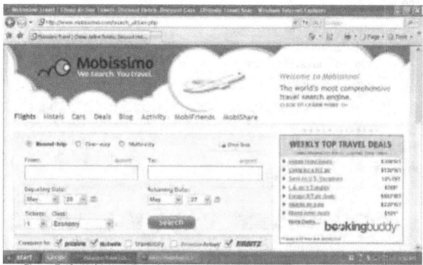

Figure 7-18. Mobissimo Travel is a travel search engine offering a full range of travel amenities.

SeatGuru

www.seatguru.com

Learn about affiliates and partners, what planes the airlines use, available amenities, seating details — the works. SeatGuru.com (Figure 7-19) is the site to visit if you want to learn anything about any airline you might use during your travels. Through a comprehensive listing of world airlines, you can discover everything from seat width and pitch to what kind of peanuts they serve. Click on an airline and type of plane you will use, and you can utilize the seat map to decide which seat you want to reserve. Icons describe inflight amenities so you know what to expect.

The site

- is a little large for small screens;
- includes tons of inflight information that makes up for any web site inconvenience;
- provides airline phone numbers to make communication a snap; and
- tells you what to expect on those lengthy international flights.

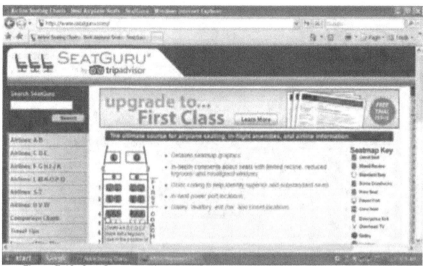

Figure 7-19. SeatGuru provides everything you want to know about practically every airline in the world.

Sandemans New Europe: The Home of the Free Tour

www.neweuropetours.eu

Sandemans walking tours (see Figure 7-20) are the perfect holiday activity for people who want to really see a place. This means walking. Take a tour in any of the 13 cities they cover, and you'll get to see virtually everything you want to, and nothing that you don't want to. You have the insider's edge on finding the beautiful, serene, and authentic souls of the cities. The tours are guided and narrated by a knowledgeable Sandemans staffer.

Use the site to

- book safe, scenic walks;
- plan a tour and have fun, make friends, and learn your way around;
- find information on hostels; and
- get reports on weather, year round.

Figure 7-20. Hook up with Sandemans for a free, guided two- or three-hour walking tour.

TravelPost

www.travelpost.com

TravelPost.com (Figure 7-21) is a hotel search engine that researches thousands of hotels and provides over a million hotel reviews. Hotel reviews on TravelPost's homepage include hotels worldwide, navigable by a world map. You can also search for hotel reviews by theme: click on everything from beach hotels to pet-friendly to boutique, luxury hotels and everything in between. TravelPost.com also lists about 50 top destination hotel reviews.

The site

- has a clean and easily navigable homepage;
- fits and fills small screens;
- features hotels from obscure to famous; and
- is great for finding a place to stay en route.

Figure 7-21. Once you get there, where will you stay? For those who like to know the best place to lay their head before leaving home, TravelPost.com is the web site to help find that information.

XE Currency Converter

www.xe.com/ucc

Not sure how much you are spending (or ought to be spending) when on holiday? It can be difficult when constantly faced with buying decisions using unfamiliar currency. And, given the state of the world economy, the exchange rate can fluctuate significantly in a few days time. Xe.com (Figure 7-22) is updated hourly to reflect values of world currencies.

Use the site to

- convert to and from any currency;
- understand exactly how much you are spending; and
- be aware of the impact of fixed exchange rates at merchant locations.

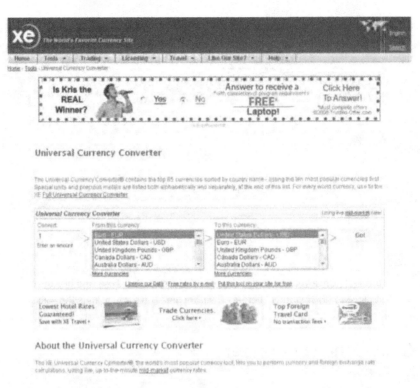

Figure 7-22. Check the exchange rate every day, and give yourself a spending allowance based on that day's currency valuations.

Babelfish Quick Translator

http://babelfish.yahoo.com

Want to know how to say or write more than a word or two in a foreign language? As long as you have a reasonable amount of phonetic proficiency with a language, Babelfish (Figure 7-23) can be almost as helpful as having your own translator. It can even translate whole web pages for you, which is really helpful if you are trying to get around or get things done in a country where your language skills are not tops.

Use the site to

- translate whole sentences;
- get proper gender, tense, and colloquial grammar rendered for you; and
- read translated web pages.

Figure 7-23. Babelfish is a really helpful tool for getting more than a word or two correctly translated.

DeepTravelers

www.deeptravelers.org

Overview

Deep Traveling is a different way of thinking about your visits to other countries. Instead of taking a vacation and sitting on a beach for a week, or sticking to tried and tested tourist spots, deep traveling is all about experiencing the real thrill of meeting new people and a new culture. The site is a forum of like-minded people who relate the stories of their travels, and how their lives were changed by the people they met and the experiences they had.

- Full of exciting and inspiring travel experiences unlike any other
- Make a change in the country you visit
- Collaboratively author "How-Tos" with other activist travelers

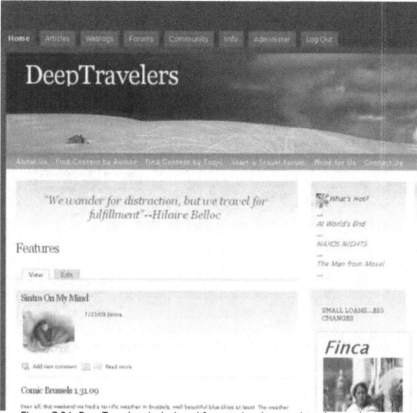

Figure 7-24. DeepTravelers is designed for people who travel to change the world, change themselves, or both. It offers insight, forums for travelers and educators, and support for fundraising for members' causes.

Entertainment and Humor

The Internet has entertainment sewn up, no matter which way you look at it. Whether you want to study entertainment or you want to be entertained, you'll find what you're looking for. You can find what's on guides and in-depth analysis on obscure classic movies, or you can just use the Net to catch up on the latest series of *Lost*. Whatever tickles your funny bone, you'll also find it on the Internet. From spoof news sites to daily comics, from cartoon animations to your favorite primetime shows, it's all here.

The Internet Movie Database

www.imdb.com

The Internet Movie Database (IMDb) is a meticulously compiled archive of every imaginable detail about thousands of productions of all kinds (Figure 7-25). This is the sort of hardcore movie buff stuff that only the true aficionado can appreciate: who was in it, who made it, where it was filmed, pertinent reviews and alternative fan sites, and just plain trivia. IMDb began as an open source project, run by an international group of (and this is the only description that really fits) movie nuts. The site retains that sensibility. The paid staff is drawn from far-flung locations in United States and Europe, and they are probably the site's most demanding users.

The site includes

- a huge list of pretty much every movie ever made (and many that are still in production);
- detailed information including plot summaries, cast lists, and showing times; and
- reviews that help you choose which films are worth watching.

Figure 7-25. If it has to do with movies, whatever you want to know, you'll find it here.

Live365 Internet Radio

www.live365.com

This site aggregates thousands of radio stations and literally makes the world of music available to you. Live365 gives you online access to broadcasts 24 hours a day and has content that includes music, talk and news (Figure 7-26). You can also use Live365 as a platform to create your own radio station. The site provides bandwidth, disc space, royalty coverage, and other critical items. You can broadcast your favorite music, do live sports coverage for your team, or start an Internet radio station for your organization. Anyone can listen to Live365's stations for free, but the subscription membership gives listeners CD quality audio.

The site

- has over 240 genres of music from which to choose;
- enables you to set up to broadcast on your own; and
- permits you to listen to stations using either the Live365 Player, Windows Media Player, or Adobe Flash Player.

Figure 7-26. Choose from more than 6,000 free online radio stations at Live365.

People.com

www.people.com/people

People magazine is the quintessential celebrity news and gossip mag, and the web-based version has everything the paper edition has, plus archives (Figure 7-27). Daily updates make the dish always current, so you don't have to wait for your next trip to the nail salon or the supermarket checkout stand to get the 411 on the most recent gossip.

Here you will find

- All the news and gossip from *People* magazine at the click of a mouse; and
- a search tool to find stories about your favorite stars.

Figure 7-27. *People* on the Web. No explanation necessary.

SideReel.com

www.sidereel.com

SideReel.com (Figure 7-28) is an entertainment guide and community site for television and film enthusiasts. Members of the SideReel social network write the guide, and participation is the key distinguishing feature of this site, as opposed to other online content sites where you simply download and watch videos. SideReel's forum page has dozens of ongoing conversations at any given time, covering everything from what happened in the last episode of *Ice Road Truckers* to member rants about the unfairness of end-of-season cliffhangers. SideReel doesn't actually host the content on its site; it indexes content from other sites and then provides links you can follow to other sites like Hulu, ABC, NBC, and other major content providers. SideReel members can create almost any type of content hosted on the site, including news, reviews, and favorites picks. You can start a discussion, add information about the cast or crew of a show, or create a new form of community feedback content.

Here you can

- catch up on cult shows;
- talk to like-minded fans; and
- read up-to-date news and gossip.

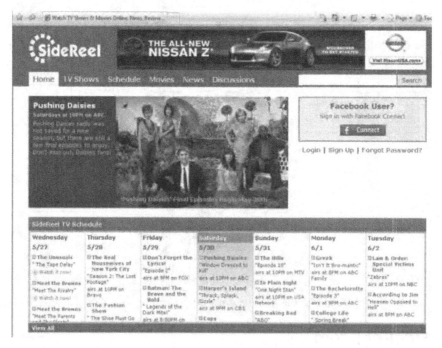

Figure 7-28. Like to talk to your friends about what you're watching? Like to hear their picks and pans? SideReel is a virtual water cooler, where there is always ongoing discussion about entertainment and news content.

Comedy Central

www.comedycentral.com

The original Internet mental health break, Comedy Central is the place to go when what your day really needs is a laugh (Figure 7-29). You can see popular TV comedy shows, watch a little stand up from your favorite comedian, or just check out a joke or two if your time budget says "no" but your funny bone says "now".

You can find

- your favorite Comedy Central shows;
- a huge range of hilarious footage; and
- something for all tastes.

Figure 7-29. Comedy Central is online and provides humor and relaxation with a mouse click. Faster than a Martini, and you can drive afterwards.

The Onion

www.theonion.com

This one comes with a content rating: PG13-R.

The Onion (Figure 7-30) is a satirical newspaper that lampoons real people, events, and society in general. It can be described as *National Lampoon* meets *New York Times,* and for the wry sensibility, it is completely hilarious. It can also be a bit raunchy, so is not appropriate for younger children (or even tweens) and you should definitely be judicious about when and where you view it (for starters, take work and school off the list). It is intelligent and incisive, deliciously skewering the pretentious and the pompous.

The site is

- one of the first and best spoof news sites on the Internet;
- laugh-out loud funny; and therefore
- best not to read somewhere you can't laugh out loud.

Figure 7-30. *The Onion* is very funny, but also extremely coarse.

Best of Craigslist

www.craigslist.org/about/best/all/

This one comes with a content rating: PG13-R.

Craigslist.org (Figure 7-31) is an online classified ad service that is free to readers. There is an interesting mix of cool items worth buying, hilarious personals, and just some generally funny stuff. The "Best Of" page ranges from useful to hilarious, and are voted on by readers each day. Aside from being a great place to find an apartment or sell those unwanted back country skis, the site is known for a free-wheeling personals section, and here you can find some really surreal entries.

The "Best Of"

- is culled from the hugely popular Craigslist Personals section;
- contains both spoof and real posts on a variety of topics; and
- can be very racy, and is not suitable for minors.

Figure 7-31. Truth is not only stranger than fiction, but at the Craigslist Best Of page, it's a whole lot funnier, too.

XKCD

xkcd.com

And, saving the best for last, we have XKCD (Figure 7-32). This is the web comic of an MIT grad who worked for NASA until he started supporting himself with his cartooning. It's really poignant. He mixes dry humor with the occasional math joke. However, it is also quite philosophical, and will leave you thinking about it for hours or days after you check it out. You may need to be sort of a geek to get a thigh slapping, milk-coming-out-of-your-nose laugh out of this stuff, but if you even know a few genuine geeks, this will give you a warm chuckle on almost every visit.

The site contains

- funny, touching, and addictive cartoons; and
- some excellent jokes that are roll-overs, so don't forget to hold your mouse pointer over each cartoon.

Figure 7-32. Attention techies: some feel-the-love geek humour.

Health and Fitness

Sitting at the computer and health and fitness may seem strange bedfellows, but there's an awful lot of informative and inspiring advice out there if you're looking to get fit or keep trim. The portability of netbooks is a huge advantage here, as you can easily take your netbook to the gym and download a fitness plan, or locate the nearest spa while you're out on vacation. The Internet is also a massive repository of recipes of all kinds, whether your cooking for special diets, or just looking for something different to try on a Saturday night.

Fitness Magazine

www.fitnessmagazine.com

If you want motivation, inspiration, a fitness community, and plans for getting and staying fit, fitnessmagazine.com is a good place to start (Figure 7-33). Especially while traveling, it's tough to keep with the routine. This site can give you a quick workout plan that you can pull together in a hotel room or on a road trip. It offers diet and health pointers, recipes, and beauty information for the person on the go.

Visit the site to

- get a motivation transfusion;
- take the hassle out of planning a workout; and
- get ideas that keep your fitness routine fun and fresh.

Figure 7-33. One-stop shopping for planning a fitness routine, healthy meals, and making it fun at the same time.

The Biggest Loser

www.biggestloser.com

If you are trying to lose weight, nothing is more affirming and inspirational than the example of people who are doing it just the way you are, one honest pound at a time. This web site (Figure 7-34) is a companion to the popular television show of the same name, and the great thing about it is that you can get your fix of determination and solidarity whenever you need it.

Visit the site to

- do your dieting along with real people;
- find tips that work about how to change your habits; and
- read about refrigerator makeovers you won't mind.

Figure 7-34. Weight loss for real people, with real people.

Cooking Light

www.cookinglight.com

Here's a key resource for effective meal planning. This site (Figure 7-35) has tons of great tasting healthy recipes that are fast and easy to make and won't bust your budget. It includes a variety of seasonal options and cuisine styles for almost every taste. If you need to shed a few pounds, this is a great way to make it fun. Even better, if a family member of significant other needs to shed a few pounds, using these methods you can put them on a diet and they won't even know it.

The site includes

- recipes that are value oriented and usually inexpensive to prepare;
- shopping tips that help you avoid traps at the grocery store; and
- great ideas for light, elegant entertaining menus.

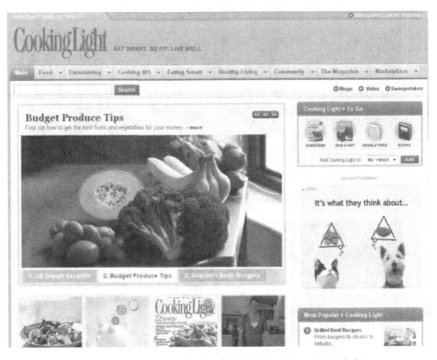

Figure 7-35. Find tips and recipes for healthy, budget oriented meals here.

Gluten-Free Girl

glutenfreegirl.blogspot.com

Wheat allergy is probably one of the cruelest of all food allergies. What gluten-sensitive person hasn't had to turn down birthday cake, holiday cookies, or sourdough bread? There is so much to go without, because gluten seems to be everywhere once you can't eat it. This blog is written by an award-winning cook who faced these issues and came up with wonderfully delicious solutions (Figure 7-36). Even people who can eat gluten all day will love these recipes, which is great for families where one member is gluten intolerant.

Visit here to

- find recipes for waffles, breads, and cakes;
- build an arsenal of dishes you can take to potlucks and everyone will enjoy; and
- learn what products substitute easily for white flour.

Figure 7-36. A big quality of life boost for gluten-sensitive people and their families.

Home and Family

Along with the big name sites, the Internet has also given voice to many individuals who might not otherwise have been noticed. These people keep "blogs", regular postings of their observations and reflections that are full of warmth, wit, and wisdom. The portability of a netbook makes it easy to check your favorite blogs whenever you have a spare minute – it also makes them the perfect tool for writing your own blog if the mood takes you.

Design.Discovery.com

http://design.discovery.com

If you're a do-it-yourselfer with a fairly refined sensibility and are willing to put a little sweat equity into your surroundings, you can get a giant leg up on you projects with this site (Figure 7-37). Simulations let you evaluate the impact of various choices of material, professional designers provide guidance on how to achieve the effect you want, and real-life project scrap books show you how other people have solved challenges like the ones in your space.

You'll find coverage of projects such as

- lighting;
- flooring;
- wallcoverings;
- window treatments;
- outdoor living; and
- digital home.

Figure 7-37. Find in-depth coverage of various home projects here.

Photograzing

http://photograzing.seriouseats.com

So if you were a big customer of the diet sites in the Health and Fitness section, you might need to treat this site like pornography. This is a photo gallery of lovely beautiful food that changes constantly (Figure 7-38). The images stand on their own. There are no recipes, no restaurant names, and no instructions. However, if you want to get some great ideas about presentation, beautiful combinations of ingredient, or you just want to imagine digging into something luscious, you'll enjoy visiting this site regularly.

Visit here to

- graze guilt-free at food photography; and
- get ideas for food presentation.

Figure 7-38 The beautiful food photography at this site will make your mouth water, and it may be enough just to get to look at it.

Scribbit-Motherhood in Alaska

http://scribbit.blogspot.com

In this blog (Figure 7-39), a mom shares the ordinary but wonderful experiences of raising her four kids. This woman's appeal is nearly universal and her readership is very large. As a consequence, she gets all sorts of kid products and services that she writes about and evaluates. She has written an e-book on blogging for women.

Visit here to

- read about and relate to funny, everyday stories of motherhood; and
- read reviews on kid-related products and services.

Figure 7-39. Charming, fun, and occasionally educational reading for anyone interested in motherhood.

Project Foodie

www.projectfoodie.com

Projectfoodie.com is the ultimate site for foodies (Figure 7-40). It's all here. This stuff isn't all for the low-budget, health-conscious, or time-constrained cook, but if you think of the kitchen as an art studio where one work in the medium of food, you'll visit this site often.

You'll find

- thousands of recipes from television programs and magazines; and
- blogs and articles covering all things "foodie."

Figure 7-40. Project Foodie lets you search more than 95,000 recipes collected from magazines, newspapers, television programs, and cookbooks.

The Kitchn

www.thekitchn.com

Thekitchn.com is about the kitchen from the floorboards up (Figure 7-41). You can tour the gallery of marvelous kitchen makeovers (sorry, no before, but the afters are really fantastic), find recipes, learn cooking techniques, or shop for equipment. You can see beautiful place settings and food presentations and read clever, engaging blogs. This site is sophisticated, eclectic, and just the sort of thing that you'll enjoy checking in on to see what is new.

You'll find

- recipes and photographs of kitchen makeovers; and
- tips on kitchen accessories and tools.

Figure 7-41. The recipes are great, but the kitchen tours are not to be missed.

The Ultimate Wedding Blog

www.stylemepretty.com

Who doesn't love a wedding? Stylepretty.com is a marvelous exposition of just how romantic, memorable, and beautiful that ritual can be (Figure 7-42). While some of the weddings pictured here obviously had a budget greater than the GDP of some of the world's less affluent countries, the site also has tips and how-tos for a variety of styles and bankrolls.

Their wedding themes include

- beautiful budget;
- casual elegance;
- contemporary;
- do-it-yourself inspired;
- traditional elegance;
- vintage chic; and
- whimsical.

Figure 7-42. If you are tying the knot, or a key figure in someone else's plans to do so, you want to see this site.

Lifestyle

When you get used to the idea of carrying your netbook around, and having the Internet with you whenever you need it, you'll find yourself using it for all aspects of your life, including some aspects you didn't know you had before! If you want to download the latest music, catch up on hot gossip, view a friend's photos, or sell some of that old stuff in your basement, the Internet can help you get it done.

Amazon.com MP3 Downloads

www.amazon.com/MP3-Music-Download

Most netizens are familiar with Amazon.com's comfortable way of searching for retail products, and will have no trouble finding music they are looking for at Amazon.com MP3 Downloads (Figure 7-43). Amazon.com provides a daily deal, offers MP3 albums at discounts, and encourages browsing by most popular, by price, and by genre. For those not sure what they're looking for, suggestions of top albums, songs, and artists are easy to follow.

Amazon.com

- is familiar and user friendly at all levels;
- provides great viewing and browsing on small screens;
- has competitive pricing for music downloads; and
- simply offers a ton of music.

Figure 7-43. Amazon.com enjoys a solid reputation as one of the Internet's most successful retailers. It is no surprise that it offers a wide selection in multiple genres of the latest new music and the best of classic music.

BuzzFeed

www.buzzfeed.com

Buzzfeed.com (Figure 7-44) solicits information on just about everything from its subscribers. Potential buzz items post first in the site's "Raw" category, and if the material does "buzz," it appears on BuzzFeed's homepage. From there, it spreads virally throughout a network of linked sites. Submissions include links, articles, photos, games, videos, commentary — anything anyone feels might create a buzz. BuzzFeed is the fastest way to view newest and latest information from all over the world. Some of it is useful, some not. What a concept.

The site

- is clean and easy to view on small screens;
- represents the next evolutionary step in social networking;
- provides an almost incomprehensible diversity of information; and
- is viral and flat-out fun

Figure 7-44. BuzzFeed takes advantage of the viral nature of information, and takes social networking to a new and timely level.

Craigslist.org

www.craigslist.org

Craigslist.org is a shopaholic's delight (Figure 7-45). Looking for something from anywhere in the world? You can find it here. Craigslist offers job listings, housing and other wanted items, stuff for sale or barter, personal ads, and services. Craigslist also offers access to communities and forums to discuss what you want, who has it, and where to find it, and practically everything about anything else, whether you are looking for it or not.

The site

- is easily navigable and viewable on small screens;
- secures your anonymity with an in-house email system; and
- enables sellers to post pictures of items.

Figure 7-45. Craigslist is one of the most popular online forums for buying, selling, advertising, posting personal ads, and finding deals, jobs, and entertainment on the Internet.

Dopplr

www.dopplr.com

Dopplr is a relatively new entry in the travel lifestyle and social networking world (Figure 7-46). Dopplr is conversant in multiple, worldwide destinations, and provides travelers with a social network to complement travel and planning.

Dopplr.com helps travelers plan trips together with friends or separately, and lets you know when a friend or colleague is visiting the same destination. Travelers can Twitter to Dopplr, or the web site will import your travel information from any web-based calendar. Dopplr.com recognizes the importance of privacy while traveling and allows members to pick and choose who is aware of who you are, where you're going, and what you're doing.

The site

- Is clean and easy to view on small screens;
- maintains a personal log of your travels; and
- keeps track of your friends so you can meet at exotic destinations.

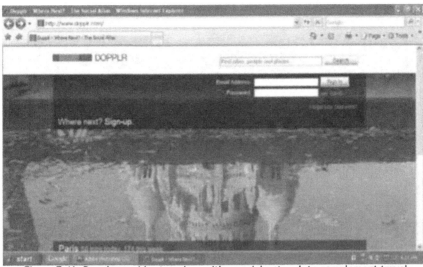

Figure 7-46. Dopplr provides travelers with a social network to complement travel and planning.

Facebook

www.facebook.com

Facebook is an online community site that can be used and enjoyed in a vast number of ways (Figure 7-47). Some people use their Facebook presence to promote businesses or causes. Others use it to contact and catch up with people they haven't seen in years. Still others use Facebook simply to communicate with friends and workers on a day-to-day basis. Facebook is great for travelers to keep in touch with friends back home, and conversely to let people know all your latest adventures.

Facebook features

- a fun and easy user interface that is accessible to small screens;
- ability to make and keep your information as public or private as you want;
- a huge online community is full of surprises; and
- worldwide online accessibility that makes travelers feel right at home.

Figure 7-47. Facebook is an online community with millions of members worldwide. Facebook helps you communicate with friends, make new friends, and catch up with those you haven't seen in years.

Flickr

www.flickr.com

Flickr.com is the place for photographs (Figure 7-48). Whether you are an amateur, professional, or "pro-sumer," Flickr provides easy upload capabilities, lots of storage capacity, and your own private showcase. Great news for travelers: Flickr lets you upload from anywhere, and store photos to protect against loss. Don't worry about carrying external hard drives and other photo storage devices that are easily lost. Upload to Flickr, and then organize and edit when you get home.

Flickr features

- fast and easy access on small computer screens;
- clear, simple, and straightforward instructions;
- tools that let you set up photo albums around your own special themes; and
- ability to allow access to friends or the viewing public...or not

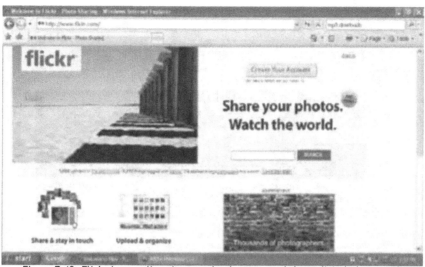

Figure 7-48. Flickr is an online site to upload, store, and share digital photographs. Top of the line in membership and user ease, Flickr is ideal for travelers to store photos during their travels.

Last.fm

www.last.fm

Last.fm is a treasure to find (Figure 7-49). Looking for the latest music, but don't know how to find it? Do you want to know what it sounds like before you buy it? Do you want to watch a music video by your favorite artist? Last.fm is the web site to visit for music to go with you wherever you travel. Pick and choose or let the web site do the work for you. Last.fm provides more music, new and classic, than you can listen to in a lifetime.

With last.fm you can

- search by artist or genre;
- access the latest music news and videos; and
- choose your genre and turn on the radio.

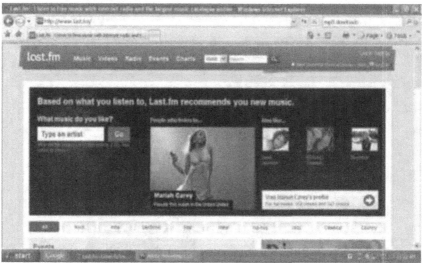

Figure 7-49. Last.fm is radio of the future, a place to find the latest tunes, news, and music information.

Sittercity

www.sittercity.com

Sittercity is an ideal service for people on the go (Figure 7-50). Hook up with Sittercity and arrange someone to look after the home front while you're on the road.

Sittercity.com is a perfect online place to find help at home while you are on the go. At sittercity.com, you can find a babysitter, nanny, dog walker, petsitter, senior caregiver, tutor, or housekeeper to help keep things on an even keel at home while you are globetrotting. Getting home late? Arrange help through Sittercity. Need someone to look after the pets? Sittercity can arrange that for you. Sittercity screens their caregivers, provides free client access to background checks, lists sitter profiles, and provides video interviews.

Here you can

- Search what you seek by ZIP code;
- view sitter profiles; and
- avail of a broad range of services while you're on the go.

Figure 7-50. Sittercity is an ideal service for people on the go. Hook up with Sittercity and arrange someone to look after the home front while you're on the road.

Twitter

`twitter.com`

Twitter is perhaps the fastest growing and most "tomorrow" online community on the Internet (Figure 7-51).

Those not familiar with Twitter are in a growing minority. Twitter is the latest quintessence of online contact and communication. Members know what each other is doing before they are even done doing it. If you don't know what you are doing, ask someone on Twitter. They are sure to know.

With Twitter you can

- read and post "tweets;"
- access a large online network of friends, family, and coworkers;
- enjoy practically instantaneous conveyance of news and events; and
- get firsthand descriptions from friends about anything that is happening.

297

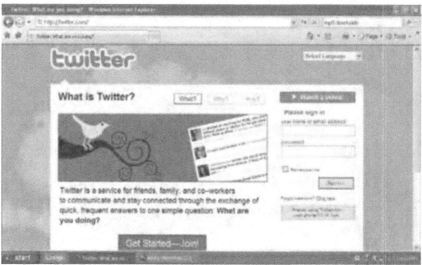

Figure 7-51. Twitter lets you know what's going on with online friends, travelers and coworkers, at any given time all the time.

Ultimate Guitar Archive

www.ultimate-guitar.com

This site offers and unbelievably vast number of guitar music tablatures, reviews, and commentary (Figure 7-52). Every hobbyist of up-and-coming rock star can find something of interest here. More particularly, it's a place to contribute music you've written, connect with others who have similar tastes and interests, and learn new riffs and techniques.

The site is

- a great source of music; and
- by musicians, for musicians.

Figure 7-52. Ultimate Guitar is a social networking site for serious musicians.

YouTube

www.youtube.com

You know there is buzz when presidential candidates supplement their campaigns with YouTube video coverage (Figure 7-53). Somehow, practically everything under the sun finds its way onto YouTube. Say, for example, you are traveling and unable to keep up with lifestyle features on television. No worries: visit YouTube so you don't miss anything. YouTube hosts searchable videos of every kind of music, television event, political gathering, or speech...stuff you can't even imagine why someone would capture it on video. Some of it takes your breath away; some illustrates mundane day-to-day life and demonstrates that we are all members of the human community. It's all there and it's all video.

YouTube is

- loaded with videos that display well on small screens;
- fun to browse, even if you aren't looking for anything in particular;
- easily searchable to find something specific; and
- bound to have something for everyone.

Figure 7-53. YouTube is probably the most populated video sharing community on the internet.

Summary

I hope you found something in that list to your taste. Whether it's the slow charms of XKCD or the frenzied updates of Twitter, the Internet has something for everyone when it comes to entertainment. All of your favorite magazines and television shows are likely to have their own web site dedicated to them full of gossip and extra information. No matter what you like, you can guarantee there'll be someone else out there who likes the same thing and has written a blog about it!

That concludes our tour of the best of the Net, but in the next chapter I'll turn back to the serious side of the Internet. Along with all the great things that the Internet offers, there are also some dangers out there. In the next chapter, we'll look at how to make sure your data is kept secure when you're browsing the Web, and how you can protect children on the Internet.

Chapter 8

Maintaining Privacy and Security in a Pervasively Connected World

Note: portions of this chapter are reprinted with the permission of Faulkner Information Services FACCTS series from previous works by Nancy Nicolaisen.

Explaining online privacy is actually fairly straightforward: you have none. That part is definite. The impact of and remedies for this are considerably less clear-cut, but one thing is certain: whether at home or at work, everything that you, your friends, your employees, your partners, and your customers do online is both transparent and readily available to a host of others. Virtually every site that offers free services, online networking, or shopping captures your activity, amalgamates it with data from other tracking sources, and sells it to someone. Or even many someones. There are no federal statutes in the United States that protect online privacy, and no effective controls over the use of personal information gathered by online surveillance.

There are a few strategies one can implement to limit the access trackers have, but defending yourself is fairly difficult and the available shields are limited in their actual ability to create boundaries around your personal information and behavior. Ultimately, the question is what is at stake for you and how much do you care. Perhaps the easiest and most realistic way to approach this situation without investing a lot of time and effort is to consider the connected world a *public* place. Just as there are things we don't customarily do or say in a shopping mall or at a library, there are similar considerations for using the Web to conduct your social life or personal business transactions.

Maintaining Your Personal Privacy on the Internet

Google, MSN Search, Yahoo, AOL, and most other search engines collect and store records of user queries. They are, in effect, using the free services they provide as market research tools, and as a result, are ever more successful at targeted advertising. It's clever. It's efficient. And it's modern. But the scale and precision of this sort of market research should give us pause. In August 2008, the New Jersey State Supreme Court issued a ruling that may have important implications in ongoing legal disputes over whether an IP Address can be considered "personally identifying information." This is a key point, because Internet privacy activists have long maintained that ensuring privacy is a two-part process: regulating *what* can be collected and regulating *how* collected data can be used. The court seems to have said that for now, IP addresses should be considered private information, but it left the door open for future modification of its position.

It seems a shame, really, that a freedom enshrined in two centuries of United States' constitutional law has largely been fobbed off in favor of free webmail. This is indeed the state of affairs, however, because in practice, most of us have made a de facto decision to relinquish our personal privacy when we use the Web. Forestalling collection of personal data requires consistent, specific attention, and not a small amount of inconvenience. Still, given the potential for what some observers have described as a "privacy Chernobyl," it seems as though the situation may eventually come to the attention of legislators in the United States. The EU recently committed $15.8 million, joining forces with IBM, to develop means of protecting the privacy of users of social networking and community sites. In April 2008, an EU Privacy Panel announced it would exert pressure on the likes of Google and Yahoo to delete user data after six months.

Ultimately, it may be technology that rescues us from technology. Proposed features of Internet2, a collaborative venture including key academic researchers, major industry players, and government to redesign the Internet and its underlying infrastructure and protocols, would make it possible for users to employ secure, private means of data transmission when using web-based applications and communications. This would eliminate the need for "cookie"-like strategies, and give individuals control over the degree of privacy in which net communications are conducted.

For now, however users have few advocates and even less legal protection when it comes to online privacy. One of the lonely but effective activist voices defending your right to be free of net meddlers is The Electronic Frontier Foundation (EFF). Established in 1990, the EFF editorializes, organizes, lobbies, and sues its way through confrontations with industry and government over online privacy and freedom of speech. EFF recommends the following to individuals who wish to rigorously protect their personal information while using the Internet:

- *Don't put personally identifying information in your search terms.* Don't search for your name, address, credit card number, social security number, or other personal information. These search queries create a map that leads to your doorstep and potentially exposes you to identity theft. If you want to "vanity search" for your own name, use a different computer than the one you typically use for searching.

- *Don't use your ISP's search engine.* Your ISP is able to link your personal identity to your searches *and* able to link all your individual queries into a comprehensive search history.

- *Don't log in to your search engine or related tools.* Search engines sometimes give you the opportunity to create a personal account and login. Many engines are affiliated with other services, such as Google with Gmail and Google Chat and MSN with Hotmail and MSN Messenger. When you log into the search engine, your searches can be linked to each other and to you personally, *across the affiliate sites.* If you use the same company's search engine and webmail (or other service), it will be significantly harder to protect your search privacy

- *Block "cookies" from your search engine.* Search engines can link your searches together using cookies and IP addresses. Since cookies are stored on your computer, they allow sites to track you even when you are using different Internet connections in different locations. Or, allow only short-lived "session" cookies, which expire when you quit your browser. Search engines can't use session cookies to construct search histories

- *Vary your IP address.* When you connect to the Internet, your ISP assigns your computer an IP address. Search providers and other online services can see your IP address and use it to link together all of your searches. IP addresses are particularly sensitive, because they can definitively identify you. Unlike cookies, your IP address does not follow your computer wherever it goes.

- *Use web proxies and "anonymizing" software.* To hide your IP address, you can use other computers as proxies. You send your communication to the proxy, the proxy sends it to the intended recipient, and the intended recipient responds to the proxy. Finally, the proxy relays the response back to your computer.

Understanding the Privacy Policies of Sites

At the very least, you should understand, and make sure your children, students, employees, and colleagues understand, what to expect from the Internet when it comes to the privacy and security of your interactions. In the most minimal practical sense, you have to do the following things in order to live the connected mobile lifestyle relatively prudently and responsibly.

Most websites that ask you to *register* or *join* (and by this I mean provide explicit, personally identifying information in return for membership or some sort of benefit), save, and actively use the information you provide. *With respect to your privacy on the Web, the first thing to remember is that "free" services are actually an exchange, not a gift.* The information you provide, both actively and passively, is used to market products and services to you. Sometimes this is more invasive than others, and a prudent person should never forget this when considering what information they share about themselves, their lifestyles, their health matters, and their finances on the Internet. Visualize a drop of ink landing on the surface of a moving stream. There is no way to get the ink back, no real way to predict where it will go, no way to know who will eventually trap individual ink molecules, or how they will use them.

Here's an excerpt from the Google privacy overview. Note that Google isn't necessarily more diligently invasive than other search marketers. However, pretty obviously, they are far and away the best at it.

Uses

We may use personal information to provide the services you've requested, including services that display customized content and advertising.

We may also use personal information for auditing, research and analysis to operate and improve Google technologies and services.

We may share aggregated non-personal information with third parties outside of Google.

When we use third parties to assist us in processing your personal information, we require that they comply with our Privacy Policy and any other appropriate confidentiality and security measures.

We may also share information with third parties in limited circumstances, including when complying with legal process, preventing fraud or imminent harm, and ensuring the security of our network and services.

Google processes personal information on our servers in the United States of America and in other countries. In some cases, we process personal information on a server outside your own country.

—www.google.com/privacy_highlights.html

Google does more than just comb through your emails for advertising keywords to latch onto. If you use the Google toolbar as you surf the Web, information about the pages you visit is tracked in real time and sent to Google for analysis of page viewing patterns. It may sound like I'm singling out Google here, but that's not the case. The important thing is that you understand that in many cases on the Web, there really is no such thing as a free lunch (or search service). Google isn't providing one of the most powerful search engines out of the goodness of their hearts. It's a business, and what it takes as payment in exchange for its service is your data. The data is used for, among other things, providing targeted advertising and improving Google's search capabilities, and as long as you're happy with the way your data is used, there's no reason why you shouldn't carry on using Google. The important thing is that you understand that they're providing a service, and you're paying for it.

Using "Opting-out" Programs

Sometimes search and web tool providers offer their users "opt-out" programs. One might assume from the name that this means that if you don't want to be tracked or have your mail and activities monitored, you can just say so. In certain cases this is actually true, but rarely. More likely, if you read the opt-out policy, you'll find that it offers you very little in the way of protecting your privacy. In the interest of fairness, this time let's examine the fine print of Yahoo's opt-out policy for *ad matching*. (Yahoo!'s ad matching policy analyzes your web use to target ads to your likely interests.)

They (interest matched ads) are ads we show you that are based on your interests. And "interest-matching" is a process of trying to determine what interests you so that we can show you advertising and content that is more relevant. Many people and companies call this practice "behavioral targeting" or "online behavioral advertising."

Yahoo! creates interest segments (categories of interest) based on a number of things. We consider which pages you visit and which links you click, which ads you see and click on, and the categories of search terms you enter. We observe these interests on Yahoo! and across our partner sites and then we create interest categories. Partners may also give us data to use on their behalf for interest-matched ads. Your opt-out applies to all these forms of interest-based matching.

Yahoo! may also use other information for additional customization, such as geographic data based on the IP address we receive when you visit, ZIP codes provided on some of our products, and your age and gender from your Yahoo! account. **If you opt out of receiving interest-matched ads, we will still collect this information.** (Emphasis added)

– info.yahoo.com/privacy/us/yahoo/opt-outfaq/

So again, the important thing is to understand that these "free" services are very rarely free at all. You may be able to lessen the use web sites can put your data to, but they'll still store your data and use it for their own analysis. That's part of the exchange for using their services, and it's something that you, as a good netizen, should be aware of. If you want to take absolute care of your privacy, then you need to be sure to read all of the small print on the Web, even for things such as search engines that you may have thought would be innocuous.

Knowing What Should and Shouldn't Go in Email

Having one's mail scanned for keywords is probably one of the more appalling invasions of privacy imaginable, but we seem as a society to have accepted this idea as long as it is impersonally and anonymously done by search engines and advertisers. If we stipulate that a lot of people feel that this is a *benign* invasion of privacy, and balanced by the benefits, there is still a whole class of problems that can stem from email that falls into the wrong hands by accident or design.

Unless you make specific provisions to the contrary, email is sent as *clear text*, meaning that if anyone can intercept the stream of data sent from your browser to the mail server, they can read what it says. This makes compromised email a rich source of information for identity thieves and cybercriminals who create programs that monitor traffic through a compromised email transmission route and recognize certain kinds of patterns (think credit card numbers, social security numbers, and the like).

Always Avoid Putting These in Email

The following should never be included in an email:

- credit card numbers
- financial account numbers
- driver's license numbers
- social security numbers
- health insurance membership numbers
- passport numbers
- password and login combinations
- sensitive health, lifestyle, or personal information or images
- passwords for various web accounts

Use Common Sense When Putting These in Email

Include the following in email, but exercise caution:

- *Automatic signature lines:* Most email programs let you insert automatic signature blocks at the bottom of your emails. These typically contain full contact and physical address information. Great for business contacts, but if this information is indiscriminately distributed it can help identity thieves. Use a signature block only when appropriate and necessary, and disable automatic insertion.

- *Lengthy, visible recipient lists:* If you routinely mass-email friends, family, and colleagues with jokes or links to interesting stories, you run the risk of exposing their addresses to spammers. Use blind carbon copy (BCC) facilities to hide long lists of addresses from recipients of mass mailings.

- *Business intelligence and proprietary information:* Undiscerning use of webmail to relay or discuss business related information exposes you to all sorts of risks and unpleasant consequences. Use secure communication channels for critical business communications.

Personal Privacy and Social Networking Sites

Because you are reading this book, it is a safe assumption that you are part of an emergent, connected mobile culture. Social media sites and social networking sites are the foundation of this culture, and they provide people an engagement and circle of friends that adds value and richness to day-to-day life. But what is rarely considered (and perhaps not fully understood by most people) is that, unlike all the other forms of information dissemination in the history of humankind until now, this one has no natural, built-in coefficient of friction to eventually slow or stop the circulation of information. (*If you don't believe this, two words: Paris Hilton.*)

Basically, you have to assume that when you place information about yourself in the public domain (for example LinkedIn or MySpace, or even from your company's web site)

- you have relinquished all control over that information and its distribution; and
- that information may, and probably will, live on forever if it is lewd, funny, or potentially embarrassing.

For social media aficionados, the most alarming thing about this should be that *employers now routinely do web searches of this sort of information in the job screening process*. There are tons of things a potential employer can never ask you in an interview, because privacy and discrimination laws forbid it: history of substance abuse, sexuality and sexual preferences, health status and pre-existing conditions, religious practices, and so on. But there are *no* legal or practical limits on their use of information culled from the public domain. If you are being considered for a responsible, professional job, it is highly likely that what you've put out there about yourself is going to be gathered and reviewed. Probably by unsympathetic eyes, or at least by people who you may want to see you in a somewhat different light than the one in which your Facebook friends do.

It is trivial for a knowledgeable, determined or devious person to break the "privacy" of social networking sites like Facebook or LinkedIn. In a survey published by ExecuNet, a professional organization for executive recruiters, 77% of the recruiters said they use web searching to research and qualify candidates for executive jobs. *Thirty-five percent said that they had disqualified candidates based on things they found using web search techniques*. And here's one more example of where reading a site's privacy policy may temper your enthusiasm for unfettered online self-disclosure: *Facebook allows limited member profile information to be searchable using ordinary web search engines.*

In early 2009, several news stories surfaced not about job applicants, but *employees,* who lost jobs or were disciplined for making negative comments online about employers. At least in large organizations, it is a safe assumption that social media activities of employees are routinely monitored by the companies and institutions for which they work.

Common Sense Tips for Protecting Privacy on Facebook

Facebook is a lot of things to a lot of people, but underneath its multifaceted exterior is a powerful, sophisticated content management system that offers users fine-grained control over the visibility of the information they disclose on the site. Fundamentally, Facebook makes all of its users publishers, and publishing is a *job.* Put another way, setting up an appropriately limited and configured Facebook page requires planning, attention to detail, and ongoing maintenance. Here are a few tips that will help you avoid some of the most common pitfalls of the Facebook experience:

- Use multiple Friend Lists to create easy and obvious boundaries of privacy when you are granting access to content that you wouldn't necessarily want all of your family, colleagues, and acquaintances to see. Multiple Friend Lists offer a flexible solution to communication management because

    - individual friends can be added to multiple lists;

    - each list can have its own custom privacy settings; and

    - friend groups can be used as tags.

- Facebook lets you limit the extent to which you are visible in their search results. Use the Facebook Search Visibility control to limit who can find profile information about you. This setting controls visibility inside Facebook searches. (Find this under Settings > Account Settings > Privacy > Search.)

- Facebook also lets you opt out of having your profile information indexed for display public search results (Google, Yahoo!, MSN and the like).

- You can limit the visibility of embarrassing or unflattering tagged images and videos posted on Facebook by visiting the Profile Privacy Page and putting visibility limits on them using the Photos Tagged of You setting control.

- Control the visibility of your photo collections on an album-by-album basis using the Facebook Photos Privacy Page.

- Consider very carefully whether or not you want to treat your *"Relationship Status"* as news feed item (Changes in status are announced to some or all of your Friends via an RSS feed mechanism). This and other News Feed settings can be controlled form the News Feed and Wall Privacy Page. *Relationship Status* also appears as an element of Basic Information on your profile page, and if you wish to be completely discreet in this respect, disables its display there as well.

- Facebook add on applications that publish stories can be embarrassing if they feed sensitive information to a broader spectrum of friends than you intend. Not every Facebook add on is trustworthy or behaves as expected. Uses common sense and reasonable caution when visiting unknown Facebook applications

- Not everybody you meet on Facebook is who they seem to be. Be discriminating about how liberally you display your contact information and particularly how you distribute you physical address. A February 2009 DigitalWire story report that of the 90,000 registered sex offenders MySpace evicted from its user base, over 8,000 of them have re-registered on Facebook. Last year Facebook made a deal with 49 state attorneys general to aggressively work to identify and remove registered sex offenders from the site.

- Joining Facebook groups that identify your ethnicity, political leanings, religious practices, and sexual orientation give screeners information they can't get legally in an interview process, but *can* use if you make a public disclosure.

- Consider your Facebook Friends' needs for privacy when making wall posts, tagging photos, and exposing their identities in Friend Lists. Remember that they, like you, may someday be subject to personal scrutiny where the memorialized indiscretion of weeks, months, or years past could have tremendous negative consequences.

ExplainED

Treat Facebook like any other public place, but add a little caution, because not only are images and interactions more or less public, even deleting them doesn't make them go away. They may downloaded, copied, and archived, reappearing unpredictably and inconveniently for years to come. Be wary of adding people you don't know to your friends list,

Staying a Step Ahead of Identity Thieves

Forget the Hollywood stereotype of a smart twenty-something living in his Mom's basement, subsisting on microwaved foods and hacking the Pentagon. (Though it was a really entertaining movie.) Today, hacking (and identity theft is only a subset of this pursuit) is a business staffed by very knowledgeable, motivated, sophisticated professionals. Various factors including the international governance of the Internet, the obsolescence of its underlying design, and the difficulty of detecting the source of cybercrime make it easy for the bad guys to stay in the game, and often to prosper.

Sometimes, no matter how cautious you are, your personal information can be stolen from your computer. Any computer, of course, but netbook users are, perhaps, more vulnerable to the determined thief or hacker, because highly mobile computing is inherently less private and less secure than stationary computing. The mere fact of convenience and ultra portability tends to give a person the feeling that netbook computing is more casual than working at a desktop machine in the privacy of your home or office. In fact, it is even more important to observe sensible disciplines and precautions using a netbook, because you are far more likely to be observed, eavesdropped upon, or to physically lose a netbook.

Recognizing that you have been compromised as early as possible and being prepared to act to limit the exposure are key to your privacy and security.

Recognizing the Symptoms of Identity Theft

If any of these things happen, immediately get and review copies of your credit report, credit card, brokerage and bank statements:

- You are refused a loan or credit card due to the information in your credit report.

- You are contacted by a collection agency for obligations you don't recognize.
- You receive a bill for an account you didn't open.
- Financial statements and bills don't arrive on time.
- You receive notification that online banking or financial services accounts have been established in your name, without your prior knowledge.
- You receive notification that passwords or PINs have changed and you didn't change them.
- Your credit card, debit card, or check is declined unexpectedly.

ExplainED

Throughout this book, there are tips for protecting your netbook from tampering, securing data, protecting yourself from spyware and malware, and maintaining your online privacy. Sometimes identity theft is random, simply a matter of ill luck. More often, though, you can do a great deal to prevent it. It's worth the effort and attention.

Like other kinds of enterprise, cybercrime operates at various levels. Sometimes thieves steal an identity in order to use it immediately, for example to go on a spree with a stolen credit card. More insidious though, are wholesale operations, where large quantities of identity and account information are stolen in a single sting, and then resold, possibly more than once.

If you are a victim of identity theft, don't assume it is a closed chapter after you discover the theft or you have taken steps to limit your exposure as described in the accompanying sidebar. A professional operation that wholesales stolen identities may retain your information for a considerable period of time. Carefully monitor your accounts and statements for at least six months after the discovery of a compromise.

What to do if you think your identity has been stolen

- Be prepared to act immediately. Keep a record of your credit card numbers in a safe place, along with each of their Customer Service Numbers for reporting lost and stolen credit cards. It is okay to put this information on paper, as long as your assured of storing it in a completely safe place (a filing cabinet in your home, for example).

- Alert your financial institutions and ask that they extend your fraud alert protection. Credit reporting bureaus can do this for up to seven years. Much stolen identity information isn't used directly by the thieves. Rather, it is often aggregated and resold, so impacts from the loss of your information could occur many months after you've been snooped. You need to keep your guard up for a considerable period of time.

- Here are the numbers of the three major United States' credit reporting bureaus. Call them immediately if you think your identity has been stolen, because they can prevent thieves from opening additional accounts in your name or successfully processing mortgage, auto or student loan applications.

    - **Equifax**

        Web: www.equifax.com
        For Fraud Alerts, call: 800-525-6285 and write:
        P.O. Box 740241, Atlanta, GA 30374-0241
        Hearing impaired call 1-800-255-0056 and ask the operator to call the Auto Disclosure Line at 1-800-685-1111 to request a copy of your report.

    - **Experian**

        Web: www.experian.com
        For Fraud Alerts, call: 888-EXPERIAN (398-3742) and write:
        P.O. Box 9530, Allen TX 75013
        TDD: 1-800-972-0322

    - **Trans Union**

        For Fraud Alerts, call: 800-680-7289 and write:
        Fraud Victim Assistance Division,
        P.O. Box 6790, Fullerton, CA 92634
        TDD: 1-878-553-7803

Safety for Netkids

The Internet is a wonderful resource for teachers, students, friends, family, and all sorts of communities of constructive, creative common interests. But you know that already. Unfortunately, it's something else as well, and you probably know this, too. For the young and the naïve, it can be a pathway that leads to dangerous people.

For parents, teachers, and other adults that are responsible for children, it is absolutely necessary to recognize and understand common patterns of Internet interactions that typify developing exploitative relationships involving a minor.

For preteens and younger children, it is important to know when to go to an adult for help and how to recognize when net friends might not really be who they say they are.

It is also important for older teens to know when to ask for help, to recognize when they may be putting themselves at risk, and to develop a bit of "net smarts" about people who are excessively charming, attentive, and flattering. Older kids deal with other social Internet challenges as well: identity thieves, bullying on social networking sites like MySpace and Facebook, establishing appropriate boundaries in terms of information and images they share with friends over the internet, and using extreme caution when converting relationships that were initiated on the Internet to real flesh-and-blood encounters.

Do's for Preteens

Learn about sites where you can find resources that help with schoolwork or offer age-appropriate games, music, sports, and video entertainment. Find sites that help you develop skills or where kids who have the same hobbies and interests as you share their experiences.

Do's for Preteen Parents and Caregivers

Help your kids develop lists of age-appropriate favorite sites, and set up bookmarks for these sites. For kids twelve and under, buy and set up "web nanny" software that limits the display of lewd content and embargoes sites which could be unsafe for kids. Routinely check web browsing history and know where your child spends time online.

Don'ts for Preteens

Be wary of chat rooms. Most people who exploit children first discover them in web chat rooms, IRC chats, and the like. Turn down invitations to go to private chat rooms. Don't masquerade as an older kid in order to gain access to more adult social media and social networking sites. Last year, law enforcement and MySpace operators made a deal where MySpace had to promise to evict all registered sex offenders from their site. In order to be a registered sex offender, you have to have been *convicted* of a sex crime. MySpace hired a detective company to find sex offenders' accounts on their site, and there were over 90,000 of them! After these people were kicked off MySpace, 8,000 of them later turned up registered at Facebook.

Don'ts for Preteen Parents and Caregivers

Don't allow your ignorance of the risks of the Internet to put a child in danger. It's not a pretty picture, but get to know how child exploiters operate. Child sex offenders who use the Internet typically find their victims in chat rooms. Demographically speaking, they are people of all ages, genders, income levels, and educational backgrounds. They are patient and sometimes enjoy the long, slow process of ensnaring a victim by gradually gaining trust. While some exploiters "cut to the chase" almost immediately, initiating sexually explicit conversations or sending pornographic imagery (or directions on how to find it), others are much more subtle in their tactics. They are empathetic, often playing on concerns or resentments of a child. They listen. They are students of youth culture and trends. They show kindness and generosity, and frequently provide gifts or send letters. Gradually and insidiously, this sort of devoted attention will lower the defenses of a vulnerable adolescent. For these reasons, limit or monitor very closely preteens' use of chat rooms. Given the dangers, it is absolutely necessary to talk to preteens and, in an age-appropriate way, make common sense rules governing their socializing on the Internet.

Most teens have a long history of exposure to Internet culture and should be reasonably savvy about the risks of developing relationships on the Web. Just the same, take all of the cautions that apply to younger kids to heart. Not everyone out there is who they say they are or what they seem to be.

Do's for Teens

Engage in connected mobile culture, use the Web to comparison shop and investigate learning opportunities like online college courses and technical training.

Do's for Teen Parents and Caregivers

If you've done a good job teaching teens about Internet safety as younger children, your job at this point may run more to teaching the responsibilities of good network citizenship and how to avoid identity theft.

- Help them to understand that the Internet is fundamentally a public place. Posting compromising pictures of themselves or others, creating or forwarding content that is of questionable taste, or behaving in an aggressive or harassing way is a bad idea. Employers, teachers, other people's parents, and ultimately, law enforcement, can all gain access to online information that kids may assume is "private." Even worse, such things can and do surface much later, when the impact can be really dreadful. Kids should assume that whatever they put on the Web could ultimately become a permanent part of their future resume, and that it may be accessed by people evaluating their fitness for jobs, loans, scholarships, various honors and recognitions, membership in clubs, and the like.

- The place where teens are most likely to be naïve is with respect to identity theft. Both the student loan industry and the credit card industry target youth with aggressive marketing. This behavior has spawned an industrious criminal enterprise that targets 17 to 25 year olds. It works well for the crooks because youth are less likely to experience the symptoms of an identity theft, and so the theft goes undiscovered for a much longer period. By the time it is discovered, the trail to the thieves is stone cold and the few consumer protections that apply have lapsed. Educate teens about what kinds of information should and shouldn't be shared on the Internet.

- Netbooks are fun, attractive, really convenient and oh-so-portable. This makes them appealing targets for thieves. Everything in the previous two bullet *points* about what is and isn't safe on the Internet goes *double* for data stored on a netbook. Unless your netbook is really well secured (and I'll tell you how to do this later in this chapter), when your netbook gets lost or stolen you have to assume the data stored on it just became public. Use best practices for securing your netbook against tampering. Store sensitive data in an online web repository that guarantees complete privacy, on a removable storage that is kept separate from the netbook, or using encryption if necessary to keep it stored on the netbook.

Don'ts for Teens

On the Internet, boundaries matter. In terms of personal behavior and self-expression, understand that just because there are a lot of people out there who seem to have few inhibitions, this neither makes poor judgment okay nor eliminates the consequences for inappropriate self disclosure. The Internet is far more public than you can possibly imagine, and far more insecure than you probably want to imagine. What seems (pretty reasonably) like it should be your business and no one else's simply isn't. Remember these things, and think about the consequences before you click "Send:"

- Even between consenting individuals of similar ages, using the Internet to solicit sex with a person under 18 is a *federal crime*.

- Exchanging or receiving sexual imagery of persons under 18 is a *federal crime*.

- If you even forward a sexual picture of someone underage, you can be held accountable. You are considered as legally responsible for the image as its original sender. You could face child pornography charges, go to jail, and have to register as a sex offender.

- You have no control over where images you post or forward may later be sent or posted. What you send to a boyfriend or girlfriend may well end up with their friends, and friends of friends, and friends of friends of friends.... Apply the same propagation model to parents, teachers, coaches, potential employers, and just about anyone else. Young people have been kicked off of sports teams, endured painful and damaging humiliation when others shared pictures widely, lost educational opportunities, and have been deemed unfit for jobs when inappropriate images have come to light.

- Because web hosting providers and email providers keep detailed logs of the traffic that passes through their networks, very often there is solid, incontrovertible evidence of how files were shared among people, who had them, who forwarded them, and when. For this reason (and the ones stated previously), if you receive pictures with sexual content you should report them to an adult you trust. *Don't delete the message or cover up, because this will tend to make you appear to be a collaborator in a crime. Assume there is a record that you got the message.* These records are easy for forensic cybercrime investigators to find. If you are under 18 or the person in the picture is under 18, get your parents or guardians, teachers, and school counselors involved immediately.

- Email is not private, and identity thieves routinely scan compromised email data streams for patterns that allow them to discover information like account numbers, social security numbers, driver's license numbers, and the like. Don't make it easy for identity thieves by placing sensitive information in email you send. Also, remember that if you use webmail just because *you* delete an email, that doesn't make it go away. Webmail hosts save your mail for their own use for months or even years, in order to figure out what ads they should display on the browser pages they send you.

- If you receive email that claims it is from a bank or other financial institution and asks you to confirm information like account numbers or social security numbers, *it is a fraud*. Banks never ask customers for these things by email, precisely because they are well aware of the risks. This sort of scam is known as *phishing*, and there are a variety of approaches Internet criminals use to get access to credit cards, bank accounts, or information that allows them to apply for loans in your name. *Never respond to emails that ask for personal information, not even to say that you aren't fooled.* Even responding to refuse their request gives them information about your computer and lets them know they have used a valid email address to contact you.

- Prospective employers, colleges, and professional organizations hire search firms that scan the Internet to qualify (or disqualify) candidates for jobs, scholarships, memberships, and the like. In 2008, 77% of the professional executive recruiters surveyed said they routinely used this technique to find out more about job applicants. Half of them used the information they found online (often at social networking sites like Facebook and MySpace) to eliminate candidates.

- After several high-profile incidents of online bullying, many school districts across the United States have adopted policies where such behavior is punishable *at school* by suspension, loss of privileges (like athletic eligibility) and referral to law enforcement.

  - If you witness online bullying, don't join in, or even to respond to the bully, because you risk escalating the conflict.

- If you are a target of online bullying, *you have choices*. You can show evidence of the bullying to your parents or school. In Colorado, there is a completely anonymous hotline which kids can call to get authorities involved in situations that, for a kid, are just "too hot to handle." This includes bullying, sexual misconduct by adults, fire starting, suicide prevention, you name it. (Visit www.safe2tell.org to get more information about this program.) Other states and localities have similar programs.

- Clinical research has shown that most cyberbullies will act out the same aggressive or abusive behaviors in real-life situations. This means that if the bully is a person you know, time is probably not on your side if you are a target of cyberbullying. In other words, waiting to report incidents of bullying *won't* make things better. The big plus in the online situation is that unlike real life bullying, which normally takes place in an isolated situation, cyberbullying happens in an extremely public place. The user agreements for most social media sites and webmail providers specifically prohibit bullying. At a minimum, you should contact the site administrator using their published contact information and inform them that you are the target of aggressive, abusive or inappropriate behavior. Then tell your parents or school guidance counselor, and show them the evidence.

- File sharing sites where people get access to music, movies. and videos for free involve you in an illegal activity: copyright violation. That is another name for stealing. Though this hasn't been much in the news recently, announcements by the motion picture industry's trade group that sales were off dramatically in 2008 due to online file sharing suggest that the lull in prosecutions is probably temporary. If you like a song enough to listen to it more than a couple of times, then pony up and pay the 99 cents. If you want to see the movie, buy a ticket like everybody else.

It is typically not difficult for responsible adults to persuade teens that abusive language, sexually inappropriate content, or other forms of antisocial behavior are not less reprehensible on the Internet than they would be elsewhere. When it comes to identity theft and credit scams, kids are a lot more vulnerable, simply because they can't imagine that they have anything someone could steal or anything to lose. Unfortunately, this makes them attractive targets for people who use stolen identities to get credit cards and loans. Kids, after all, aren't likely to monitor their credit reports, so these crimes can go undetected for long periods of time. Identity theft can blight a kid's opportunity to get student loans and the like, so make a point of helping them learn how to protect themselves from this.

- Don't let a kid shop, spend, or bank online until you are sure they understand the reality of the risk of identity theft. Kids tend to frequent sites that have a bad track record for malware downloads and identity theft. Get a credit card with a very low limit and use it exclusively for a teen's online purchases. Have the card company change the number every six months.

- Don't let kids keep files containing login/password pairs, credit card numbers, PIN numbers, and the like on computers or phones. If you write this information down don't let them carry it. Keep it in one safe place and control access to it.

- Exchanging or receiving sexual imagery of persons under 18 is a *federal crime, punishable by jail time. Those convicted of this offense may be required to register as sex offenders*. If you've been a parent or teacher for long, you know that teens explore. And their patterns of discovery often involve experimenting and pushing boundaries. Making a mistake of this kind, even if it is a byproduct of a consensual relationship, could change the course of their entire lives: career choices may be foreclosed to them, and very few college dorms, fraternities, or sororities want convicted sex offenders as residents. Before turning them loose with a netbook (or for that matter, a smartphone), give them the information they need about this. Go together to the FBI web site and read *A Parent's Guide to Internet Safety* (www.fbi.gov). Most particularly, read about and discuss the penalties for "sexting" (the practice of exchanging sexually explicit photos using camera phones or the Internet) and the exchange of sexual imagery by and of people under 18. Make it clear that this isn't just *your* rule. It's not just a parent, caregiver or teacher being judgmental. It's the law, and the consequences are real.

NetParenting Best Practices for All Ages

The following "best practices" apply to kids of all ages.

Place time limits on chat-room use and talk to your kids about who their online friends are. Perhaps the best, easiest, low-tech first step is to require your kids to use their netbooks in common, shared space like a family room or at the kitchen table. Especially for older kids, online interactions can be a source of entertainment and a way to escape the pressure of school and family.

Even so, an astonishing percentage of online interactions have sexual undertones and motivations. As a parent of any netkid, you need to help them get a little savvy, and understand that not everybody out there is who they seem to be or who they claim to be. While it is relatively easy for an exploiter to weave a deception late at night in a chat room, talking about these interactions in the cold light of day may help kids identify obvious lies, manipulation, and potential danger.

Let your kids know that you examine their browsing histories. Do this routinely, and with the knowledge that in all likelihood, you'll occasionally come across some naughty stuff. Kids are curious, and for many kids, exploration is predictable. Talk to them about whatever you find that concerns you, and be prepared for the uncomfortable moment now and then. Remember, if they *can't* talk to you about their curiosity, they are a wide-open target for a lurking exploiter. Also, don't assume that you know everything just because you do keep an eye on browsing histories. Remember that a lot of kids nowadays know how to clear their browsing history, and most modern browsers now offer a "privacy mode" which doesn't record browsing information.

Put your foot down about file sharing and downloading copyrighted material. Both the recording industry and the movie business have suffered tremendous losses due to illegal propagation of material covered by copyright laws, and they are not happy about it. In fact, they are *so* not happy that they have successfully pursued lawsuits in civil court in which they were awarded tens of thousands of dollars in damages from kids *and their parents* as a way of making the point that they don't plan to take this behavior lying down. Don't let kids of any age use file sharing software that is expressly intended to facilitate distribution of copyrighted material. Not only are you at risk if they are targeted for prosecution or a civil suit, these sites are primary vectors of transmission for malware and identity theft software.

Create a common space in your home and encourage kids to use their netbooks there Set up a single, publicly situated "charging station." It is harder to create a situation where you can easily monitor your children's web surfing habits when they are using an ultra mobile netbook device than when they use a desktop computer, but sooner or later they'll need to check in for a battery charge. Control access to the battery charger, and you are guaranteed access to the netbook every couple of days. Use these opportunities to check browsing histories and the newest file downloads of younger kids.

Make it absolutely clear, that never, under any circumstances, are they to meet with a new Internet friend in person by themselves. Generally, parental scare tactics should be reserved for the gravest matters, but this is one of them.

Make sure kids understand what good Internet boundaries are and how to create them. Kids are very likely frequent some kinds of sites that harbor malware and operate as shells for phishing scams and identity theft. Music and video download sites, peer-to-peer file sharing sites and some social networking sites are rife with threats to the integrity and privacy of the information in their netbook. The mobility of a netbook increases this threat, because most public wireless access points are unsecure as well. They need to understand the implications of the net as a public place, and that neither email nor the information they offer about themselves online is anything like private.

If your kids use netbooks for schoolwork, make it one of their family chores to do biweekly backups of their important data. The very fact that netbooks are so conveniently portable increases the risk that they will be lost, damaged or stolen, or that their data will be corrupted by a stray blast of electro magnetism. Telling a teacher or professor the "My computer crashed" is more or less equivalent to the previous generation's "My dog ate my homework" excuse. Data backups are a responsibility netkids should take seriously.

When to Sound The Alarm

If you suspect a child exploiter may have your netkid in their sights, you have to act. If you are wrong, you may embarrass yourself a little, but at least your child will know you are attentive and that you care. If you are right, you may well put the brakes on an unfolding tragedy. Remember that not all of these kinds of interactions will fit our stereotypes of them. Sometimes sexual manipulators are close in age to their intended victim. *This in no way mitigates or excuses the harm such a person may do to your child. Every combination of ages, genders and circumstances are documented among sexual predators who use the Internet to find victims.* Even if it seems outlandish, if you notice one or more of these warning signs, it is time to start paying close attention:

- A kid is spending large amounts of time online, in chat rooms, and often in isolated circumstances or late at night.
- You find pornography on your child's computer or on storage devices like thumb drives or flash cards.
- They receive phone calls at home from people you weren't aware they know.
- Their cell phone shows calls to numbers that you can't identify, don't appear to be local, or large numbers of calls to 800 or 888 numbers.
- Your child receives gifts unexpectedly and unexplainably.

- Your child receives mail from unusual sources.
- Your child turns off the computer or hides the screen quickly when you approach.
- Your child has online accounts of which you weren't aware.

The things in the following list constitute crimes, and if you discover them, you should contact state or local law enforcement, the FBI or the National Center for Missing and Exploited Children. Keep any computers involved disconnected from the Internet and turned off, because they will be used as evidence:

- Your child or anyone in your family receives pornography involving children.
- Someone who knows your child is under 18 has sexually solicited the child.
- Someone who knows your child is under 18 has sent the child sexually explicit images.

A parent's "Need-to-know" List of Chatroom abbreviations

When it comes to web chat, what you don't know *can* hurt you—or your child. This list of common chat abbreviations can help you decipher conversations in which your kid is taking part:

- 143 — I love you
- 182 — I hate you
- 411 — information
- Ana-mia – anorexia/bulimia
- ASL — age/sex/location
- BF or B/F — boyfriend
- BFF — best friends forever
- BRB — be right back
- CD9 — code 9, parents around
- EZ — easy
- F2T — free to talk
- FOAF — friend of a friend

- FUBAR — fouled up beyond all repair
- GF or G/F — girlfriend
- H8 — hate
- HW — homework
- IDK — I don't know
- IMHO — in my humble opinion
- KFY — kiss for you
- KIT —- keep in touch
- L8R — later
- LDR — long distance relationship
- LOL — laugh out loud
- MorF — male or female

- NAZ —name, address, zip
- Noob — newbie (an insult)
- OTP — on the phone
- OTW — on the way
- PAW — parents are watching
- PDA — public display of affection
- Pic — picture
- PIR — parent in room
- RBTL — read between the lines
- ROFL — rolling on floor laughing
- RSN — real soon now
- RU/18 — are you over 18?
- S2R — send to receive pictures
- SN — screen name
- SorG — straight or gay?
- SWIM — someone who isn't me
- SWIY — someone who isn't you
- SxE — straight edge (also denoted by an "x" on either side of the name); embracing hardcore music and a drug-free lifestyle
- TDTM — talk dirty to me
- TMI — too much information
- TTYL — talk to you later
- Vid — video
- X-1-10 – exciting
- Warez — pirated software

Like any aspect of youth culture, the chat idiom is in a constant state of evolution. You can check here to find new acronyms or look up ones that don't appear in this somewhat abbreviated list:

www.sharpened.net/glossary/acronyms.php

Resources for Ensuring Safety, Civility, and Appropriateness

The Internet presents our society with a complicated cultural challenge. On the one hand, we cherish free speech, unfettered access to information, and the opportunity to connect to other people who are far separated in distance and time from us. But we also want to create adequate protections for the vulnerable and hold people accountable for their actions and the probable consequences of those actions. Let's be clear about this: *The Internet is great*. My bet is that it will turn out to be the defining achievement of the twentieth century. In terms of creating peace, prosperity, liberty, and community, we have no better tool. The take home message of this section is NOT "Be afraid." It's more like this: Be smart. Be tidy. Be sensible and considerate in your interactions and diligent in your defenses. It's not that hard, doesn't cost much, and like any other set of good habits, *once they become habits*, you can't imagine doing things any other way. Table 8-1 lists some resources to help you create a healthy, rewarding connected mobile lifestyle:

Table 8-1. Useful links for keeping safe on the net

Web Site	Services and Information:
www.fbi.gov/parents.htm	FBI's basic information on safe internet use, laws that apply to internet conversations, and links to law enforcement information.
www.us-cert.gov/ reading_room/	The U.S. Computer Emergency Readiness Team provides response, support, and defense against cyber attacks the executive branch of the U.S. government. They develop guidelines for safe, secure, productive Internet use, which are updated regularly, easy to understand, and available as a free download.
www.nsba.org/	National School Boards Administration is active in developing templates for school internet policies and student safety.
www.netsmartz.org	This is a web site published by the National Center for Missing and Exploited Children that provides educational resources and support for kids of all ages, parents, schools and law enforcement.
www.facebook.com/help/ contact_generic.php	Contact Facebook administration to report abuses.
cms.myspacecdn.com/ cms/SafetySite/documents/ SchoolAdministratorGuide.pdf	*The Official School Administrator's Guide to Understanding MySpace and Resolving Social Networking Issues*
www.youtube.com/	Contact YouTube in writing to document concerns or issues: YouTube, LLC, 901 Cherry Ave, San Bruno, CA 94066 USA; Phone: +1 650-253-0000; Fax: +1 650-253-0001
www.flickr.com/ report_abuse.gne	Contact Flickr to report abuse or issues.

Ensuring Privacy, Integrity, and Availability of Your Data

A good deal of the privacy, integrity, and availability of the data you keep on a netbook is a simple matter of doing some "chores" on a routine basis. The good news is that a lot of these things can be automated. For both Windows and Linux netbooks, lots of great open source and proprietary solutions are available to manage backups, secure data against accident or intentional disclosure, and increase productivity by sharing files between mobile devices and larger systems.

Making Backups

Backups are copies of a computer's file system that are made frequently and stored in a safe place so that they can be used to recover from hardware failures, accidental file deletion, or file corruption problems. They are generally a "last line of defense," so use these guidelines to ensure they'll be there and ready to use when you need them:

- Backups should be made in a documented fashion, using the same tools every time.

- Backups should be made on a routine basis, using a scheduler that automatically triggers the backup process during a time when you don't typically need access to your computer.

- Backups should be labeled clearly and thoroughly, with the date of creation, what kind of backup it is (partial or full), what tool made the backup, what person made the backup, and who owns the data on the backup.

- Backups should be stored safely. This means that even if your backup utility lets you copy to a local disk, you should save them off to some other place: a network repository, a DVD or CD, a thumb drive, or a removable external hard drive. You need to make sure that if you lose or damage your netbook, those all-important backups don't disappear with it. Small business users should consider having a safe place to store backups off the computer and away from home or office. This protects you in the event of a fire, flood, tornado, and the like.

- Backups should be periodically validated, so that you know the data they contain is complete and readable. Occasionally the backup process goes awry and aborts, important files are left open and so are missed by the backup process, or the storage medium is either defective to begin with or degrades over time.

- Full backups contain a snapshot of your system, so remember that any sensitive or private material they contain makes you vulnerable if they fall into the wrong hands. Make sure all of your back up storage is appropriately secure.

Table 8-2 lists some third-party backup tools.

Table 8-2. Third-party backup solutions

Third-Party Backup Utilities for Windows and Linux Netbooks	Services and Information
www.educ.umu.se/↩ ~cobian/cobianbackup.htm.	**(Windows) Cobian Backup** is a multi-threaded program that can be used to schedule and backup your files and directories from their original location to other directories/drives in the same computer or other computer in your network. FTP backup is also supported in both directions (download and upload).
www.hiteksoftware.com/jaba/	**(Windows) JaBack** automates Backups of important files and folders. The backup set is created in standard ZIP format, which allows flexibility in restoring the data using any zip software to unzip the backup set. JaBack transfers your backup set to a remote location using either FTP or email. Provides a scheduler and email notification of task failure based on task exit code.
www.mondorescue.org/↩ about.shtml	**(Linux) Mondo Rescue** is reliable. It backs up your Linux Netbook to tape, CD-R, CD-RW, DVD-R[W], DVD+R[W], NFS or hard disk partition. In the event of catastrophic data loss, you can restore all of your data [or as much as you want], from bare metal if necessary. Mondo is in use by Lockheed-Martin, Nortel Networks, Siemens, HP, IBM, NASA's JPL, the US Dept of Agriculture, dozens of smaller companies, and tens of thousands of users.

Encryption and Passwords

To encrypt a file, you use special tools to turn it into a code comprised of a series of letters, numbers, and symbols. The file can only be read by a person (or software program) that can crack the code. Generally the person or program that initiates the encryption process knows a secret *encryption key* (you can think of this as a password). When the encryption program processes your files, it uses the key to generate a unique encoding. In order to *decrypt* the file (decryption is the process of turning the file back into something readable), you have to have this key. Encoding is a very effective tool for keeping private, sensitive information from falling into the wrong hands.

Given the occasionally "wild west" nature of the Internet, it's a good idea to *make sure that any sensitive data you physically store on you netbook is kept in encrypted files and folders*. This goes double for sensitive information stored or transported on a USB stick, which are easy to lose. Here are some resources and information about using file encryption to protect your mobile data:

- Microsoft tools for encrypting files on Windows XP:
  http://support.microsoft.com/kb/307877
- Microsoft discusses Vista file encryption and related techniques:
  http://technet.microsoft.com/en-us/magazine/cc160980.aspx
- Linux File Security and Privacy:
  http://linuxreviews.org/howtos/security/

Making Passwords Unbeatable

Everybody has had the experience of forgetting an important password and being "up the creek" when they can't find a way to recover it easily. (Well, maybe not everyone, but I've certainly had this experience more than once.) The reason this happens is that there are very few combinations of 8 characters involving letters and numbers that are easy for the typical person to remember. There are only two really easy solutions to this problem: use something painfully obvious (like your birthday or your kid's name) or write your password/login combinations down in some handy form and carry this information around with you. *Both these things are absolutely terrible practices*, and in many cases are forbidden by repositories of sensitive information (such as financial institutions and the like). The point of a password is to protect your privacy, and by taking the easy way out, you undermine your own defenses. There are various tools available that you can use to check or improve the strength of your passwords. One of the more popular tools is Microsoft's free Password checker. You can try out potential passwords at http://www.microsoft.com/protect/yourself/password/checker.mspx (Figure 8-1).

For this example, I entered my first name, capitalizing the first letter. Obviously not a very secure choice, and this tool isn't even taking into account that a real password hacker would probably already know my name if the privacy of my email, computer, or web surfing habits had been compromised.

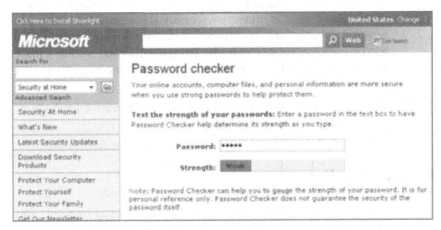

Figure 8-1. Checking password strength using Microsoft's password checker.

Password Do's

To a cracker, a strong password seems random. This makes sense when you consider that password cracking programs are really looking for patterns or matches. If they know your name, birthday, or phone number, they'll first try combinations involving these things. Aside from the fact that it's easy, there is a good reason that they do this: it works a lot of the time. Use these strategies to make your passwords harder to break:

- The longer a password is, the harder it is to break. Depending on the numbers, letters, and symbols used in your password, it can become thousands of times harder to guess for each additional character. Passwords should be a minimum of 8 characters in length; 14 characters or more makes them very strong.

- Some systems allow you to create a *pass phrase*, or something a lot like a sentence (ThiS I$ a SAMP1e Pa$$pHrAse). Pass phrases are typically easier to remember than passwords, and far more secure owing to their length. If you have this option, use it.

- Combine letters, numbers, and symbols, and use the entire keyboard if the system allows it. The fewer types of characters in your password and the shorter it is, the easier it is to crack. If you cannot create a password that contains characters other than letters and numbers, make it as long as the system allows to increase its strength.

- Writing password/login combinations on paper for safekeeping may strike you as an insecure thing to do, but at least if you do this, you are in sole control of them. Be sensible about how and where you record passwords, and be cautious about where you store them. A good guideline is for safe password storage is that you shouldn't leave them anywhere that you wouldn't want to leave the information that they protect.

- Change your passwords fairly frequently. The stronger a password is, the longer you can assume it is safe.

- Use password strength checkers to see how safe your passwords are.

Password Don'ts

The following are password practices you should definitely avoid.

- Don't use the same password at every online site you frequent. This vastly multiplies the chance your password will get cracked.

- Don't pick passwords because they are easy to type (for example, *qwerty* is composed of 6 consecutive keys from the top row of an English language keyboard). Don't use sequences or repeated characters (12345678, 11111, *xyz*).

- Don't use *spoof characters* to make the password easier to remember. Crackers always try these with combinations of the personal information they have about you. (For example, J0hn, D1anne, $teve, M@tt).

- Don't use your login id, any part of your name, birthday, social security number, phone number, physical address, children's names, or children's birthdays. First, because these are obvious, and second, because you'll have confirmed for a password cracker that the other information they have about you is correct.

- Don't use legitimate words *from any language*. Remember that crackers are basically running an intensive pattern matching process on your password. There are numerous, complete online dictionaries available for them to use as databases to power these attacks, and they take advantage of these as a matter of course.

- Unless you are using your own computer (and here is a really big advantage of netbooks), don't use your sensitive password-protected accounts in public places like Internet cafés, computer labs, shared systems at work, conferences, or airports. Assume you have a minimum amount of privacy in these situations.

- Don't give other people your passwords, even if you intend to change them immediately.

- Don't put passwords in email. Any email that wants your password or asks that you visit a Web site to verify your password is most likely a fraud. If you are concerned that such a request is legitimate, contact the institution that is ostensibly making the request by phone.

- Don't store passwords online.

- Don't fall for a *spoof site* and give your password to crackers. Spoof sites are designed to look exactly like the legitimate site, and are used in conjunction with email phishing scams to get you to disclose sensitive information like passwords. Two key symptoms let you know you are at a spoof site:

    1. *The browser's address bar doesn't display a small picture of a lock.* This symbol should always be present if you are being asked to enter sensitive personal or financial information. Also, be very sure that the web address that appears in the browser bar begins with **https://**.

    2. When you closely examine the site's address, it doesn't exactly match the address of the site it seems to be. It may contain spoof characters, for example a zero in place of a capital "O" or a capital "I" in place of a lower case L.

- If you find yourself lured to a spoof site, close the browser. When you reopen it, clear your browsing history and erase and stored cookies in case the spoof site managed to store data on your system. In most browsers you can find options to delete your browsing history under Tools or Safety headings.

File Sharing Netbooks with Desktop Computers

Many people who use netbooks to extend their workday, study in places away from their desktop system, or collaborate with others face a dilemma when it comes to synchronizing files. These situations raise the possibilities that you could accidentally overwrite newer files with older ones, spread viruses and malware from one device to the other, and miss important data when you make backups. Basically, if you have a netbook that you plan to pair with an existing laptop or desktop computer, you have just entered the career field of network administration. Welcome!

Not to be glib, but this is a challenge for which you have to plan, and there are several approaches. The easiest of them is simply to designate certain files and folders on each device as things that should stay in "sync." Here are some online resources where you can find tips and tools for file synching between computers:

- Go to www.microsoft.com/downloads and search SyncToy.
- Go to www.ubuntu-news.net/tag/netbook/ and read about built in Linux tools for file synch.

Privacy and Security Risks for Corporate and Institutional Networks

If you are an enterprise user, you may be surprised and dismayed to learn that your corporate network administrator, database administrator, and systems administrator are not necessarily thrilled that you now have your own personal netbook. On the one hand, it sounds to you like a perfect solution. You can do little e-errands, check personal email, and take work home without ever removing anything from the office. You're more productive and aren't using corporate resources for personal activities, so what's the problem?

The problem comes in two parts. First, *taking work home*. While it's true you aren't taking a computer out of the office, you are most likely taking *data* out of the office. For that specific information, it means that the entire corporate security infrastructure is only as good as the security measures you've implemented on your netbook. If you work with sensitive information, this could make you an attractive target for a *social engineering attack*. Social engineering is basically the name for an "inside job" in the hacker world. A person approaches you, and using social skills (pleasant conversation, apparent innocence, or vulnerability) and either distracts you long enough to tamper with your device or gets you to disclose valuable information.

Problem number two arises from the fact that netbooks are amazingly good at the job for which they are designed. *They can connect to just about anything, anytime, anywhere*: Wireless Internet, the Web, ftp, Bluetooth, infrared. Very often, they are configured to do this *automatically*. This means that if you are in a public place and a Bluetooth hacker is within 10 meters of you, they may be able to pair with your device and browse freely through your files without your knowledge. It's slightly less likely, but the same is true of IR pairing. If you use your netbook to log on to the corporate network, it is a potentially undefended opening through which someone could gain access to files and facilities for which you have permission, but they do not.

Without intending to, you could do tremendous harm by using a netbook that is not properly configured and defended either to access enterprise assets or to carry sensitive proprietary information about with you. This is one of those instances where the old line "it's easier to get forgiveness than permission" just doesn't apply. If you plan to have your netbook with you at the office, let the appropriate people know and get their advice, guidance, and blessing before using it for any work-related tasks.

Protecting Your Netbook from Malware

Malware can destroy your data, slow your computer's performance, cause a crash, or allow spammers to send email using your computer. It is a reality, and not a very pleasant one, but nevertheless, one you must take into account if you want to fully participate in the connected mobile lifestyle. Here's what you need to know.

What Is Malware?

Malware is a general name for software that does bad things intentionally. There are several distinct types, and this matters because you have to do different things to defend yourself against each of them. Here are the major types and their characteristics:

- *Email scams (phishing):* Email is less popular than it once was with online criminals, primarily because spam monitoring and eradication has gotten much more effective. In addition, there have been several successful, high-profile prosecutions of known spammers. Recently a collaboration of government, industry, and academia resulted in an investigation that shut down a rogue network of thousands of malware-infected computers that accounted for *fully 85% of spam worldwide.* Spam email is often used in fraud schemes known as *phishing.* Phishing scams forge email to create official-looking messages from legitimate banks or e-commerce companies. The email includes embedded links to *spoofed* web pages. Spoofed pages look like real sites, but are actually fakes, where the spammers prompt victims to provide their account information. They harvest passwords, account numbers, and personal information that they then either use in identity theft frauds or wholesale to other thieves.

- *Viruses, worms, and Trojan horses:* These are all names for software programs that surreptitiously find their way onto peoples computers. Often they come as email attachments, which is why you should never open an email attachment unless you are certain you know what is in it, even if it came from someone you know. A common strategy for spreading a virus is to program it so that it will be sent to everyone in an infected computer's contact list. Because many people use web mail, which has very effective tools for identifying viruses, worms and Trojans in mail or attachments, hackers have developed techniques to download viruses when you visit web pages, install browser plug ins, or download shared files like music or video. Techniques of attackers are various, subtle and ever-changing, so the only realistic defense against this type of malware is to use anti-virus scanners very frequently.

- *Spyware and adware*: To my way of thinking, adware and spyware are the most concerning and deplorable of all kinds of malware (though definitely not everyone agrees with me on this). In most cases, the software programs that spy on your every keystroke and track you like bloodhounds as you browse around the Internet *do so with your permission*. The user agreement of sites like Yahoo Mail, Google, Facebook, and MySpace specify that they will collect information from your web mail files, web searches, and web navigation and use it to personalize the ad content they embed in web pages you visit. The two important things to know about spyware and adware programs is that, one, they can download themselves onto your computer. The more unsavory ones do this without your permission (often when you visit an unsafe web site). And two, they are powerful programs that can make your computer do things you don't want it to do, including using your active Internet connection to report all sorts of information back to their sources.

- *Botnets*: Botnets are a cute name for an insidious problem. It is very difficult (actually, pretty close to impossible) to make an ordinary Internet-connected computer 100% secure against malware. It takes time, attention to detail, and expense to really defend a computer used to surf the Web, and most people either don't want to take the trouble or don't appreciate the threat. Computers like these are easy to compromise, and hackers systematically hunt them out, infect them, and aggregate them into large networks over which they exercise remote command and control. Botnets make excellent tools for *brute force attacks*. Basically you can think of brute force attacks this way: if you want to do something bad and have thousands or maybe tens of thousands of computers with which to do it, you can accomplish a lot very quickly when you make your Botnetwork attack. An example of this type of attack is called a *Denial of Service*. Here's how it works. Say you want to deny the United States' State Department the use of its network and computing assets. You tell the entire botnet to start sending masses of spam email to the target of the attack, all at the same time. This cause a *flood* of network traffic, so that legitimate accesses can't make it to the target system, and the target system is so overwhelmed that it crashes or stalls. (In either case, it can't work effectively at the job for which it is intended.) It is difficult to trace the source of the attack, because individually, the bots appear to be randomly located around the Internet and the command and control center isn't directly or obviously associated with them. CNN, eBay, and various government agencies have all been victims of denial of service attacks. Most people whose computers have been co-opted into a botnetwork have no idea they are participating in an attack.

Best Practices for Preventing Infections

Even though 2008 was a banner year for perpetrators of all sorts of malware attacks (according to Sophos, a leading web security monitoring firm, there was a new infected page *every five seconds* last year), millions and millions of people surfed the Web, conducted business and research, and enjoyed fuller, happier lives by using the Internet, suffering no ill effects in the process. The point here is this: if you make a point of doing a few simple start-up tasks when you first get your netbook, and develop good security habits, you can make it much harder for even a determined attack on your computer to succeed.

Setting Up Your Web Browser to Defend You

All modern web browsers are built to do a great deal to provide security, but unless you proactively take advantage of such features, only the default settings will be in place, and these, though helpful, fall far short of all a well configured browser can provide. This takes a bit of effort and knowledge, because simply setting your security for the highest level possible will probably prevent many web pages from loading or behaving properly. The best approach is to adopt the highest level of security and only enable features when you require their functionality. Browsers vary tremendously in how they can be configured and what they can do, but here are some general things to keep in mind:

- Have your browser warn you if Javascript, Java, or Active X controls are about to be downloaded. These are executable programs and can be used to attack your computer or to install spyware.

- Browser plug-ins are programs that let browsers provide some new functionality, and are often necessary to see or use certain types of content. Before you install a plug-in, examine its source carefully and be sure it is both necessary and prudent to continue. These can be particularly insidious, because they have automatic access to the Internet to both send and receive data using your computer, Internet connection, and even your identity.

- Let your browser block pop-up windows by default, and prompt you for a decision about whether to let them launch. This allows you to let legitimate ones display themselves, but to easily discard any that you don't want to see.

- Control the amount of time you let *"persistent cookies"* remain on your computer. *Cookies* are actually small files containing items of information that can help make your browsing experience more convenient and efficient. For example, cookies store your email address so it can be displayed by default when you open your email account or fill out a form. Persistent cookies are stored between browser launches and system shutdowns. Cookies are stored in a public directory, so typically an attacker combs through these files to gather your personal information. Setting a default expiration time on them means that you may have to re-enter information at sites you visit from time to time, but you will reduce the risk of having a large amount of potentially sensitive information hanging around indefinitely in a public place.

- On a Windows Netbook using Internet Explorer, you can adjust security and privacy setting using Tools >Internet Options and using the settings contained on the Tools and Privacy Tabs.

Looking Out for Email Scams (Phishing)

Much of this information was covered in detail in the "Do's for Teens" section of this chapter, but there are some additional points to make here.

- Install anti-virus software, firewalls, and email filters, and keep them current by setting them to automatically update themselves every night. This is key, because industry security researchers discovered tens of thousands of instances of new malware attacks in 2008. Malware attackers have professionalized, are well informed, well equipped, and well capitalized. The inherent weaknesses of the Internet's aging design give them the edge. You are only as safe as the currency of your defenses. Good products for this purpose are available from McAfee, Norton, and others.

- Use junk mail filters that come with your mail client program, and don't open the trapped emails unless you are certain they were mistakenly filtered. Delete trapped spam email regularly.

- Never forward bad spam to friends or colleagues. Aside from exposing them to the risks of malware or identity theft, your own "sending reputation" may be tainted if network monitoring infrastructure detects that you have an apparent relationship with a known spammer or malware distributor. This can trigger a number of consequences, including having your mail refused and bounced by smart mail gateways and having warning messages displayed to friends and colleagues when they try either to send or receive mail which has you address in the header.

- Report phishing scams to the proper authorities. *Without opening the email or any of its attachments*, forward it to the U.S. Computer Emergency Team, using this email address: phishing-report@us-cert.gov

Getting, Installing, and Using Anti-Virus Software

Anti-virus software is actually more like a service than a product. Because of the changing nature of the threat, an effective anti virus tool constantly consults online libraries that are updated by malware researchers as new malware threats emerge. These online libraries of threat profiles contain a *signature,* or set of identifying characteristics (much like a fingerprint) for each known virus, Trojan, or worm. Your anti-virus program checks for malware signatures by scanning for these signatures in the files on your computer, your incoming email, or files you are downloading either intentionally or as a side effect of web browsing. When it finds suspected malware, it quarantines suspicious files, reports this fact to you, and then optionally deletes the bad stuff. At a minimum, good malware defense systems will do the following things:

- *Update routinely and automatically with signatures of the latest malware threats.* The exact time of update should be configurable, because when anti-virus software is running, it can make the computer extremely slow and unresponsive. Aside from being merely annoying, this will tempt you to cancel downloads of new information about threats and abort scans of your computer as the anti-virus software looks for potential infections. Most commercial anti-virus software includes a feature to download updates automatically when you are on the Internet.

- *Quarantine any infected files it discovers, but give you the option of deleting them.* If you scan routinely, chances are your anti-virus software will identify things on your computer it thinks are threatening. If you don't get around to looking at the scan results every single morning, at a minimum, you want the bad stuff disabled until you have the opportunity to make a judgment as to whether it should get the toss. This behavior is called *"quarantining"* and effectively prevents any program code the suspicious files contain from being executed, either by you or by a remote agent. This is important, because there are a lot of innocent (and very necessary) kinds of programs that an anti virus scan might detect that are actually okay. You don't want it to *automatically* delete everything it sees as suspicious.

- *Reverses certain kinds of predictable malware attacks.* Sometimes malware attacks a computer with the intention of using it as part of a larger scale, ongoing attack (See the description of botnets in the introduction to this section), or with the intention of returning to the same computer many times to steal personal information. Smart anti-virus software reestablishes your computer's defenses after it discovers this kind of attacker

Spyware and Adware

The bad news story about spyware and adware is that there's no good news. Some sorts of spyware are invasive and annoying. Other sorts are very nearly impossible to remove without entirely wiping your hard drive, but may be subtle and silently invasive. There are a lot of definitions for Spyware but typically, it tracks where you travel on the Internet, reports this back to a marketing enterprise, and, if well designed, does so without ever arousing your defenses. By contrast, *adware* spawns pop-up windows advertisements in your web browser (such as Internet Explorer), often several at a time, and often difficult to close. Spyware and adware often interact to tune the content of the ads to your browsing history and apparent interests. Like all advertising gambits, these are creative, novel (but not in a good way), and very often well-funded operations. For this reason, it's worth having and using more than one anti-spyware program, because it is very difficult for even the best malware defense programs to keep up with all of the possible ways a very determined snoop can invade your computer.

Like anti-virus software, the spyware defense tools you purchase from McAfee, Norton, or another vendor should be used very frequently, and preferably automatically launched at a time when you are not typically using your computer. Ridding your computer of spyware can dramatically improve its performance and responsiveness, particularly on the Internet. If you notice any of the following things, suspect that you have a spyware infection:

- You see a noticeable increase in pop-up windows and popup ads.
- You type one address into your browser address bar, but are redirected to web sites other than the one you intended.
- You have new, unexpected toolbars in your web browser, but you haven't upgraded the browser or added the tool bars.
- You see new, unexpected icons in the task tray at the bottom of your screen.
- Your browser's home page suddenly changed or seems to contain odd content, controls, or links.
- Your default search engine has been changed.
- Your keyboard behaves differently or some keys no longer work in your browser (for example, you can no longer use the tab key to move among fields within a form).
- You suddenly start seeing Windows error messages that have never been there before.
- You notice that your computer has become very slow when opening programs or doing routine tasks.

Secure Web Surfing Practices

Most malware infection occurs as byproduct of routine web surfing. You can shortstop malware infections by being aware of the signs of suspicious activity by websites. Here are a few "best practices" that will help you avoid inadvertently opening the door to spyware programs:

- *Don't click on links or buttons displayed within pop-up windows, even if the captions say things like "Close" or "Exit".* Pop-up windows are often a tool of spyware, and clicking inside the pop-up's window frame may install spyware on your computer. To close the pop-up window, click on the "X" icon in the title bar, or right-click on the pop-up's caption tile in the status bar at the bottom of your browser. When the standard fly-out menu appears, select Close.

- *Select "No" when asked unexpected questions.* Pay attention to dialog boxes asking whether you want to run a particular program or perform another type of task, and don't ignore warnings about programs trying to access the Internet from your computer and programs that want to change local settings. Always select "no" or close the dialog box in the ways described in the previous tip.

- *Don't download any content from sites you don't trust, and understand that even trusted sites are using incentives to plant spyware so they can send customized ad displays to you.* Free download sites have the worst track record as sources of malware. This includes things like images, video, and file sharing, as well as executable programs. Another frequent source of spyware is customized toolbars, web 2.0 gadgets or other "fun" browser add-ons. Spyware is often bundled with other legitimate install elements, so at the very least, be sure to look over a list of files in a potential download and uncheck the box for suspicious or unrequested items.

- *Learn to recognize the symptoms of a social-engineering attack.* To employ a social engineering attack, an attacker uses human interaction (social skills) to get you to disclose information about an organization, its computer systems, networks, security policy, or areas of potential vulnerability. The attacker may seem harmless or even clueless, possibly claiming to be a new employee, repairperson, friend of a friend, or researcher. They may offer credentials or identification to support their claims about who they are. These probes may come as emails or chat room conversations, but they could also be phone calls or even personal contacts if the attacker already has enough information to believe that you might be able to give them information that would allow them to breach the defenses of networks or targets to which you have access. Any stranger that is extremely inquisitive about how to use specialize computing resources to which you have access should arouse your suspicion.

- *Remember, in a lot of cases, you'll get what you pay for.* If you follow email, web, or pop-up links claiming to offer free anti-spyware software, the links may actually install the spyware it claims to be removing.

Table 8-3 presents more resources for defending yourself against malware attacks.

Table 8-3. Resources for Guarding Against Malware

Website	Services and Information
www.antiphishing.org	Anti-Phishing Working Group is a nonprofit collaboration dedicated to wiping out Internet scams and fraud.
http://securitylabs.websense.com	Websense provides in-depth security information about various active threat sources for the global Internet.
www.us-cert.gov/cas	The U.S. Computer Emergency Readiness site is a government-funded operation that documents Internet threats and provides information about how to avoid or mitigate them. It offers information for typical home users, parents, educators, small business, and major enterprise IT operations.

Here's a summary of how to work and play safely on the Internet:

- Take the time to learn how the Web and the broader Internet generally operate.
- Password-protect your netbook, and if it contains highly sensitive data, use two-factor authentication for logon.
- Create a contingency plan in case a netbook is lost stolen or compromised. This may include implementing a utility to remotely lockdown, encrypt, or wipe user files.
- Be aware of the symptoms of identity theft and be prepared to act against thieves quickly to limit the damage they can inflict.
- Read the privacy policies of sites where you expose significant amounts of personal information.

Protecting Your Netbook from Physical Tampering

Security experts generally agree that there is no attack against which it is more difficult to defend than the "inside job." Basically, if someone gains physical access to a device and can logon as a legitimate user, or even the all-powerful user, the game is lost. They can steal files, introduce malware, reset important configuration values, and the like. Anything goes. This is always a consideration for people, enterprises, and institutions that use portable computers, but it is of particular concern for users of netbooks. Our computers aren't merely portable. They are *ultra-portable*. *Ultra-mobile*. Netbooks aren't just tools, they are a whole lifestyle that weighs in at under a kilo and stays on the job for a whole day on a single battery charge. They go where we go.

This kind of mobility so dramatically increases the risk of lost, theft, or compromise that we have to be exceptionally prepared to fend off physical tampering. To do this we use authentication, and we have a contingency plan in place, in case of loss or theft.

Restricting Access to a Netbook Using Two-Factor Authentication and Biometrics

Authentication is the process of proving that a person or process like a computer program is who it claims to be. Logging onto a web mail account or banking web site is a type of authentication known as *challenge/response* authentication. The web site challenges you to tell it your login ID and password and you give it the proper information to gain access. Given a reasonable degree of caution by password holders, and very strong passwords (see the section earlier in the chapter, "Ensuring Privacy, Integrity and Availability of Your Data"), this is a good form of defense because it is minimally intrusive and many levels of password-protecting are available on a typical Netbook. You can protect the whole device with a start screen password, or protect individual files and applications. At a minimum, you should consider doing this when you are travelling or using your netbook in places where there is a likelihood that it will be on and unattended, even if only for very brief periods of time. This isn't an infallible method because passwords can be stole, shared, and cracked by hackers. If you need to be very sure that no one can physically tamper with your netbook, you want to use either *two-factor authentication* or *biometric authentication*.

An authentication factor is something that can be used *independently* to provide confirmation of your identity. For example, when you go through security at the airport, the TSA staff looks at your airplane ticket *and* your driver's license or passport. The ticket is an authentication factor because you *have* it. Presumably you had a checking account or credit card you used to buy it, so this is a form of assurance that a financial institution believes you are who you say you are. (We won't even talk about how people who buy airline tickets with cash are scrutinized these days.) The passport or driver's license shows your picture. This kind of authentication is called an *inherent* factor. It would be inherently obvious that I am *not* who I say I am if the picture on my passport was of, say, Nelson Mandela. Two-factor authentication for computing works more or less this same way. It takes two kinds of proof to gain access to something protected in this fashion. There are three kinds of factors that can be used to implement this sort of defense:

- **Ownership Factors** are something the user *has*. Examples include RFID-enabled wristbands, ID cards that encode access keys using magnetic stripes or embedded RFID chips, or watches and cell phones equipped with embedded RFID tags and USB keys. RFID tags are familiar to most consumers. They are the small rectangular tags often sewn into clothing or embedded in packaging and used as anti theft devices in expensive consumer products. RFID chips can be activated when they come into contact with a reader, which interrogates the chip and discovers stored information. They are ideal for use in two-factor authentication, because information can be encrypted before being stored which makes them secure. Because they are activated by the reader, they don't need a power source of their own.

- **Knowledge Factors** are something the user knows. In most cases this would be a password, but it could also be something like an employee number or the ability to work out the answer to a challenge question.

- **Inherence Factors** are also called *biometric identifiers*. Biometrics are measurements and observations of a person's physical characteristics, such as photographs, fingerprints, retinal scans, DNA sequences, and the like. These are considered the most failsafe of all authentication factors, but are also the most invasive.

Currently, there are netbooks available that include fingerprint readers for use in two-factor logon authentication. There are also a number of companies that provide add-on products for non biometric two-factor authentication. These typically use USB tokens that have to be plugged into the netbook in order for it to function and card swipe devices.

Visibility of Data and Information on the Web

One of the reasons that the early Web worked so well is that the protocol, HTTP, was designed for *"stateless"* applications. Basically, this means that when a web *client* asks to see something (a "web page" of content), the web *server* assembles whatever is necessary to show that individual page, packages it, sends it off to the client, *and then the server forgets the whole thing ever happened*. In this example, the *web client* is your browser (Internet Explorer, Firefox, Safari, and so on), and the *web server* is the computer (or group of computers) you are connecting to somewhere out there on the Internet.

This strategy made perfect sense when most connections were slow (dial-up), most content was completely static (web "brochures"), and most browsers were fairly primitive and inflexible "viewers." However, the game changes radically if a user needs to conduct any sort of meaningful, ongoing interaction. For example, you don't want your bank's web site to forget who you are between the time you logon and when you want to see your checking account balance. You don't want the game you are playing to forget your last move or forget about the points you racked up. And you don't want your chat session to make you log back in every time you want to send a new message. Vastly more than 90% of the web use today consists of exactly these kinds of user interactions, so the old way just isn't adequate.

This is all another way of saying modern web apps require a great deal of *state management*. Practically speaking, *state management* means web apps have to remember a lot of things: who you are, what you are doing, with whom you are engaging, and the like. That sort of awareness simply isn't supported by HTTP as it was originally conceived.

Workarounds that address the problems of statelessness are what makes it easy and convenient to book a flight or buy a pair of shoes on line. Unfortunately, they also make it easy for our activities to be tracked, recorded, and analyzed by the people who want to sell us things, or worse. There are two legitimate types of state tracking information that tend to compromise personal privacy on the web: *cookies* and *server logs*.

Cookies

Cookies are files that are permanently stored on the web client computer (that is, the one on which you are running the browser and surfing the Internet). Cookies are saved on your computer by web sites you visit. A cookie stores information, both during and between your visits, allowing the site to build page views quickly, remember where you were last, and alert you to things that are likely to be of particular personal interest. For example, a travel site may use stored state and page navigation history data to automatically provide information about fare sales for flights that depart from the airports you typically use. Multiplayer games remember moves, strategy, and customizations of your play experience. As a matter of principal, most browsers allow users to refuse cookies, or to be alerted when a cookie is being sent. In practice however, web applications are frequently so reliant on cookie-based state storage that many won't work at all without them. And most people would find it impossibly cumbersome and annoying to supply the same information again and again in their absence.

Over time, sites you frequent have the opportunity to develop fine-grained information about you, your finances, your web viewing and interaction habits, and your lifestyle. And, very typically, they save all of this down to your local hard disk in the form of cookies. The problem with this is that *cookies typically reside in a public directory on a web client machine, have standard kinds of names, and are pretty much easily available to any browser based app, whether you intentionally launched it or not.* This makes them vulnerable to disclosure and misappropriation.

Server Logs

Server logs are an indispensible tool for *webmasters*, the saintly types who run the backend infrastructure that puts the web pages onto your browser screen. (I wasn't kidding about the saint part. This is not a job for you if you like things like vacations and regular sleep.). Typically, web hosting operations and busy web sites record *every* user page request. A page request includes, at least, an exact specification of content being retrieved, *Internet Protocol (IP)* of the requesting client, browser type, browser language, the date and time of the request and optionally, one or more cookies that may uniquely identify the user. In sum, everything in your browser's web page request, plus a couple of items of information you had no idea you were providing. While this sounds invasive, there are good reasons for keeping server logs. Some form of logging is necessary to *page caching algorithms.*

Your IP address is a very important piece of information, because it uniquely identifies the computer you are using to access the Internet. Every computer connected to the Internet has its own specific IP address, and assignment of these addresses is controlled by an international Internet governance body (the Internet Assigned Numbers Authority, or IANA). IANA assigns addresses in country-based blocks, which typically makes it possible to identify the country of origin of a web message.

Page caching saves a copy of a fully rendered web page, so that if you visit the same page repeatedly, the web server doesn't have to rebuild it from scratch each time. Believe it or not, even a relatively ordinary web page can take *thousands* of computing operations to create, so page caching dramatically improves the web client experience (what you see in your browser and how quickly). It also reduces load on backend server infrastructure.

Aside from the performance impacts of keeping track of what pages a user asks to view, server logging provides webmasters one of the best tools available to detect and stop malicious activities and software. Additionally, it gives web hosting operations a way to measure server and network performance.

Unfortunately, server logs also provide absolute visibility into specific individual activities. This becomes particularly invasive in the context of *web searching*, because in practice, you have little opportunity to limit the capture and resale of information that is gathered about you. Most search portals (MSN, Google, Yahoo, and such) attract users by providing "free" services, most particularly email. Here's something that will likely come as a surprise: *the content of your email is routinely processed in order to identify keywords which allow advertizing content to be more effectively targeted to your interests*. These techniques are not secret, and many of the top search engines use them.

Web Bugs: Legal, but Not Nice

Web bugs are images, usually almost invisible. They are used to monitor access to web page content and validate addresses in bulk email lists, and are tools of spammers, online marketers, and snoops. They take their name from the familiar spy craft device used for electronic eavesdropping. Here's how they work: HTML pages or email can embed references to images that aren't available on the same web server as the one sending the bulk of the page or the mail document. When the requested page is loaded or the email is opened, the user's browser or email client contacts the server where the image is stored, and asks that server to send it down to the browser. Recall what you learned about the content of an HTTP page request in the exploration of cookies and server logs. The HTTP request for the missing image identifies the IP address of the requesting device, includes a timestamp, specifies the type of browser, and optionally, provides a description of cookies left on the client device by the server that sent the web page body or email message. This can be insidious for two reasons:

- *Web bugs are almost invisible.* The image is often either completely transparent or a 1×1 pixel gif, so it is unlikely to be noticed by the user. If a web-bugged email contains no embedded advertising, it is unlikely that the bug will be detected by mail filters, effectively defeating their protection without giving the user any warning.

- *Web-bugged email messages reveal personally identifying information*, as well as specifics about how an email message was routed, whether it went to a mailing list, and valid email addresses for all of the recipients.

This information is very useful to spammers and identity thieves, because it allows them to validate email lists, find out what mail is beating spam filters, and to know who read what messages, when, and on what computers. It is possible to shortstop web bugs by configuring email clients not to display images in an HTML email where the image is denoted by a URL. Gmail, Yahoo, Mozilla Thunderbird, and Opera provide this facility, as do a number of other open source and proprietary email clients.

How to Find a Web Bug in a Suspicious Web page

For the curious, here's how to look for a web bug in a suspicious page:

- From the browser toolbar, choose "View Source" to see the raw HTML used to construct the page.

- Look for IMG tags where both HEIGHT and WIDTH are set to 1.

- If the URL for such tags is different from the one that was the source of the page, most probably the image is a web bug.

ExplainED

You don't need to assume that all web bugs are placed with malicious intent. Some web bugs are used by web metrics tracking tools so web publishers can establish and validate page view statistics. In essence, this means they are spying more on themselves than on their page visitors. These numbers are used to determine how much advertisers have to pay to place ads and incentives on the publisher's content.

347

Understanding How Data Moves from Place to Place

The Internet as we know it can be thought of as a sort of communication wonder drug that turned out to have hundreds of beneficial off-label uses, never contemplated or even imagined by its creators. However, as is so often the case with wonder drugs and the law of unintended consequences, the benefits have come at a cost: invented in the early 1970s, the Internet is showing signs of age. As a result, today's Internet functions in a state of extreme precariousness, though this is very seldom apparent to the average person enjoying its benefits.

As you read this, a huge effort called the Clean Slate Internet Project is underway. Arguably, some of the smartest people on the planet are involved in this consortium, which is more or less tasked with a "remodeling" of the Internet. Clean Slate is intended to solve many of the most nagging, persistent and costly security problems of the today's net. That's the good news.

Here's the not-so-good news. In the meantime, until they finish this job, the Internet is straining both under the weight of its own immense success and sharp divergence from the usage model for which it was initially designed.

At the time the Internet's architecture was first generally articulated, there were very few computers in the world, and virtually all of them lived in highly secured environments where a very small number of people had physical access to them. This makes perfect sense when you recall that in 1971, a smallish computer lived in an 800-square-foot locked room with heavy duty cooling, a false floor to accommodate hundreds of feet of cabling, backup generators for power outages, and a special fire suppression system that would kill all the people but save the computer if it ever deployed. In today's dollars, these installations each cost well into the many millions, and not just anyone could whip out a checkbook and buy one. *As a result, original Internet protocol designs always assumed that every host computer was trustworthy, that it stayed where it started out, and that a specific individual was responsible and answerable for its maintenance and good behavior.* Reasonable at the time, because there was no possible way for them to be otherwise. The important thing to note here, is that we *still* use all of those protocols and designs for everyday web access.

Now consider today's reality. There are millions of computers in amazingly diverse and even improbable places, most of which are at least intermittently attached to the Internet. Quite a few of them are extremely untrustworthy, and the vast majority of them are, at best, minimally secured. They are engaged in a dizzying variety of uses.

Clearly, some current popular uses of the Internet rely on kinds and rates of data transmission that still fit initial Internet design assumptions. For example, think email and file transfers. These require absolute accuracy, but it doesn't matter a whole lot how quickly they get delivered to a recipient. Relative to other kinds of things passing over the Internet, the volumes of data involved are small. Now consider Internet radio and Internet-based telephony. These demand really fast, massive movements of data, but a little bit of data loss or corruption is acceptable because temporary loss of some sound quality is acceptable to most people in exchange for a free service or the convenience and mobility of these tools. Finally, think about Internet applications that demand both high rates of accuracy *and* high data transmission rates, the bona fide business-class travelers on the Internet's data airline. This would include remote medical applications and emergency response support.

Given these three distinct kinds of Internet applications, all of which take place on the web on a daily basis, all over the world, it is easy to see that no matter what kind of model for data transfer you choose, it won't work well for everyone all of the time. So, what you need to know about the web is how the trade-offs of the Internet as we know it affect *you*, and most particularly how much risk you are taking with your data, your personal privacy and your financial information when you enjoy and embrace the connected mobile lifestyle. To make an informed judgment, about that you need to understand the basic nature of the Internet Protocols on which the web relies: HTTP (HyperText Transport Protocol) and HTTPS (HyperText Transport Protocol Secure); and to understand the advantages and disadvantages of some other popular methods for networking that a lot of netbooks support.

Where your netbook is most vulnerable to intrusions

Well. It's a jungle out there. Really. And even though you think you know what the riskiest sorts of websites are, you are most probably only partly right: Almost everyone approaches sites that offer lewd content, gambling or controlled substances with an appropriate amount of caution, and it is wise to do so. What most people don't appreciate about the risk of malware infection is that the threat has massively and dramatically professionalized over the last two years. Blame the economy. Blame careless web programmers. But according to the 2008 Sophos Security Report, the number one place to get infected with malware in 2008 was *Google's Blogspot.com* service.

The prominent threat monitoring enterprise Sophos published these findings in their report on malware trends in 2008:

- *Blogspot.com accounted for a whopping 2% of all malware contaminated pages on the Internet.* This situation is largely a side effect of the fact that each page displays a link entitled "Next Blog," which routes a reader to a random blog post. Infected blog posts play on the trusting and credulous reader to get them to download malware or follow links off the page to dangerous sites.

- *Over 90% of the pages containing malware were actually legitimate corporate websites that had been hacked using a technique called SQL injection.* This includes many in the ranks of Fortune 500.

ExplainED

SQL is the name of the program language typically used in database applications. SQL injection is a favorite tool of hackers who use programs that comb the web, probing until they find a site with vulnerabilities. This particular attack involves using a data entry form on a web site (like one where you enter your name or other information to "join" the site) to enter program code that then "breaks in" and manipulates the database behind the web site. Successful SQL injection gives the hacker full access to the database. This is actually even worse than it sounds, because these databases don't only store data: personal information, business intelligence, financials, and the like. SQL databases can store program code, as well, so the injection stores itself and takes over. A site hacked through SQL injection can be thoroughly compromised, and no longer even under the control of the site owner.

- In 2008, Sophos detected a page with embedded malware *every five seconds*. This is a threefold increase in malware contagion over the prior year. As of July 2008, the company identified 11 million unique occurrences of web-based malware.

- Social networking sites including Facebook and LinkedIn have been attractive targets for well-organized, well-funded, savvy cybercriminals. Once these bad actors gain access to legitimate user profiles, they can use them to crack barriers around corporate directories. They target the new and the naïve, with "spear-phishing" attacks, where they offer enough correct information to cause victims to let down their guard and disclose key personal or corporate information to people posing as legitimate contacts.

- Email attachment attacks have fallen dramatically, because web attacks are so much easier and more effective. The typical successful email attack promises salacious content about celebrities.

What to do if you suspect your netbook has been infected or compromised

First, if you are certain that your computer is infected, immediately disconnect from the Internet. You can be sure that you have a problem if your Internet service provider, your POP email provider, or people in your contact list notify you that you or your machine are the source of mischief. This can be especially embarrassing if the malware with which your machine is infected uses your contact list in malicious ways or sends inappropriate content to your contacts. If even one person notifies you that something like this has happened, you must assume that every entry in your contact list has been exposed. *Resist the urge to send a broad-spectrum apology to your entire list, because this could further spread the infectious agent.* While you are still connected to the Internet, a local private network like a corporate intranet, or a mail server you are still at risk of further damage, and you expose all other parts of you network as well. Disconnect completely, and then attempt to run a full scan. Follow these steps:

1. If you have Bluetooth enabled, turn it off.

2. Manually turn off the wireless antenna in your netbook.

3. If you connect to a network or router using an Ethernet connection, physically unplug the cable from the back of your netbook.

If you are uncertain that your computer is infected, but have reason to suspect it might be, run a full scan using the malware detection and removal tool or tools you have installed. Malware scanners often take advantage of databases of known threats. Because these threats are constantly evolving, malware threat databases are updated frequently and the scanners often need access to the Internet to completely and thoroughly diagnose problems. There are several well known and respected commercial tools (McAfee, Norton, Kaspersky, and others) that do this job, and a reasonable number of freeware/shareware tools as well.

Really, Really Bad Malware

Some of the most pernicious types of malware will actually block access to known anti-malware sites and prevent their removal using automatic scanning tools. If you try to run a scan of your computer and it repeatedly fails, terminates before finishing or crashes, you may need to take steps to manually find and remove bad programs infecting your computer. When malware programs are very sophisticated and difficult to defeat, it can be because they are masquerading as legitimate *device drivers* and loading themselves when Windows "boots" or starts itself up. In the case of Linux, they may install themselves as a similar tool. In that case, they are called *rootkits*.

A device driver is a small but highly privileged program responsible for operating the most basic elements of a system, for example, the keyboard, the mouse, the screen or the printer. These elements are often called *peripherals*, because they are "add-ons" to the basic, bare-bones computer, typically used to provide extra or *peripheral* capabilities of a particular user's choosing (Think headsets, modems, flash card readers and the like). Device drivers have direct access to a computer's hardware and to parts of the operating system that ordinary user programs can't touch, and they are loaded as the system starts and before an ordinary user has any control over the system.

Windows (and in fact DOS, before it) was designed to discover any new devices when it starts a computer. It adds device driver software for each item it discovers to the basic operating system, and then lets drivers take care of whatever magic they choose to undertake. It is not necessary for an actual, physical device to be attached to the system. Sometimes device drivers do things that *emulate* (or pretend to be) real devices. For example, sometimes device drivers map out a section of the computer's main memory and treat as though it were a disk drive. This makes it possible to "save" and "retrieve" things very rapidly, and is a favorite tactic of software developers and image processing programs like Adobe Photoshop. The result of this scenario is called a *virtual device*, meaning the device only *seems* to be there: this is a powerful feature of the PC architecture that makes Windows-based computers almost endlessly customizable. There is, however, one real flaw in this strategy.

Windows is relatively undiscerning when it loads drivers, so if a malware program can manage to find its way into a system disguised in a way that allows it to be loaded as a device driver at system startup, it is both extremely dangerous and extremely difficult to remove. It's not a sure bet that you can beat a really determined and destructive adversary of this kind, but sometimes these steps work to get rid of malware that installs itself during the Windows load process.

1. Shut down the computer normally if possible, but if you can't do this, turn it off.

2. Restart the netbook in Windows Safe Mode. For Windows XP, press the F8 key before the Windows Splash Screen appears. (The first screen you see, displaying the Windows logo and product name.) It is all right to press F8 more than once, but if you are too late, the computer will proceed with the normal startup process and you will need to try again. For Vista users, hold the F8 key down while the computer starts. When you get to the Safe Mode start up screen, select Safe Mode with Networking from the available choices.

3. Because Safe mode only installs the minimum working set necessary to run the computer, it is very unlikely that the malware has gotten access to any resources yet. Your virus scanning software should be able to run successfully at this point. In addition, run any tools you have that detect spyware.

4. Remove any infected programs or files and restart Windows normally.

Best Practices for Maintaining the Availability, Integrity, and Security of Your Netbook

Table 8-4 summarizes the measures you should take to ensure your netbook is secure, private, and stable.

Table 8-4. Best Practices for Netbook Protection

Practice this:	To accomplish this:
Use virus-scanning tools and anti-spyware tools. Run them nightly and review results before you begin using your computer.	Defense against malware and identity thieves.
Use automatic in-file backup tools. Keep labeled and dated backups on CD or DVD for a full year.	Protect data integrity and ensure recoverability in the event of hardware failures or loss of computer.
When not using the netbook, keep it in a protective case.	Prevent damage due to dust, spills, and minor drops. Reduce opportunities for physical tampering that could impact privacy and security.
Take the time to learn how the web and the broader Internet work.	Knowledge is the best defense against security and privacy compromises.
Password-protect your netbook, and if it contains highly sensitive data, use two-factor authentication for logon.	Make your data theft- and tamper-proof.
Create a contingency plan in case a netbook is lost, stolen, or compromised. This may include implementing a utility to remotely lockdown, encrypt, or wipe user files.	Limit the risks of making data highly mobile.
Be aware of the symptoms of identity theft and be prepared to act against thieves quickly to limit the damage they can inflict.	Make yourself a difficult target for cyber criminals.
Read the privacy policies of sites where you expose significant amounts of personal information.	Recognize risks and vulnerabilities inherent in "free" services and social media.

Summary

It somehow seems strange to me to write so extensively about something as important as the need to safeguards one's personal privacy, but we seem to live in a time when few people value it much until it is lost. If for no other reason than sheer economics, think seriously about the things in the chapter, and take action to preserve those elements of your privacy that you can ill afford to do with out. If you shop or bank online, take special note of how to create strong passwords. If you must store sensitive data on your netbook, then buy one that does two-factor authentication.

No matter what you do with your netbook, buy and use good tools for malware detection and eradication. And if you are a parent, raise your kids to be safe, respectful, and reasonably impulse-controlled about their uses of the web and social media in general.

Notebook Specification Sheets.

Lowest Cost Entry-Level Connectivity

Must-Know Specs for Shopping the Key Features

			Standard Features						Emerging Standard Features			
Category		Specification	Long Battery Life	Multiple Connectivity Types	Work from Anywhere	Solid State Local Storage	Ruggedized	Excellent Media Experience	High Fidelity Audio	Easily Securable	Support for VoIP Calling
System Characteristics		Windows	●					●			
		Linux						●		●	
		Main Memory (RAM)	●					●	●		
		Local Storage Size & Type	●			●	●	●	●		
		External Device Support		●				●		●	
Physical Characteristics		Dimensions		●				●			
		Weight		●							
		Battery Type & Size	●								
		Screen Size & Type	●	●				●			
		Keyboard Size		●							
Connectivity		WiFi (802.11b/g)		●	●			●			
		WiFi (802.11n)	●	●	●						
		Bluetooth		●							
		IR		●							
		USBs		●	●	●				●	
		External Memory		●				●		●	
		Headset			●			●			
		External Monitor						●	●		
Media Support		Screen Size	●					●			●
		Screen Resolution	●					●			●
		Screen Colors	●					●	●		●
		Audio Quality	●		●			●	●		●
		Web Cam			●						●

Figure A-1. Lowest Cost Entry-Level Connectivity

Lightest, Smallest, and Leanest

Must-Know Specs for Shopping the Key Features

Requirement		System Characteristics					Physical Characteristics					Connectivity								Media Support				
	Group	Windows	Linux	Main Memory (RAM)	Local Storage Size & Type	External Device Support	Dimensions	Weight	Battery Type & Size	Screen Size	Keyboard Size	WiFi (802.11b/g)	WiFi (802.11n)	Bluetooth	IR	USBs	External Memory	Headset	External Monitor	Screen Size	Screen Resolution	Screen Colors	Audio Quality	Web Cam
Long Battery Life	Must Haves	●		●	●				●	●			●							●	●	●	●	
Ultra Portable	Must Haves						●	●	●															
Solid State Local Storage	Must Haves		●		●																			
Touch Screen	Nice to Have	●					●			●														
Ruggedized	Nice to Have		●		●																			
Fast Data Transmission	Nice to Have												●	●	●									
Integrates Easily with External Devices	Nice to Have					●						●	●	●	●	●	●							
Environmentally Friendly	Nice to Have															●								
Multiple Connectivity Types	High End	●	●	●	●	●	●					●	●	●	●	●	●							
Excellent Media Experience	High End	●	●	●	●					●		●							●	●	●	●	●	

Figure A-2. Lightest, Smallest and Leanest

Entertainment: Music, Movies, TV, Sports and News

Must-Know Specs for Shopping the Key Features

		System Characteristics					Physical Characteristics					Connectivity								Media Support				
		Windows	Linux	Main Memory (RAM)	Local Storage Size & Type	External Device Support	Dimensions	Weight	Battery Type & Size	Screen Size & Type	Keyboard Size	WiFi (802.11b/g)	WiFi (802.11n)	Bluetooth	IR	USBs	External Memory	Headset	External monitor	Screen Size	Screen Resolution	Screen Colors	Audio Quality	Web Cam
Must Have	Long Battery Life			●	●				●	●			●							●	●	●	●	
	Ultra Portable						●		●															
	Watch from Anywhere	●	●	●	●	●	●	●		●	●	●	●	●	●	●		●					●	●
	Excellent Media Experience		●	●	●	●	●	●		●		●		●				●	●	●	●	●	●	
	Fast Data Transmission												●		●									
	Lots of Local Data Storage			●	●	●										●	●							
Nice to Have	Environmentally Friendly															●								
High End	Multiple Connectivity Types											●	●	●	●	●	●							
	Integrates Easily with Other Consumer Electronics					●						●	●	●	●	●	●							

Figure A-3. Entertainment: Music, Movies, TV, Sports and News

Kids and Family

Must-Know Specs for Shopping the Key Features

		System Characteristics					Physical Characteristics					Connectivity								Media Support				
		Windows	Linux	Main Memory (RAM)	Local Storage Size & Type	External Device Support	Dimensions	Weight	Battery Type & Size	Screen Size	Keyboard Size	WiFi (802.11b/g)	WiFi (802.11n)	Bluetooth	IR	USBs	External Memory	Headset	External Monitor	Screen Size	Screen Resolution	Screen Colors	Audio Quality	Web Cam
Must Have	Long Battery Life	●		●	●				●											●	●	●		
	Ruggedized				●																			
	Work from Anywhere					●	●	●			●	●	●	●	●	●		●					●	●
	Larger Screen						●				●									●				
	Larger Keyboard						●				●													
	Good for Web Surfing					●	●			●														
	Fast Data Transmission						●						●		●		●			●				
	Excellent Media Experience	●	●	●	●	●	●			●		●						●	●	●	●	●	●	
Nice to Have	Ruggedized				●											●								
	Accessibility Features																							
	External Keyboard Support					●																		
	External Monitor Support																		●					
	Support for VoIP Calling																	●					●	
	Support for Live Video Conferencing																●	●					●	●
	Low Cost		●							●		●												
	Environmentally Friendly																							
High End	Multiple Connectivity Types											●	●	●	●	●	●							
	Built-in Web Cam		●															●	●	●	●	●	●	●
	Easily Securable				●	●																		
	Integrates Easily with Other Consumer electronics					●						●	●	●	●	●	●							

Figure A-4. Kids and Families

Travelers

Must-Know Specs for Shopping the Key Features

	Feature	Windows	Linux	Main Memory (RAM)	Local Storage Size & Type	External Device Support	Dimensions	Weight	Battery Type & Size	Screen Size & Type	Keyboard Size	WIFI (802.11b/g)	WIFI (802.11n)	Bluetooth	IR	USBs	External Memory	Headset	External Monitor	Screen Size	Screen Resolution	Screen Colors	Audio Quality	Web Cam
		System Characteristics					**Physical Characteristics**					**Connectivity**								**Media Support**				
Must Have	Long Battery Life	•		•	•				•	•			•							•	•	•	•	
	Ultra Portable	•	•				•	•	•															
	Easily Securable	•	•			•																		
	Support for VoIP Calling											•	•	•		•	•	•					•	•
	Multiple Connectivity Types											•	•	•	•	•	•							
	Excellent Media Experience			•	•		•			•								•	•	•	•	•	•	
	Fast Data Transmission												•			•	•							
	Lots of Local Data Storage			•	•	•										•	•							
Nice to Have	Environmentally Friendly			•																				
	Integrated Web Cam									•								•			•		•	•
High End	Multiple Connectivity Types			•								•	•	•	•	•	•							
	Integrates Easily with Other Consumer Electronics	•	•			•						•	•	•	•	•	•							
	Biometric Logon	•	•			•										•	•							

Figure A-5. Travelers

Students and Teachers

Must-Know Specs for Shopping the Key Features

	System Characteristics					Physical Characteristics					Connectivity								Media Support				
	Windows	Linux	Main Memory (RAM)	Local Storage Size & Type	External Device Support	Dimensions	Weight	Battery Type & Size	Screen Size	Keyboard Size	WiFi (802.11b/g)	WiFi (802.11n)	Bluetooth	IR	USBs	External Memory	Headset	External Monitor	Screen Size	Screen Resolution	Screen Colors	Audio Quality	Web Cam
Must Have																							
Long Battery Life	•		•					•	•										•	•	•		
Low Cost		•				•	•		•		•								•	•	•	•	
Work from Anywhere				•		•	•		•	•	•	•	•	•	•		•					•	•
Larger Screen						•				•									•				
Larger Keyboard						•				•													
Good for Writing						•			•					•		•							
Fast Data Transmission												•	•	•									
Lots of Local Data Storage				•	•											•							
Nice to Have																							
Ruggedized				•											•								
Accessibility Features																							
External Keyboard Support					•											•							
External Monitor Support																•	•	•	•				
Support for VoIP Calling																	•					•	•
Support for Live Video Conferencing																						•	•
Open Source App Development Community		•																					
Environmentally Friendly																							
High End																							
Multiple Connectivity Types											•	•	•		•	•							
Integrated Web Cam				•															•				•
Easily Securable	•	•			•										•	•			•				•
Ease of Remote Administration															•	•							
Supports Recording Equipment															•	•			•	•	•	•	

Figure A-6. Students and Teachers

Field Research

Must-Know Specs for Shopping the Key Features

Category	Feature	Windows	Linux	Main Memory (RAM)	Local Storage Size & Type	External Device Support	Dimensions	Weight	Battery Type & Size	Screen Size (Phys.)	Keyboard Size	WiFi (802.11b/g)	WiFi (802.11n)	Bluetooth	IR	USBs	External Memory	Headset	External Monitor	Screen Size (Media)	Screen Resolution	Screen Colors	Audio Quality	Web Cam
Must Haves	Long Battery Life	•		•	•				•	•			•							•	•	•	•	
	Work from Anywhere					•	•	•		•	•	•	•	•	•	•		•					•	•
	Seamlessly Integrates with Exisiting Infrastructure	•	•	•	•	•						•	•	•	•	•								
	Supports Recording Equipment						•				•					•	•		•	•	•	•		
	Good for Writing									•	•						•			•				
	Fast Data Transmission																•							
	Ruggedized		•		•																			
	Ease of Remote Administration												•			•								
	Remote Provisioning of Apps and Data		•	•	•							•	•	•	•	•	•							
	Open Source App Development Community		•																					
Nice to Have	Low Cost	•										•												
	Flexible Connectivity						•			•														
	Integrates Easily with Specialized Devices and Sensors					•												•					•	•
	Lots of Local Data Storage					•	•							•	•	•	•	•	•	•	•	•	•	•
High End	Multiple Connectivity Types											•	•	•	•	•	•							
	Integrated Web Cam																•	•	•	•	•	•	•	•
	Support for Live Video Conferencing																							•
	Solid State Local Storage				•																			

Figure A-7. Field Research

Backpack Journalists

Must-Know Specs for Shopping the Key Features

		System Characteristics					Physical Characteristics					Connectivity								Media Support				
		Windows	Linux	Main Memory (RAM)	Local Storage Size & Type	External Device Support	Dimensions	Weight	Battery Type & Size	Screen Size	Keyboard Size	WiFi (802.11b/g)	WiFi (802.11n)	Bluetooth	IR	USBs	External Memory	Headset	External Monitor	Screen Size	Screen Resolution	Screen Colors	Audio Quality	Web Cam
Must Have	Long Battery Life	●		●	●				●	●			●							●	●	●	●	
	Work from Anywhere					●	●	●		●	●	●	●	●	●	●		●					●	●
	Larger Keyboard						●				●													
	Supports Recording Equipment																							
	Good for Writing						●				●					●	●			●	●	●		
	Fast Data Transmission												●	●	●		●			●				
	Lots of Local Data Storage				●	●									●		●							
Nice to Have	Low Cost		●				●			●		●						●	●	●	●	●	●	
	Ruggedized				●											●								
	Easily Securable		●			●										●								
	Extra Monitor Support																●		●					
	Environmentally Friendly																							
High End	Multiple Connectivity Types											●	●	●	●	●	●							
	Integrated Web Cam																		●	●			●	●
	Biometric Logon Authentication					●										●								
	Solid State Local Storage				●																			

Figure A-8. Backpack Journalists

Gamers: Multiplayer Mobile Gaming

Must-Know Specs for Shopping the Key Features

	System Characteristics					Physical Characteristics					Connectivity								Media Support				
	Windows	Linux	Main Memory (RAM)	Local Storage Size & Type	External Device Support	Dimensions	Weight	Battery Type & Size	Screen Size & Type	Keyboard Size	WiFi (802.11b/g)	WiFi (802.11n)	Bluetooth	IR	USBs	External Memory	Headset	External Monitor	Screen Size	Screen Resolution	Screen Colors	Audio Quality	Web Cam
Must Have																							
Long Battery Life	●		●	●				●	●			●							●	●	●	●	
Ultra Portable						●	●	●															
High Fidelity Audio			●	●																	●	●	
Support for VoIP Calling																●	●	●	●	●	●	●	●
Support for Live Video Chat																●	●		●	●	●	●	●
Fast Data Transmission												●	●	●		●							
Nice to Have																							
Touch Screen	●	●				●			●														
Integrated Web Cam			●						●								●		●	●		●	●
Ruggedized				●											●								
Solid State Local Storage				●																			
Environmentally Friendly																							
High End																							
Multiple Connectivity Types											●	●	●	●	●	●							
Solid State Local Storage				●																			

Figure A-9. Gamers

Eldercare

Specs for the Key Features

Feature	Windows	Linux	Main Memory (RAM)	Local Storage Size & Type	External Device Support	Dimensions	Weight	Battery Type & Size	Screen Size (Physical)	Keyboard Size	WiFi (802.11b/g)	WiFi (802.11n)	Bluetooth	IR	USBs	External Memory	Headset	External Monitor	Screen Size (Media)	Screen Resolution	Screen Colors	Audio Quality	Web Cam
Must Have																							
Long Battery Life	●		●	●				●	●			●							●	●	●	●	
Integrated Web Cam			●						●										●	●		●	●
Accessibility Features																				●		●	
High Fidelity Audio			●	●													●				●	●	
Larger Keyboard										●						●	●	●					
Support for VoIP Calling																	●		●	●	●	●	●
Support for Live Video Conferencing						●											●		●	●	●	●	●
Remote Provisioning of Apps and Data	●	●	●	●							●	●	●	●	●	●							
Ease of Remote Administration	●	●	●	●							●	●	●	●	●	●							
Fast Data Transmission		●										●	●		●								
Nice to Have																							
Touch Screen	●	●							●														
Ruggedized				●		●			●														
Biometric Logon	●	●			●																		
Ease of Remote Administration	●																						
External Monitor Support	●				●									●	●	●		●					
External Keyboard Support					●										●	●							
Environmentally Friendly																							
High End																							
Multiple Connectivity Types											●	●	●	●	●	●							
Integrates Easily with Specialized Devices and Sensors					●						●	●	●	●	●	●							
Solid State Local Storage				●							●	●	●	●	●	●							

Figure A-10. Eldercare

Public Safety/Public Service Delivery

Must-Know Specs for Shopping the Key Features

Column groups: **System Characteristics** (Windows … External Device Support) · **Physical Characteristics** (Dimensions … Keyboard Size) · **Connectivity** (WiFi 802.11b/g … External Monitor) · **Media Support** (Screen Size … Web Cam)

Feature	Windows	Linux	Main Memory (RAM)	Local Storage Size & Type	External Device Support	Dimensions	Weight	Battery Type & Size	Screen Size (Phys.)	Keyboard Size	WiFi (802.11b/g)	WiFi (802.11n)	Bluetooth	IR	USBs	External Memory	Headset	External Monitor	Screen Size (Media)	Screen Resolution	Screen Colors	Audio Quality	Web Cam
Must Have																							
Long Battery Life	●		●					●	●										●	●	●	●	
Ultra Portable						●	●	●	●													●	●
Work from Anywhere				●					●		●	●	●	●	●	●	●						
Ruggedized				●		●																	
Ease of Remote Administration	●				●						●	●	●	●	●	●							
Larger Keyboard										●													
Easily Securable	●	●									●	●	●	●	●	●							
Ease of Asset Management	●	●									●	●	●	●	●	●							
Large Number of Security Apps		●																					
Solid State Local Storage				●																			
Nice to Have																							
Integrate Easily with Existing Systems	●				●						●	●	●	●	●	●							
Integrates Easily with Specialized Devices and Sensors					●						●	●	●	●	●	●							
Integrated Web Cam																			●	●	●	●	●
Support for VoIP Calling																	●					●	●
Support for Live Video Conferencing																	●		●	●	●	●	●
Open Source App Development Community		●																					
Environmentally Friendly																							
High End																							
Seamlessly Integrates with Exisiting Infrastructure	●	●									●	●	●	●	●	●							
Two-Factor Authentication	●	●			●											●							

Figure A-11. Public Safety/Public Service Delivery

Mobile Productivity

Must-Know Specs for Shopping the Key Features

	System Characteristics					Physical Characteristics					Connectivity								Media Support				
	Windows	Linux	Main Memory (RAM)	Local Storage Size & Type	External Device Support	Dimensions	Weight	Battery Type & Size	Screen Size	Keyboard Size	WiFi (802.11b/g)	WiFi (802.11n)	Bluetooth	IR	USBs	External Memory	Headset	External Monitor	Screen Size	Screen Resolution	Screen Colors	Audio Quality	Web Cam
Must Have																							
Long Battery Life	●		●	●				●	●			●							●	●	●	●	
Larger Screen						●			●										●	●	●		
Larger Keyboard						●				●													
Support for VoIP Calling											●					●	●		●	●	●	●	●
Fast Data Transmission												●	●	●									
Easily Securable	●	●			●							●	●	●									
Large Number of Mobile Productivity Apps	●	●													●	●							●
Support for VoIP Calling																●	●		●	●	●	●	
Lots of Local Data Storage			●	●																			
Nice to Have																							
Integrated Web Cam																	●	●	●			●	●
Support for Live Video Conferencing									●								●	●	●	●	●	●	●
Integrates Easily with Specialized Peripherals					●	●									●	●							
High End																							
Excellent Media Experience	●	●				●					●							●	●	●	●	●	●
Flexible Connectivity	●	●							●		●	●	●		●	●		●				●	●
Two-Factor Authentication	●	●														●							
Ruggedized				●																			

Figure A–12. Mobile ProductivityT

Business: Lowest TCO

Must-Know Specs for Shopping the Key Features

	System Characteristics					Physical Characteristics					Connectivity								Media Support				
	Windows	Linux	Main Memory (RAM)	Local Storage Size & Type	External Device Support	Dimensions	Weight	Battery Type & Size	Screen Size	Keyboard Size	WiFi (802.11b/g)	WiFi (802.11n)	Bluetooth	IR	USBs	External Memory	Headset	External Monitor	Screen Size	Screen Resolution	Screen Colors	Audio Quality	Web Cam
Must Have																							
Long Battery Life	●		●	●				●	●			●							●	●	●	●	
Work from Anywhere			●		●	●	●		●	●	●	●	●	●	●		●					●	●
Larger Keyboard						●				●													
Easily Securable	●	●			●																		
Ease of Asset Management	●																						
Large Number of Enterprise Ready Apps	●																						
Lots of Local Data Storage			●	●																			
Nice to Have																							
Flexible Connectivity											●	●	●	●	●	●	●	●				●	●
Two-Factor Authentication	●	●			●							●				●							
Ease of Remote Administration	●	●														●							
Remote Provisioning of Apps and Data	●	●	●	●							●	●	●	●	●								
Environmentally Friendly					●										●								
High End																							
Seamlessly Integrates with Existing Infrastructure	●	●	●		●							●											
Integrated Web Cam																●	●		●	●	●	●	●
Support for VoIP Calling																●	●		●	●	●	●	●
Support for Live Video Conferencing																●	●		●	●	●	●	●

Figure A-13. Business: Lowest TCO

System Characteristic	Windows	Yes
	Linux	Yes
	CPU	Intel Atom
	Main Memory (RAM)	512MB -1.5GB
	Local Storage Size & Type	NAND flash module or hard disk drive for internal storage
		NAND flash module: 8 GB
		Hard disk drive: 120GB
		Storage expansion: SD™ Card reader
Physical Characteristics	External Device Support	Three USB 2.0 ports
		External display (VGA) port
		Headphone/speaker/line-out jack
		Microphone-in jack
		Ethernet (RJ-45) port
		DC-in jack for AC adapter
	Dimensions	249 (W) x 170 (D) x 29 (H) mm (9.8 x 6.7 x 1.14") for SKUs with NAND flash module and 3-cell battery pack
		249 (W) x 195 (D) x 36 (H) mm (9.8 x 6.7 x 1.42") for SKUs with hard disk drive and 6-cell battery pack
	Weight	995 g (2.19 lbs.) for SKUs with NAND flash module and 3-cell battery pack
		1.26 kg (2.78 lbs.) for SKUs with hard disk drive and 6-cell battery pack
	Battery Type & Size	24 W 2200 mAh 3-cell Li-ion battery pack
		57 W 2600 mAh 6-cell Li-ion battery pack
		3-hour battery life for SKUS with NAND flash module and 3-cell battery pack
		7-hour battery life for SKUS with NAND flash module and 6-cell battery pack
	Screen Size	8.9"
	Keyboard Size	84-key keyboard with 1.6 mm (minimum) key travel
		- Touchpad pointing device with two buttons
		- 12 function keys, four cursor keys, one Windows® key for Windows® XP Home or one Home key for Linpus™
		- Linux® Lite version, hotkey controls, embedded numeric keypad, international language support
Connectivity	WiFi(802.11b/g) WiFi(802.11n) Bluetooth	Acer InviLink™ 802.11b/g Wi-Fi CERTIFIED® network connection, supporting Acer SignalUp™ wireless technology2
	USBs	Three USB 2.0 ports
	External Memory	Multi-in-1 card reader: Supporting Secure Digital™ (SD) Card, MultiMediaCard (MMC), Reduced-Size Multimedia Card (RS-MMC), Memory Stick™ (MS), Memory Stick PRO™ (MS PRO), xD-Picture Card™ (xD
		Supported storage cards with adapter: miniSD™, microSD™, Memory Stick Duo™, Memory Stick PRO Duo™
	Headset	Headphone/speaker/line-out jack
	External monitor	External display (VGA) port
Media Experience	Screen Type	WSVGA high-brightness TFT LCD LED backlight
	Screen Resolution	1024 x 600 pixel resolution
	Audio Quality	High-definition audio support
		Two built-in stereo speakers
		MS-Sound compatible
		Built-in digital microphone
	Web Cam	Integrated Acer Crystal Eye webcam, supporting 0.3 megapixel resolution
	Suggested Vendors:	Amazon.co.uk
		Amazon.com (USA)
		Buy.com USA
		Newegg USA
		PCWorld.co.uk
		Play.com (UK)
		TigerDirect - Canada

Figure A-14. Acer Specs

System Characteristics	Windows	Yes
	Linux	Yes
	CPU	Intel Atom
	Main Memory (RAM)	512MB-2GB
	Local Storage Size & Type	Depending on the model, SDD of 16-64 GB; HDD of 80-160GB; Hybrid models use internal flash with external hard disk to provide 38GB total storage
Physical Characteristics	External Device Support	Two PCI Express Mini Card connectors
	Dimensions	Smallest: 170mm(L) x 225mm(W) x 34mm(H)
		Largest:266mm(W) x 191.2mm(D) x 28.5mm~ 38mm(H)
	Weight	Lightest: 922g (2.04lbs)
		Heaviest: 1450g (3.20lbs)
	Battery Type & Size	High End Systems: Li-polymer battery; Estimated Battery Life: 6 hrs
		Longest Life Model: 6-Cell Li-ion Battery; Estimated Battery Life: 9.5 hrs
	Screen Size	7-10.1"
	Keyboard Size	8.9-10"
Connectivity	WiFi (802.11b/g)	Yes
	WiFi (802.11n)	Yes
	Bluetooth	Yes
	USBs	3 USB 2.0 ports
	External Memory	MMC/SD (HC) card reader
		USB2.0/eSATA port
Media Experience	Headset	Headphone jack
	External monitor	VGA out
	Screen Type	LED Backlight
	Screen Resolution	On high end and mid range models: 1024x600 (WSVGA)
		On lower end models: 800X480 (WVGA)
	Audio Quality	Realtek ALC662 Hi-Definition Audio 5.1 CODEC
		Built-in stereo speakers
		Built-in microphone
	Web Cam	On lower end models: 0.3 megapixel; up to 640×480, up to 30 frame/s
		On premium models:1.3M Pixel
	Suggested Vendors:	Use the Asus Comparison Chart to find the model you want before shopping third party vendors.

Figure A-15. Asus Specs

System Characteristics	Windows	Windows XP Home Edition SP3
	Linux	Ubuntu Linux version 8.04.1
	CPU	Intel Atom
	Main Memory (RAM)	Up to 1GB
	Local Storage Size & Type	Up to 16GB configured with a solid state drive and Genuine Windows XP Home Edition
		Up to 32GB configured with a solid state drive and Ubuntu Linux
Physical Characteristics	External Device Support	USB 2.0 (3)
		Integrated 10/100 LAN (RJ45)
		15-pin VGA video connector
		Audio jacks (1-line out, 1 mic-in)
		3-in-1 media card reader
	Dimensions	Width: 9.13" (232mm)
		Height: 1.07" (27.2mm) front / 1.25" (31.7mm) back
		Depth: 6.77" (172mm)
	Weight	Weight: Starting weight of 2.28 lbs. (1.035 kg) (8.9" display, 4 cell battery). Weights will vary depending on configurations and manufacturing variability.
	Battery Type & Size	4-cell 32WHr Li-Ion battery
	Screen Size	8.9"
	Keyboard Size	92% the size of a traditional laptop keyboard
Connectivity	WiFi(802.11b/g)	802.11g mini-card
	WiFi(802.11n)	
	Bluetooth	Bluetooth® Internal (2.0) mini-card
	USBs	USB 2.0 (3)
	External Memory	Play CDs and DVDs with an optional external optical disk drive.
	Headset	Audio jacks 1-line out, 1 mic-in
Media Experience	External monitor	15-pin VGA video connector
	Screen Type	WXGA Truelife widescreen Backlit LED display
	Screen Resolution	1024X600 (133 dpi)
	Audio Quality	One external speaker
	Web Cam	Optional 0.3MP or 1.3MP webcams
	Suggested Vendors:	http://configure.us.dell.com/dellstore/

Figure A-16. Dell Specs

System Characteristics	Windows	Genuine Windows Vista Home Basic 32
		Genuine Windows Vista Business 32
		Genuine Windows Vista Business downgrade to Genuine Windows XP Professional installed
	Linux	SuSE Linux Enterprise Desktop 10
	Other OS	FreeDOS
	CPU	VIA C7-M ULV
	Main Memory (RAM)	1024MB or 2048MB
	Local Storage Size & Type	120/160GB 5400 rpm SATA Hard Drive
		120/160GB 7200 rpm SATA Hard Drive
Physical Characteristics	External Device Support	Hard drives are customer removable and will withstand multiple insertion/removal cycles. Up to 10GB is reserved for the system recovery software.
		Up to 32-bit per pixel color depth
		VGA port supports resolutions up to 2048 x 1536 at 75 Hz, and
		lower resolutions at up to 100 Hz
		Supports ExpressCard/54 and ExpressCard/34
	Dimensions	1.05 (at front) x 10.04 x 6.5"
		27 (at front) x 255 x 165 mm
	Weight	Starts at 2.8 lbs (1.27 kg)
	Battery Type & Size	3-cell (28 WHr) high capacity Li-Ion. Battery Life: Up to 2 hours 15 minutes
		6-cell (55 WHr) high capacity Li-Ion; Battery Life: Up to 4 hours 30 minutes
		Standby time: Up to 1 week
	Screen Size	8.9"
	Keyboard Size	Spill-resistant keyboard is 92% of full size, 101/102-key compatible with isolated inverted-T cursor control keys, both left and right control and alt keys, 12 function keys, and hotkey combinations for audio volume, power conservation, brightness, and other features. U.S. and international key layouts are available.
Connectivity	WiFi(802.11b/g)	Integrated support for 802.11a, b, g, and n draft 2.0*
		Up to 300 mbps data rate
	WiFi(802.11n)	Wi-Fi CERTIFIED*
		Cisco Compatible Extensions support (Version 4.0)
		Wired Equivalent Privacy (WEP) support up to 128-bit keys
		Wi-Fi Protected Access (WPA) and WPA2 support
		802.1x authentication support, including EAP-TLS, EAP-TTLS, PEAP-GTC, PEAP-MSCHAPv2, and LEAP
		Advanced Encryption Standard (AES) support
		WiFi certified for WPA2, WMM
		Dual antennas integrated in the display enclosure
	Bluetooth	Bluetooth Specification v2.0 compliant
		Works with a wide range of Bluetooth devices
	USBs	Two USB 2.0
	External Memory	Via optional HP External MultiBay II (9.5-mm):
		MultiBay II DVD-ROM Drive
		MultiBay II DVD/CD-RW Combo Drive
		MultiBay II DVD+/-RW SuperMulti DL Drive
Media Experience	Headset	Stereo headphone/line out Stereo microphone in
	External monitor	Up to 32-bit per pixel color depth
	Screen Type	VGA port supports resolutions up to 2048 x 1536 at 75 Hz, and
		lower resolutions at up to 100Hz
	Screen Resolution	1024 x 600
		1024 x 600
	Audio Quality	ADI1984HD High Definition CODEC
		24-bit DAC
		Integrated stereo speakers
	Web Cam	
	Suggested Vendors:	hp.com

Figure A-17. HP Specs

		Clamshell Model	Clamshell/Tablet Convertible Model
System Characteristics	Windows	Windows XP	Windows XP
	Linux	Mandriva Linux Discovery 2007:Low resource version of Fedora Linux with the Sugar GUI and mesh networking	Mandriva Linux Discovery 2007: Low resource version of Fedora Linux with the Sugar GUI and mesh networking
		Ubuntu Education Edition for Classmate PC: Low resource version of Ubuntu Linux plus bundled open-source education applications	Ubuntu Education Edition for Classmate PC: Low resource version of Ubuntu Linux plus bundled open-source education applications
	CPU	Intel Atom N270 1.6GHz Processor	Intel Atom N270 1.6GHz Processor
	Main Memory (RAM)	512MB - 1 GB	512MB - 1GB
	Local Storage Size & Type	16GB/ 8GB / 4GB / 2GB Flash	16GB/ 8GB / 4GB / 2GB Flash
		1.8" HDD	1.8" HDD
	External Device Support	1 SD slot	1 SD slot
			VGA port for external monitor
Physical Characteristics	Dimensions	238 x 251 x 42 mm, including handle	238 x 251 x 42 mm, including handle
	Weight	1.25kg-1.49kg	1.25kg-1.49kg
	Battery Type & Size	6-cell battery (6 hours)	6-cell battery (6 hours)
		4-cell battery (4 hours)	4-cell battery (4 hours)
	Screen Size	8.9"	8.9"
		7"	
Connectivity	Keyboard Size	9" water-resistant, easy-to-clean keyboard	9" water-resistant, easy-to-clean keyboard
	WiFi(802.11b/g)	802.11b/g support	802.11b/g support
	WiFi(802.11n)		802.11n support
	Bluetooth		
	USBs	2 x USB 2.0 ports	2 x USB 2.0 ports
	External Memory		
Media Experience	Headset		
	External monitor		VGA port for external monitor
	Screen Type	Color LCD	Color Touch Screen
		Color LCD	
	Screen Resolution	8.9": 1024 x 600	
		7": 800 x 480	
	Audio Quality	Integrated 2 channel audio	Integrated 2 channel audio
		2 built-in speakers and microphone	2 built-in speakers and microphone
	Web Cam	.3 MP	1.3 MP camera, capable of 30 frame/second video at a resolution of 640x480
	Suggested Vendors:	http://2gopc.com/	
		http://www.equuscs.com/edu	
		http://www.shopmanda.com	
		http://www.howardcomputers.com/	
		http://www.britecomputers.com/	

Figure A-18. Classmate PC Specs

374

System Characteristics		
Windows	Windows XP Home	
Linux	Novell SUSE Linux Enterprise Desktop	
CPU	Intel Atom Processor N270 with single-core	
Main Memory (RAM)	512MB or 1GB std / 1.5GB max7	
Local Storage Size & Type	80GB (5400 rpm) or 160GB (5400 rpm) HDD	
External Device Support	One slot (ExpressCard/34)	
	4-in-1 reader (MMC, Memory Stick, Memory Stick PRO, Secure Digital Card)	
	Two USB 2.0, external monitor (VGA DB-15), ethernet (RJ-45)	
	One Mini PCI Express slot	

Physical Characteristics		
Dimensions	With 3-cell battery: (WxDxH): 9.8" x 7.2" x 0.9-1.1"; 250mm x 183mm x 22-27.5mm	
	With 6-cell battery: (WxDxH): 9.8" x 7.7" x 0.9-1.4"; 250mm x 196mm x 22-36mm	
Weight	3-cell: starting at 2.65 lb (1.2 kg)	
	6-cell: starting at 3.09 lb (1.4 kg)	
Battery Type & Size	Lithium Ion, 3-cell 2600 mAH or 6-cell 4800 mAH	
	3-cell: up to 2.5 hr; 6-cell: up to 5.0 hr	
Screen Size	10.1"	
Keyboard Size	6-row, 80-key, 85% size, Fn keys, Novo key, wireless on/off button; Two-button touch pad with scroll feature and multi-touch	

Connectivity		
WiFi (802.11b/g)		
WiFi (802.11n)		
Bluetooth	Bluetooth 2.1 wireless, LED indicator (optional)	
USBs	Two USB 2.0	
External Memory		
Headset	Stereo headphone jack (3.5 mm), microphone input jack (3.5 mm),	
External Monitor	VGA DB-15	

Media Experience		
Screen Type	WSVGA, TFT color, LED backlight	
Screen Resolution	1024x576	
Audio Quality	High Defi nition (HD) Audio, RealTek® ALC269 codec / two stereo speakers (1.5 watt) /	
Web Cam	Camera on top of screen, 1.3-megapixel, fi xed focus	

Suggested Vendors:	http://shop.lenovo.com	

Figure A-19. Lenovo Specs

System Characteristics	Windows	Windows XP Home Edition
	Linux	
	CPU	Intel Atom N270
	Main Memory (RAM)	1GB
	Local Storage Size & Type	160GB HDD
Physical Characteristics	External Device Support	PDA's, digital cameras, digital video cameras, digital MP3 Players, Global GPS Systems and the like connecting through USB 2.0 Port
	Dimensions	10.23"(L) x 7.08"(D) x 0.748"~1.24
	Weight	2.6 lbs (6 cell)
	Battery Type & Size	Lithium Ion 6 Cells; Estimated Battery Life - 5.5 hours
	Screen Size	10"
Connectivity	Keyboard Size	10"
	WiFi(802.11b/g)	
	WiFi(802.11n)	Built-in 802.11b/g/n WLAN card
	Bluetooth	Yes
	USBs	USB2.0 Port X 3
	External Memory	4-in-1 Card Reader, SD/MMC/MS/MSpro
	Headset	Mic-in Port X 1, Headphone Output X 1
	External monitor	VGA (15-pin, D-Sub) X 1
Media Experience	Screen Type	WSVGA LCD
	Screen Resolution	WSVGA LCD
	Audio Quality	SoundBlaster compatible, Internal speaker x 2
	Web Cam	1.3 MP Web cam
	Suggested Vendors:	http://www.msimobile.com/

Figure A-20. MSI Wind Specs

Index

Zoho Show, 181–183
Zoho Wiki, 183-184
Zoho Writer, 174–175
    Go Offline link, 174
    help and advice, 175
    languages, 177
    sharing documents, 174
    working offline, 174
ZumoDrive, 126–128
    photo albums, 127

You Need the Companion eBook

THE EXPERT'S VOICE™

233 Spring Street, New York, NY 10013